T0139704

All the Sonnets of Shakespeare

How can we look afresh at Shakespeare as a writer of sonnets? What new light might they shed on his career, personality, and sexuality? Shakespeare wrote sonnets for at least thirty years, not only for himself, for professional reasons, and for those he loved, but also in his plays, as prologues, as epilogues, and as part of their poetic texture. This groundbreaking book assembles all of Shakespeare's sonnets in their probable order of composition. An inspiring introduction debunks long-established biographical myths about Shakespeare's sonnets and proposes new insights about how and why he wrote them. Explanatory notes and modern English paraphrases of every poem and dramatic extract illuminate the meaning of these sometimes challenging but always deeply rewarding witnesses to Shakespeare's inner life and professional expertise. Beautifully printed and elegantly presented, this volume will be treasured by students, scholars, and every Shakespeare enthusiast.

Paul Edmondson is Head of Research and Knowledge and Director of the Stratford-upon-Avon Poetry Festival for the Shakespeare Birthplace Trust. He is the author, co-author, and co-editor of many books and articles about Shakespeare, including *Shakespeare's Sonnets* (with Stanley Wells, 2004), *Twelfth Night* (2005), *Shakespeare: Ideas in Profile* (2015), Shakespeare Beyond *Doubt: Evidence, Argument, Controversy* (2013) and *The Shakespeare Circle: An Alternative Biography* (2015) (both with Stanley Wells, Cambridge University Press), *Shakespeare's Creative Legacies* (with Peter Holbrook, 2016); *Finding Shakespeare's New Place: An Archaeological Biography* (with Kevin Colls and William Mitchell, 2016), and *New Places: Shakespeare and Civic Creativity* (with Ewan Fernie, 2018). He is a priest in the Church of England.

Professor Sir Stanley Wells, CBE, FRSL, is Honorary President of the Shakespeare Birthplace Trust. His many books include *Shakespeare: For All Time* (2002), *Looking for Sex in Shakespeare* (2004), *Shakespeare & Co.* (2006), *Shakespeare, Sex, and Love* (2010), and *Great Shakespeare Actors* (2015). He edited *Shakespeare Survey* for almost twenty years and is co-editor of *The Cambridge Companion to Shakespeare on Stage* (with Sarah Stanton, Cambridge, 2002), and *The New Cambridge Companion to Shakespeare* (with Margreta de Grazia, Cambridge, 2010). He is also the general editor of the Oxford and Penguin editions of Shakespeare.

All the Sonnets of Shakespeare

EDITED BY

Paul Edmondson
The Shakespeare Birthplace Trust

Stanley Wells
The Shakespeare Birthplace Trust

CAMBRIDGE
UNIVERSITY PRESS

Shaftesbury Road, Cambridge CB2 8EA, United Kingdom

One Liberty Plaza, 20th Floor, New York, NY 10006, USA

477 Williamstown Road, Port Melbourne, VIC 3207, Australia

314–321, 3rd Floor, Plot 3, Splendor Forum, Jasola District Centre,
New Delhi – 110025, India

103 Penang Road, #05–06/07, Visioncrest Commercial, Singapore 238467

Cambridge University Press is part of Cambridge University Press & Assessment,
a department of the University of Cambridge.

We share the University's mission to contribute to society through the pursuit of
education, learning and research at the highest international levels of excellence.

www.cambridge.org
Information on this title: www.cambridge.org/9781108490399
DOI: 10.1017/9781108780841

First published 2020 (version 7, March 2024)

Printed in Great Britain by CPI Group (UK) Ltd, Croydon CR0 4YY, March 2024

A catalogue record for this publication is available from the British Library
Library of Congress Cataloging-in-Publication data
Names: Shakespeare, William, 1564-1616, author. | Edmondson, Paul, editor.
Wells, Stanley, 1930- editor.
Title: All the sonnets of Shakespeare / edited by Paul Edmondson, Stanley Wells.
Other titles: Sonnets
Description: Cambridge, UK ; New York, NY : Cambridge University Press,
2020. | Includes bibliographical references and index.
Identifiers: LCCN 2020026294 (print) | LCCN 2020026295 (ebook) | ISBN
9781108490399 (hardback) | ISBN 9781108780841 (ebook)
Subjects: LCSH: Sonnets, English. | LCGFT: Sonnets. | Poetry.
Classification: LCC PR2848.A2 E36 2020 (print) | LCC PR2848.A2 (ebook) |
DDC 821/.3—dc23
LC record available at https://lccn.loc.gov/2020026294
LC ebook record available at https://lccn.loc.gov/2020026295

ISBN 978-1-108-49039-9 Hardback

Contents

Acknowledgements [*page* vii]

Introduction [1]
All the Sonnets of Shakespeare? [1]
When Did Shakespeare Start Writing Sonnets? [2]
Writing Sonnets in the Plays [8]
The Originality of *Shakespeare's Sonnets: Never before Imprinted*
(1609) [14]
Setting Forth Shakespeare's Sonnets [21]
'Among His Private Friends' [26]
His Name Is Will [32]

About This Volume
How Have We Decided What to Include? [38]
The Layout of this Volume [42]
A Note on the Text [43]
A Note on Abbreviations and Abstract Nouns [44]
Some Suggestions for Further Reading [44]

All *the Sonnets of Shakespeare*
(All dates are conjectural.) [45]

Early Sonnets
Sonnets 154 and 153 (pre-1582) [47]
Sonnet 145 (1582) [49]

1589–1595
from *The Two Gentlemen of Verona* (1589–1591) [50]
Sonnets about Venus and Adonis (1590–1593) [51]
from *Edward III* (1592) [54]

Sonnets 127–144 (1590–1595) [55]
Sonnets 146–152 (1590–1595) [75]

1594–1595
from *The Comedy of Errors* (1594) [82]
from *Love's Labour's Lost* (1594–1595) [88]
from *Romeo and Juliet* (1594–1595) [89]
Sonnets 61–77 (1594–1595) [92]
Sonnets 87–103 (1594–1595) [109]

1595–1597
Sonnets 1–60 (1595–1597) [126]
from *A Midsummer Night's Dream* (1596) [187]

1598–1600
from *Much Ado About Nothing* (1598) [188]
Sonnets 78–86 (1598–1600) [189]
from *Henry V* (1599) [198]
from *As You Like It* (1599) [199]

1600–1609
Sonnets 104–126 (1600–1604) [200]
from *Troilus and Cressida* (1602) [223]
from *All's Well That Ends Well* (1605) [224]
from *Pericles* (1608) [226]

1610–1613
from *Cymbeline* (1610) [228]
from *All Is True, or Henry VIII* (1613) [230]

Textual Notes [231]
All the Sonnets of Shakespeare: Literal Paraphrases [233]
Numerical Index of *Shakespeare's Sonnets* (1609) [291]
Index of First Lines [295]

Acknowledgements

For helpful comments we are grateful to: Martin Butler, José A. Pérez Díez, Devon Glover ('The Sonnet Man'), Emily Hockley of Cambridge University Press, MacDonald P. Jackson, Andy Kesson, Jane Kingsley-Smith, Adam Smyth, Sarah Stanton, Tiffany Stern, Will Tosh, and Martin Wiggins.

Introduction

All the Sonnets of Shakespeare?

For most people the phrase 'Shakespeare's Sonnets' refers to the 154 poems published in 1609 under the title *Shakespeare's Sonnets: Never before Imprinted.*[1] These have since appeared in numerous editions in print and on-line, ranging from plain-text reproductions through illustrated gift-books to collections with varying amounts of editorial material. *Shakespeare's Sonnets* (1609) have been translated into most of the world's languages, anthologised, modernised, and set to music; they have inspired other works of art including plays, novels, other poetry, songs, ballets, and films; and they have been performed and recorded in a variety of media.

But the sonnets that appeared first in 1609 represent only a limited proportion of Shakespeare's uses of sonnet form. Shakespeare includes sonnets in his plays at many points in his career to change, vary, and heighten the dramatic mood. The manner in which he does so resembles that in which other writers of his time, such as Sir Philip Sidney (1554–86) and Robert Greene (1558–92), interspersed their prose fictions with poems, some elaborate in form, and in which dramatists, including John Lyly (1553–1606) and Shakespeare himself, dotted their plays with song lyrics. Martin Wiggins's and Catherine Richardson's multi-volumed *British Drama 1533–1642: A Catalogue* (from 2011) shows that even before Shakespeare wrote, writers of pageants and entertainments used sonnet form for set pieces such as prologues and addresses to the monarch. Shakespeare seems, on the surviving evidence, to be a pioneer in broadening the stylistic range of drama by using sonnet form for spoken dialogue in the linguistic fabric of plays.

---

1 Images of the 1609 quarto's title page: *SHAKE-SPEARES SONNETS. Neuer before Imprinted* (London: G. Eld for T.T., 1609) are easily viewable on-line. Search for 'Shakespeare's Sonnets title page' in Google, and click 'images'.

Sonnets alter the verbal and aural textures of the drama. In hearing them, his audiences may be set momentarily at a critical distance from the action, character, and story. Sometimes they can be highly comic, as in *Love's Labour's Lost*, when the King of Navarre and his Lords speak rather laboured poems of their own composition (pp. 83–8, this volume). Sonnets are used for moments of personal revelation within passages of dialogue, as in Valentine's sonnet-like letter in *The Two Gentlemen of Verona* (p. 50) and in *The Comedy of Errors* when the form reflects the inescapably transfixed and confused state of mind of Antipholus of Syracuse (p. 82). Sonnets served Shakespeare as the structure for prologues, as in *Romeo and Juliet* (pp. 89 and 91), and for epilogues, as in *Henry V* (p. 198) and the co-authored *All Is True* (*Henry VIII*) (p. 230). Romeo and Juliet famously share the speaking of a sonnet when they simultaneously fall in love at first sight (p. 90). In *All's Well That Ends Well*, Helen speaks a sonnet and writes a confessional letter to her mother-in-law, the Countess, which Shakespeare casts into the form of a sonnet (pp. 224–5). As his style of versification developed, moving away from the relative formality of his earlier work to the stylistic and rhythmic freedom of his later plays, he found less use for the sonnet structure, but even so it is present in later plays as well. The prophecies of the goddess Diana in *Pericles* (p. 227) and the god Jupiter in *Cymbeline* (p. 228) emphasise their other-worldliness through their use of the sonnet form.

This volume contains all the surviving sonnets of Shakespeare. It includes the 154 collected together and published in 1609 as *Shakespeare's Sonnets*; alternative versions of 2 of them, as well as 3 of uncertain authorship but attributed to him in the unauthorised collection published as *The Passionate Pilgrim* (1599); and 23 that he incorporated into the plays, making a total of 182 sonnets. For the first time in their history, we endeavour to arrange them, so far as current scholarship allows, in the order in which they were written.

When Did Shakespeare Start Writing Sonnets?

In the opening scene of *The Merry Wives of Windsor*, the lovelorn Abraham Slender, seeking inspiration for his wooing of Mistress Anne

Page, says 'I had rather than forty shillings I had my book of songs and sonnets here' (1.1.181–2). He is speaking of the book published by Richard Tottel in 1557 – over forty years before the play was first staged – as *Songes and Sonnettes written by the right honorable Lorde Henry Haward late Earl of Surrey, and other.* The word *sonnet* comes from the Italian *sonnetto,* meaning 'a little sound' or 'song'. The first sonnets in the now familiar fourteen-line form were written by Italian poets including Dante Alighieri (1265–1321) and Francesco Petrarch (1304–74). In early English usage the word could refer to any brief piece of lyric verse, and this meaning survived even after the fourteen-line form was introduced into English. *Songs and Sonnets* – often referred to as Tottel's *Miscellany* – the first-ever published anthology of English verse – introduced to the English reading public both the word *sonnet* and the poetic forms to which it can be applied. It includes translations of sonnets by Francesco Petrarch and other writers. Frequently revised, Tottel's *Miscellany* appeared in eight subsequent editions up to 1587 (when Shakespeare was twenty-three years old) and is one of the very few books written during Shakespeare's era to be mentioned in his writings.[2]

Most early sonnets are secular love poems, but they could also be religious in tone and subject matter. In fact the first English sonnet sequence is Anne Locke's *A Meditation of a Penitent Sinner,* published as early as 1560. In 1575 the soldier-poet George Gascoigne (1535–77) wrote: 'some think that all poems being short may be called sonnets', and John Donne's (1572–1631) *Songs and Sonnets,* printed posthumously as late as 1633, contains no poems written in regular sonnet form. Nevertheless, Gascoigne went on to write: 'I can best allow to call those sonnets which are of fourteen lines containing ten syllables. The first twelve do rhyme in staves of four lines by cross metre, and the last two, rhyming together, do conclude the whole.'[3] Two standard sonnet structures were, however, in common

---

2   Another example is Beatrice's mention of *The Hundred Merry Tales* in *Much Ado About Nothing* (2.1.120).

3   George Gascoigne, *Certain Notes of Instruction* (1575), in *Sidney's 'The Defence of Poesy' and Selected Renaissance Literary Criticism,* ed. Gavin Alexander (London: Penguin Books, 2004), 237–47 (p. 245).

use in Shakespeare's time. Both are composed of fourteen iambic pentameter lines – that is, lines having (like regular blank verse) ten syllables with five stresses. The difference between the two structures lies in the rhyme scheme. The less common form, known as the Spenserian Sonnet, because of its use by Sir Edmund Spenser (1552–99), rhymes *abab-bcbc-cdcd-ee*. More usually, an English poet would structure a sonnet around fourteen lines made up of three quatrains (four-line units) followed by a couplet, rhyming: *abab-cd-cd-efef-gg*. This has become known as the Shakespearian Sonnet and is exemplified by Shakespeare's regular use of it.

Though Tottel's *Miscellany* is not likely to have formed part of the classics-based Stratford grammar school curriculum, the teenage Shakespeare must surely have owned a copy. And it seems likely that, aged around seventeen, he attempted to further his courtship by imitating its use of sonnet form, writing for a real-life Anne – Anne Hathaway – the sonnet printed in *Shakespeare's Sonnets* as Sonnet 145.[4] It ends with a pun on her surname:

> 'I hate' from hate away she threw,
> And saved my life, saying – 'not you'.

Simple in diction and in syntax, it is untypical in its line length among his wider sonnet collection. We place this sonnet early in our chronologically ordered edition.

It is possible, however, that Shakespeare had written sonnets even earlier, when he was a schoolboy. Sonnets 153 and 154, printed last in the 1609 volume, are anomalous in several respects. They bear no clear relationship to the rest of the collection. Far from being intimate love poems, like some (though by no means all) of the other sonnets, they are impersonal narratives, and each tells the same story though in different form. Both are translations of the same six-line Greek narrative (often referred to as an epigram) by one Marianus Scholasticus (fifth to sixth centuries AD), which circulated in

---

4   This connection was not made until A. J. Gurr's 'Shakespeare's First Poem: Sonnet 145', *Essays in Criticism*, 21 (1971), 221–6.

manuscript and was first printed in Florence in 1494, and published in Latin in 1603. No one knows where Shakespeare found this widely disseminated Greek text, or whether he knew it in the original Greek or in Latin. It seems reasonable to suggest that it formed part of his early classical education, in the course of which he acquired what Ben Jonson (1572–1637) was to describe (in his memorial poem at the front of the 1623 Folio of Shakespeare's works) as 'small Latin and less Greek'. The existence of two separate versions of the same poem savours strongly of an academic exercise. May the books of exercises prescribed for the pupils of the King's School, Stratford-upon-Avon have included one in which the Greek text was set as a translation exercise?[5] And is it possible that Shakespeare exercised his budding talent for poetic composition first by translating these lines and then, dissatisfied by his first attempt – perhaps as the result of criticism from his teacher – producing a more coherent version? Rendered simply into modern prose, the Greek reads:

> Beneath these plane trees, detained by gentle slumber, Love slept, having put his torch in the care of the Nymphs; but the Nymphs said to one another 'Why wait? Would that together with this we could quench the fire in the hearts of men.' But the torch set fire even to the water, and with hot water thenceforth the Love-Nymphs fill the bath.[6]

Critics and editors – some of them apparently unaware of the classical source – have often related the poems to Shakespeare's sex life, suggesting that they tell of his personal search for medicinal baths, possibly in the city of Bath, to treat a venereal disease. But the closeness of the story told in both poems to the text of its original source surely suggests, rather, that it is an academic exercise in translation, and this impression is heightened by the fact that Sonnet 154 is clearly the earlier version, clarified and improved in Sonnet

5 'He may even have seen the Greek at school', writes David West, in *Shakespeare's Sonnets: With a New Commentary* (London: Duckworth, 2007), p. 468.

6 Colin Burrow (ed.), *The Complete Sonnets and Poems* (Oxford: Oxford University Press, 2002), p. 686.

153 — in other words, Shakespeare wrote a complete sonnet based on a Greek text, and later — but probably not much later — realised that he could do better and composed Sonnet 153, while retaining both the revised and the unrevised version among his papers.[7] Thus the two poems give us a rare (if relatively trivial) insight into his creative processes, most closely paralleled perhaps by the accidental survival in print of two versions of lines spoken by Biron in *Love's Labour's Lost* (4.3 from line 294). Their placing as the final poems in the 1609 collection acknowledges their distinctiveness.

In either late 1598 or 1599, there appeared a slim volume of twenty poems called *The Passionate Pilgrim*, said on its title page to be by William Shakespeare and published by William Jaggard — later one of the publishers of the Shakespeare First Folio of 1623. It is a catchpenny volume, clearly put together by the publisher with no input from Shakespeare; nevertheless, it sold well enough for a reprint to appear soon after the first edition. The first two poems are versions of Shakespeare's Sonnets 138 and 144. These poems used to be regarded as debased versions of the later-printed poems, but it is now thought that they are early versions of poems that Shakespeare later revised into the form in which they appeared in 1609. We include them in our edition as independent poems, earlier versions.

The Passionate Pilgrim also includes versions of passages from *Love's Labour's Lost*, which had appeared in print the previous year. We include only the later versions published in 1609 but collate the differences to be found in the 1599 texts. The remaining fifteen poems in *The Passionate Pilgrim* include some that are known to be by other writers, including Richard Barnfield, Bartholomew Griffin, and Christopher Marlowe — a version of his popular lyric 'Come live with me and be my love', to which Shakespeare refers in *The Merry Wives of Windsor* (3.1.16–20 and 22–5). There are also four poems on the theme of Venus and Adonis, one of which appears to have been written by Bartholomew Griffin be-

---

7 James Hutton, 'Analogues of Shakespeare's Sonnets 153–4', *Modern Philology*, 38 (1941), 385–403.

cause it appears in his *Fidessa* (1596). The remaining three are usually dismissed as imitations of Shakespeare rather than as examples of his work. But in a well-argued though neglected article published in 1975, C. H. Hobday[8] revived and reinforced a suggestion by Edmond Malone (1741–1812), later supported by John Masefield (1878–1967) and John Middleton Murry (1889–1957), that Shakespeare wrote the three poems as early sketches for *Venus and Adonis* (published in 1593). Finding this plausible, we place them early in our chronological ordering.

It was not until 1609, long after Shakespeare composed his first sonnets, that his non-dramatic ones appeared in print, as *Shakespeare's Sonnets* 'never before imprinted', clearly advertising itself as a retrospective publication, and with a suggestion that they were eagerly awaited – a bit of a publishing coup. By then the vogue for sonnet sequences had long passed. After the sonnets themselves appeared, 'A Lover's Complaint', a narrative poem of 329 lines which is sometimes read as being thematically connected to the sonnets.[9] The book was published by Thomas Thorpe, a reputable publisher with no other known connection to Shakespeare. Not reprinted until 1640, it had nothing like the success of *Venus and Adonis*, which went through at least ten editions during his lifetime. Nevertheless, Shakespeare's mastery of the sonnet form warranted international comparison by 1613. His friend Leonard Digges (who wrote one of the memorial poems for the First Folio of 1623) remarked that the sonnets of the Spanish playwright Lope de Vega (1562–1635) were thought of in Spain 'as in England we should our William Shakespeare'.[10]

---

8 C. H. Hobday, 'Shakespeare's *Venus and Adonis* Sonnets', in *Shakespeare Survey 26*, ed. Kenneth Muir (Cambridge: Cambridge University Press, 1973), 103–9.

9 John Kerrigan was influential in discerning a significant literary relationship between the Sonnets and 'A Lover's Complaint' in his edition: *The Sonnets and A Lover's Complaint*, The Penguin Shakespeare (Harmondsworth: Penguin, 1986), pp. 13–18. Shakespeare's authorship of 'A Lover's Complaint' has been disputed.

10 Paul Morgan, 'Our Will Shakespeare and Lope de Vega: An Unrecorded Contemporary Document', in *Shakespeare Survey 16*, ed. Allardyce Nicoll (Cambridge: Cambridge University Press, 1963), 118–20 (p. 118).

Writing Sonnets in the Plays

Abraham Slender is not the only character in a Shakespeare play to wish he could write a sonnet. In what is probably Shakespeare's first single-authored play, *The Two Gentlemen of Verona*, written possibly before 1591, when the sonnet vogue began, Proteus, enjoined by the Duke to persuade Silvia to fall in love with the foolish Thurio, advises Thurio to

> lay lime to tangle her desires
> By wailful sonnets, whose composèd rhymes
> Should be full-fraught with serviceable vows.
>
> (3.2.68–70)

The Duke agrees that this might help: 'much is the force of heaven-bred poesy'; and Proteus provides Thurio with a template for the content of a conventional love sonnet along with an account of the frame of mind that will be conducive to its composition:

> Say that upon the altar of her beauty
> You sacrifice your tears, your sighs, your heart.
> Write till your ink be dry, and with your tears
> Moist it again, and frame some feeling line
> That may discover such integrity.
> For Orpheus' lute was strung with poets' sinews,
> Whose golden touch could soften steel and stones,
> Make tigers tame, and huge leviathans
> Forsake unsounded deeps to dance on sands.
>
> (3.2.72–80)

The implication is that the writer must personally feel the emotion that he wishes to express in verse. Thurio agrees that this is good advice, and, saying 'I have a sonnet that will serve the turn', says he will go off to seek out 'some gentlemen well skilled in music' to accompany him. (This may suggest that he is thinking of a 'sonnet' in the sense of a love lyric to be set to music.) When, however, Proteus serenades Silvia it is on his own behalf, not Thurio's, and the words of his song, 'Who is Silvia?', do not fall into conventional sonnet form.

Fascinatingly, we also have a little-known scene in which Shake-speare actually shows someone trying — but failing — to write a love sonnet. This comes in a joint-authored play, *Edward III*, composed some time between 1588 and 1594. The play has only come to be included in mainstream editions of Shakespeare's works since Giorgio Melchiori's Cambridge University Press edition of 1998, and the identity of its other author or authors is unknown, but the sonnet-writing scene is now recognised as being by Shakespeare.

In it, King Edward III (who is married) falls madly in love while on a Scottish campaign with the virtuous (and also married) Countess of Salisbury as soon as he sees her, and before long is so visibly besotted that his servant Lodowick says

> Then Scottish wars, farewell. I fear, 'twill prove
> A ling'ring English siege of peevish love.

> (2.188–9)

Seeking to seduce the Countess, Edward calls for Lodowick, who he says is 'well read in poetry' (a phrase that also occurs in *The Taming of the Shrew*, 1.2.168), instructing him to bring pen, ink, and paper and to make sure that they can 'walk and meditate alone'. Privacy, it seems, is desirable for poetic composition. The King, lacking confidence in his poetical powers, says he will 'acquaint' Lodowick 'with' his 'passion, / Which he shall shadow with a veil of lawn' — a fanciful way of saying 'turn into verse' — 'Through which the queen of beauty's queen shall see / Herself the ground of my infirmity' (2.221–4). He retires with Lodowick to a 'summer arbour', then instructs him to

> invoke some golden muse
> To bring thee hither an enchanted pen
> That may for sighs set down true sighs indeed,
> Talking of grief, to make thee ready groan,
> And when thou writ'st of tears, encouch the word
> Before and after with such sweet laments
> That it may raise drops in a Tartar's eye,
> And make a flint-heart Scythian pitiful —
> For so much moving hath a poet's pen.

> (2.231–9)

(This is interestingly analogous to lines spoken by Biron in *Love's Labour's Lost*:

> Never durst poet touch a pen to write
> Until his ink were tempered with love's sighs;
> O, then his lines would ravish savage ears,
> And plant in tyrants mild humility.
>
> (4.3.322–5))

King Edward praises the Countess in extravagant, even comically hyperbolical terms, instructing Lodowick to call her 'Better than beautiful' (2.250), to 'Devise for fair a better word than fair' (2.251), saying that anything Lodowick may write is exceeded 'Ten times ten thousand more' by the value of the woman he is praising (2.256). Faced with such hyperbole, Lodowick bemusedly enquires 'Write I to a woman?', to which the King replies in exasperation 'What think'st thou I did bid thee praise? A horse?' (2.264).

Poor Lodowick says he needs more information about the woman's 'condition or state' before he can do as the King wishes, and the King embarks upon a further extended encomium of his beloved's beauty and virtue. The hapless servant gets no further with his sonnet than 'More fair and chaste than is the queen of shades' (2.307) – presumably referring to Diana, goddess of the moon and of chastity – before the King stops him, objecting both to the comparison with the moon and to praise of the Countess as chaste – common in Petrarchan love poetry – whereas he (rather crudely) says he 'had rather have her chased than chaste' (2.320). Then, in seeking to give Lodowick a sense of the kind of sonnet he wants him to write, he rhapsodises at length about the Countess, and, while so doing, speaks a foreshortened sonnet, eleven lines long (see p. 54). At last, the King permits Lodowick to start the second line of his suspended sonnet, 'More bold in constancy' (2.335), before interrupting him again – he does not wish her to be 'constant' to her husband – and finally saying he will take over the composition of the sonnet himself. He is interrupted, however, by the entrance of the Countess and pretends that he and his servant have been drawing up battle plans.

Later in this (very wordy) scene, the King declares his love to the Countess, she repudiates it, and he seeks in vain to get her father, the Earl of Warwick, to persuade her to yield herself to him. Warwick's final speech, during which he commends the Countess for her virtue, is made up of a series of aphorisms including one – 'Lilies that fester smell far worse than weeds' (2.619) – that also forms the final line of Sonnet 94. This is the only occasion on which a full line from one of Shakespeare's sonnets is duplicated in one of his plays. Though it sounds proverbial, it has not been found elsewhere. In addition to this line, Sonnet 94 includes other phrases from this scene (at lines 1, 12), as also do Sonnets 95 (line 2) and 142 (line 6).[11] The phrases are identified in the notes of this volume.

This episode of *Edward III* is based on a tale in the popular anthology of short stories known as *Painter's Palace of Pleasure*, by William Painter (1540?–94), first published in 1566–7 and revised and expanded to include over 100 stories in 1575. In Painter, as in *Edward III*, the King gets his secretary to woo the Countess on his behalf, but not by addressing a sonnet to her.

The most heavily sonnet-laden of all Shakespeare's plays is *Love's Labour's Lost*, written we believe around 1594–5, at the height of the fashion for sonnet writing. The climax of the play comes in the great scene in which one by one the King and his three friends are seen and overheard reading sonnets that they have composed which are addressed to the Princess and her ladies-in-waiting with whom they have fallen in love. As the scene opens we see Biron '*with a paper in his hand*', initially trying to resist the thought that he may be in love: 'I will not love. If I do, hang me' (4.3.7–8). But as he imagines Rosaline he capitulates: 'O, but her eye! By this light, but for her eye I would not love her. Yes, for her two eyes. Well, I do nothing i' the world but lie, and lie in my throat. By heaven, I do love, and it hath taught me to rhyme and to be melancholy' (4.3.8–12). He goes on: 'Well, she hath one of my sonnets already. The clown bore it, the fool sent it, and the lady hath it.' (4.1.14–15). He is speaking of the 'sealed-up counsel',

11 Giorgio Melchiori, *Shakespeare's Dramatic Meditations* (Oxford: Clarendon Press, 1976).

which we have not yet heard, and that he has asked the clown Costard to deliver to Rosaline (3.1.164). Now, with mischievous malice, he hopes that his fellows, too, are in love. He stands aside to see what will happen. Sure enough, the King '*entereth with a paper*' (4.3.19.1) and, thinking he is alone, reads aloud a sonnet that he has composed to the Princess. And he drops the paper in the expectation that she will find it. He too steps aside, unaware of Biron's presence, and Longueville comes forward, also with a paper. The King and Biron independently exult in the thought that Cupid has another victim. Longueville reads aloud the sonnet that he has addressed to Maria, and also 'steps aside'. Within seconds Dumaine, too, enters 'with a paper', and Biron gloatingly anticipates what is to happen:

> All hid, all hid — an old infant play.
> Like a demigod here sit I in the sky,
> And wretched fools' secrets heedfully o'er-eye.

> (4.3.75–7)

Dumaine reads aloud what he calls 'the ode that I have writ' (4.3.97). Here, however, Shakespeare provides variety by casting Dumaine's poem not into conventional sonnet form (though the stage direction calls it a sonnet) but into trochaic tetrameter couplets (lines of eight syllables with the stress on the first, third, fifth, and seventh syllables) beginning:

> On a day — alack the day —
> Love, whose month is ever May
> Spied a blossom passing fair
> Playing in the wanton air.

> (4.3.99–102)

With the lovers all independently concealed over the stage, and each unaware of the other's presence, the King comes forward, hypocritically mocking the men for the composition of their 'guilty rhymes' and joyfully anticipating how Biron will gloat over their folly. But now Biron steps forward, as he says 'to whip hypocrisy', while himself hypocritically boasting of his own constancy, but of course paving the way for the revelation that he too has broken his vows. It is a virtuoso piece of dramatic craftsmanship.

It is perhaps indicative of Shakespeare's concern in each of his plays to match the form to the content that in *Richard II*, believed to have been written straight after *Love's Labour's Lost*, and composed entirely in verse,[12] he makes no use of the sonnet form, though the highly stylised dialogue includes an exceptional number of rhymed couplets. Two passages of verse in the form of a sestet occur in *King John* (1.1.170–5 and 2.1.505–11), both of them spoken by the Bastard; and in both of them the verse form serves as a means of indicating thoughts that are private rather than public, as kinds of soliloquies. We do not include these.

The composition of a love sonnet is more light-heartedly referred to in two other plays. In *Much Ado About Nothing* (written mainly in prose), after Benedick has jokingly asked Margaret to help him pay his addresses to Beatrice, she teasingly asks 'Will you then write me a sonnet in praise of my beauty?' (5.2.3–4); he agrees to do so 'in so high a style that no man living shall come over it'.

In the same play comes the solemn scene in which Claudio hangs on the supposed tomb of Hero an epitaph which opens with the words 'Done to death by slanderous tongues' (5.3.3), and which has the rhyme scheme of a sonnet sestet (though it is written in trochaic tetrameters, not the usual iambic pentameters), and which is followed by an additional couplet. Following this, Don Pedro bids the mourners farewell in lines ('Good morrow, masters ...') that have the form of a quatrain, and the scene ends with another quatrain:

DON PEDRO
Come, let us hence, and put on other weeds,
   And then to Leonato's we will go.

CLAUDIO
And Hymen now with luckier issue speed's
Than this for whom we rendered up this woe.

                           (5.3.30–3).

And in the play's final scene, after Beatrice and Benedick have declared their love for each other but are still jokingly denying it in

---

12 *Richard II* shares this status with *King John*.

public, Claudio produces what he claims to be 'A halting sonnet of his [Benedick's] own pure brain / Fashioned to Beatrice', and Hero produces another 'Writ in my cousin's hand, stol'n from her pocket, / Containing her affection unto Benedick' (5.4.89–90).

The writing of sonnets becomes a matter of jest again – but this time a different kind of jest – in *Henry V*, when, on the eve of battle, the leaders of the French army nervously await the break of day. The absurdity of addressing a sonnet to a horse had been mentioned in *Edward III*. Now, praising his horse in extravagant terms, Bourbon says 'I once writ a sonnet in his praise, and it began thus: "Wonder of nature! –"' (*Henry V*, 3.7.40), to which Orléans deflatingly responds: 'I have heard a sonnet begin so to one's mistress' (3.7.41). 'Then did they imitate that which I composed to my horse, for my horse is my mistress', says Bourbon (3.7.42–3). This leads into bawdy wordplay sustaining the comparison between the horse and a woman with allusions to bestiality. Shakespeare himself did not, of course, address a sonnet to his horse, but he does declare that the love his beloved feels for him is 'of more delight than hawks or horses be' (Sonnet 91, line 11).

The Originality of *Shakespeare's Sonnets: Never before Imprinted* (1609)

The year 1591 saw the beginning of a sudden vogue for the composition and publication of sequences of interrelated sonnets, initiated by the posthumous publication in that year of Sir Philip Sidney's *Astrophil and Stella*. At least nineteen such collections appeared between then and 1597, when the vogue faded out, and it is likely that Shakespeare wrote most of his non-dramatic sonnets during this period. But they did not appear in print during these years, nor do they hang together in the manner of the published sonnet cycles by other writers. Though there was no obvious outlet (such as the literary magazines of later periods) for the publication of individual poems, Shakespeare, it seems, was initially writing sonnets either out of a self-generated creative impulse, or from a desire to communicate privately in poetic form, or to commission. The titles of the sonnet sequences of the 1590s often included the idealised name of a (sometimes identifiable) female loved one: Sir Philip Sidney's *Astrophil and Stella* in 1591, Samuel Daniel's *Delia* (1592), Thomas Lodge's *Phillis* (1593), Henry Constable's *Diana* (1594), William Percy's *Sonnets to Celia* (1594), Richard Barnfield's *Cynthia* (1595), Bartholomew Griffin's *Fidessa* (1596), William Smith's *Chloris* (1596), and Robert Tofte's *Laura* (1597). Barnfield, much influenced by Christopher Marlowe's homoeroticism, was original during this period in also writing sonnets addressed to an idealised male subject in *An Affectionate Shepherd to His Love* (1594).

In the first sonnet of *Astrophil and Stella* (1591), Sir Philip Sidney famously instructed writers of poetry to 'look in thy heart and write'. But the sonneteers who followed him do not seem readily to have taken up his advice. The sequences published in the 1590s are heavily indebted to European models, which Shakespeare's sonnets are not. Those making up Giles Fletcher's sequence *Licia* (1593), described on the title page as being 'poems in honour of the admirable and single virtues of his lady', demonstrate themselves to be literary exercises after Latin examples. In contrast, *Shakespeare's Sonnets* does not present a classical idealisation of love; it is not derivative of previously published sequences. Rather, it is as if he benefitted from and absorbed the other sonnet writers' work, and then made the form a vehicle for a much more unsettling and original expression of his feelings and thoughts. The number of sonnets in *Shakespeare's Sonnets* exceeds that of even the longest contemporary collection by about 50 per cent (Sidney comes second with 108 sonnets).

Whilst *Shakespeare's Sonnets* intermittently reflects his reading of classical literature, by drawing occasionally on Ovid's *Metamorphoses* (for example Sonnets 60, 63, and 114), Horace's *Odes* (for example Sonnet 55), and translating Marianus Scholasticus (Sonnets 153 and 154), it is, on the whole, a collection of often highly personally inflected poems written over at least twenty-seven years, rather than a sequence aimed at catching the mood and developing the taste for a literary fashion. His sonnets are not public poems written and published for money (like his two narrative poems, *Venus and Adonis*, 1593 and *The Rape of Lucrece*, 1594, much reprinted in Shakespeare's lifetime); they were published a decade after the vogue for sonnets had passed, printed only once, and were 'clearly a flop on their first appearance'.[13] He seems interested primarily in using the sonnet form to work out his intimate thoughts and feelings.

As a result, his collection is the most idiosyncratic gathering of sonnets in the period and includes, for example, the frankest of all sonnets about sex. Shakespeare writes vividly about the feelings and effects of lust in Sonnet 129; Sonnets 135 and 136 (with their vibrant and obsessive punning on his own name, 'Will', a polyvalent word with connotations of the male and female sexual organs, and sexual passion in general) read like witty, masturbatory fantasies – private poems which seem surprised to find themselves in the public domain; and Sonnet 151, in part describing the effects of male tumescence and detumescence, ends with a couplet that, surreally, could be spoken by his own penis:

> No want of conscience hold it that I call
> Her love 'love', for whose dear love I rise and fall.
>
> (lines 13–14)

Shakespeare's Sonnets have acquired a romantic reputation. But these are not poems for Valentine's Day, still less are they – with the exception of a handful – poems for loved ones to read to each other. Whilst the collection includes some of the most powerfully lyrical, resonant, and memorable poems ever written about what it feels like to experience romantic love (such as Sonnets 18, 29, and 116), most of *Shakespeare's Sonnets* set forth many other moods and kinds of love, including its tough edges, insecurities, doubts, and negative obsessions. They address many topics, experiences, and emotions, including restlessness and sleeplessness (43); sleepless jeal-

---

13 Stanley Wells, *Looking for Sex in Shakespeare* (Cambridge: Cambridge University Press, 2004), p. 49.

ousy (61); painful self-abasement (49); the feelings of lust (129); sin and confession (62); the memories of a loved one (122); the power of poetry (54); the immortalisation of the loved one in poetry (55); the endless fascination of a loved one (53); the trials of separation (56); the failure of poetry to praise the loved one (106); the testing of a loved one (117); being blamed for love (121); unconventional beauty (127); the lies lived out in a relationship (138); the state of the soul (146). This is only a selection of some of the concerns and feelings Shakespeare chose to write about, and most of these themes can be applied to more than one sonnet in the collection.

Whilst it is generally agreed that the order in which the sonnets were first printed in 1609 is not the order in which Shakespeare wrote them, it does (as we have shown in Table 1) demonstrate a highly ordering mind at work. Part of the originality of *Shakespeare's Sonnets* lies in the fact that it is not a sequence; it is a collection, or an anthology. But it contains within it mini-sequences and pairs of sonnets which are revealing of what Shakespeare wanted to write about. We do not know who was responsible for the 1609 order, but since whoever it was knew the poems well, we have no objection to believing it was Shakespeare himself. In Table 1 we set out the nineteen pairs and fourteen mini-sequences covering 100 out of the 154 poems within *Shakespeare's Sonnets*. The themes listed in the table augment the ones named in the preceding paragraph and illustrate further the range of subjects covered.

We do not know whether Shakespeare himself authorised their publication.[14] He is curiously referred to in the third person on the title page: *Shakespeare's Sonnets: Never before Imprinted* (as opposed to, for example, '*Sonnets*, by William Shakespeare'). The wording suggests that the publisher takes pride in announcing a coup in making

---

14 Katherine Duncan-Jones suggests that the 1609 quarto was published with Shakespeare's permission: 'Was the 1609 *Shake-speares Sonnets* Really Unauthorized?', *Review of English Studies*, 34 (1983), 151–71. She also conjectures that Shakespeare was not in London when it was being printed, hence Thomas Thorpe himself providing the dedication: *Shakespeare's Sonnets*, The Arden Shakespeare (London: Bloomsbury, 1997; rev. 2010), pp. 10–11.

Table 1: Nineteen Pairs and Fourteen Mini-Sequences (covering 100 sonnets in all) in *Shakespeare's Sonnets*

Nos. in Q (chronological order)	Thematic or content linkage	Pair linked syntactically by first word(s) of succeeding sonnet
Pair: 133 and 134	Triangular relationship	'So'
Pair: 135 and 136	Play on poet's name, 'Will'. N.B. 22, 57, 89, 134, and 143 also play on 'Will'	'If'
139, 140, 141, 142	Power of a loved one's eyes	
Pair: 141 and 142	Love and sin	'Love is my sin'
Pair: 149 and 150	Power of a loved one	'O from what power'
Pair: 64 and 65	Time	'Since'
Pair: 67 and 68	Male beauty	'Thus'
Pair: 69 and 70	Blamed for being beautiful	'That thou art'
Pair: 71 and 72	Forgetting poet after his death	'O, lest'
Pair: 73 and 74	Mortality and poetry	'But'
Pair: 89 and 90	A loved one leaving	'Then'
91, 92, 93	Loyalty	'But'; 'So'
97, 98, 99	Absence	
100, 101, 102, 103	Poetic Muse and poetry	
1–17	Procreation	
Pair: 5 and 6	Procreation	'Then'
Pair: 9 and 10	Procreation	'For shame'
Pair: 15 and 16	Procreation	'But'
Pair: 20 and 21	Love and appearances	'So'
Pair: 27 and 28	Sleeplessness	'How can I then'
30 and 31	Grief and memory	
33, 34, 35, and 36	Mistakes in love	

Continued over

Table 1: *cont'd*

Nos. in Q (chronological order)	Thematic or content linkage	Pair linked syntactically by first word(s) of succeeding sonnet
40, 41, 42	A man takes away the poet's female loved one	
Pair: 44 and 45	The four elements	'The other two'
46 and 47	Eyes and heart	
Pair: 50 and 51	On horseback	'Thus'
57 and 58	Slavery in love	
78–86	Other poets writing about the loved one	
Pair: 80 and 81	An unidentifiable poet	'Or'
82 and 83	Being truer than other poets	
109, 110, 111, 112	Temporary absences and distractions	
Pair: 113 and 114	Imagination and eyesight	'Or'
118, 119, 120	Sickness in love	

This table demonstrates how Shakespeare often wrote syntactically related, double sonnets (a 'pair'), or wrote sequels to existing ones, thereby either making a double sonnet, or forming a short sequence of two or more sonnets.

available poems that everyone knew about, but few had been able to read. It is equally curious that the printer's initials, 'T.T.' (Thomas Thorpe), rather than those of the author, should appear below the dedication: 'Mr W.H.': 'To the only begetter of these ensuing sonnets Mr W.H. all happiness and that eternity promised by our ever-living poet wisheth the well-wishing adventurer in setting forth. T.T.'[15] 'Mr W.H.' is the dedicatee of the printer ('the well-wishing adventurer'), not Shakespeare. 'Mr W.H.' may then have been the

---

15 Images of the 1609 quarto's dedication are easily viewable on-line. Search for 'Shakespeare's Sonnets dedication' in Google, and click 'images'.

procurer ('begetter') of the manuscript (the person who supplied Thorpe with the poems), which was obtained by unknown means.[16]

What kind of manuscript, and in what state? It has been plausibly suggested, based in part on spelling variations within the collection, that the manuscript submitted to the printer was the work of two scribes. Transcribing an author's manuscript for the press was a standard practice, an equivalent perhaps of our modern-day copy-editing. Had Shakespeare written individual sonnets on loose, shufflable leaves of paper which were later bound together in some way, or did he write them up into a notebook?

Interestingly – and importantly – the chronological re-ordering has not disrupted any of the pairs or mini-sequences of sonnets as collated in Table 1. Some of these sonnets are syntactically related, for example by connecting keywords which provide a sequel to the sonnet immediately before. Sometimes short sequences of interrelated sonnets are linked by theme. Thirty-six of the sonnets form part of a syntactically linked pair, which suggests Shakespeare liked writing sequels (or afterthoughts) to a sonnet, or writing what we can understand to be a double sonnet. Indeed, some of his most famous sonnets form part of a syntactically linked pair. For example, 'A woman's face with nature's own hand painted' (Sonnet 20) is followed by 'So is it not with me as with that muse' (Sonnet 21), which continues to consider the appearance of the loved one – but now in relationship to how poetry itself might convey that truth. 'That time of year thou mayst in me behold' (Sonnet 73) is followed by its far lesser-known sequel, 'But be contented when that fell arrest' (Sonnet 74). Similarly, the sonnet which begins 'Some glory in their birth, some in their skill' (Sonnet 91) is the first of three syntactically related sonnets, a mini-sequence. These pairs and groups of linked sonnets not only remain together after the chronological re-ordering but seem more prominent and compelling because of it.

---

16 Geoffrey Caveney has suggested that Mr W. H. was William Holme, a stationer, who like Thomas Thorpe had links with Chester. Holme died in 1607, which may help to explain why the dedication is laid out like a funerary inscription: '"Mr W.H.": Stationer William Holme (d. 1607)', *Notes and Queries*, 260, 1 (March 2015), 120–4.

Setting Forth Shakespeare's Sonnets

Some of the 1609 sonnets are found in manuscript collections from around 1620 onwards,[17] but the collection was not reprinted until 1640 when John Benson published most of its contents as part of *Poems: Written by Wil. Shake-speare, Gent.* (which also includes other pieces by Shakespeare and his contemporaries from the augmented 1612 edition of *The Passionate Pilgrim*). Benson gave seventy-five of the sonnets titles (thereby hinting at narratives) and combined some of them to make longer poems. So, for example, Sonnets 1, 2, and 3 are combined to form 'Loves crueltie'; Sonnets 33, 34, and 35 form 'Loves Releese'; and Sonnets 107 and 108 form 'A monument to Fame' (in which Sonnet 108's 'sweet boy' is replaced by 'sweet-love'). Benson changed some of the masculine pronouns to feminine in Sonnet 101 and changed Sonnet 104's 'friend' to 'fair love'.[18] Though Benson's edition is often maligned – and has been defended – it remains significant because it represents the first, major critical response to *Shakespeare's Sonnets* (a biographical as well as a literary one), and because of its influence on subsequent editions for more than a century. Charles Gildon prepared a volume of Shakespeare's poems based on Benson as a supplement to Nicholas Rowe's 1709 edition of the plays.

Benson's 1640 edition was reprinted with additions several times between 1710 and 1775, and the 1609 collection appeared in Bernard Lintott's *A Collection of Poems* (1711),[19] in George Steevens's *Twenty Plays of Shakespeare* (1766),[20] and, in 1780, George Steevens's and Edmond

---

17 Jane Kingsley-Smith collates, demonstrates, and discusses the limited, immediate influence of Shakespeare's sonnets from 1598 to 1622, and cites Arthur F. Marotti's observation that 'only eleven whole [Shakespeare] sonnets in twenty different manuscripts' have so far been identified across sixteenth- and seventeenth-century manuscripts. See Jane Kingsley-Smith, *The Afterlife of Shakespeare's Sonnets* (Cambridge: Cambridge University Press, 2019), pp. 40–2, and Arthur F. Marotti, 'Shakespeare's Sonnets and the Manuscript Circulation of Texts in Early Modern England', in *A Companion to Shakespeare's Sonnets*, ed. Michael Schoenfeldt (Oxford: Blackwell, 2007), 185–203 (p. 186).

18 Margreta de Grazia, 'The Scandal of Shakespeare's Sonnets', in *Shakespeare Survey 46*, ed. Stanley Wells (Cambridge: Cambridge University Press, 1994), 35–49 (pp. 35–6).

19 Kingsley-Smith, *The Afterlife of Shakespeare's Sonnets*, p. 103.

20 Kingsley-Smith, *The Afterlife of Shakespeare's Sonnets*, p. 106.

Malone's supplement to Samuel Johnson's and Steevens's 1778 edition of the Complete Works. Malone printed the 1609 text again in 1790 (with more commentary). His text and commentary formed the basis of the first American edition of the Sonnets (1796) and remained little altered until the 1864 edition from Cambridge University Press. Malone, in bringing fresh scholarly attention to *Shakespeare's Sonnets*, began an emphatically biographical way of reading them (he was working on his own – never completed – Shakespearian biography at the time). But, as Margreta de Grazia has shown, Malone's relationship with the Sonnets is complex and anxious: 'his first step was to restrict the Sonnets to two addressees'.[21] He refers to the male addressee as 'this person', and to the female as 'a lady': 'to this person, whoever he was, one hundred and twenty-six of the following poems are addressed; the remaining twenty-eight are addressed to a lady'.[22] Malone's critical and biographical anxiety about *Shakespeare's Sonnets* (1609) is residually present in many readings of them. In 1996, Heather Dubrow, considering the state of Sonnet criticism, observed that while critics might differ on many points of interpretation, they are 'nevertheless likely to agree that the direction of these poems can be established with certainty: the first 126 sonnets refer to and are generally addressed to the Friend, while the succeeding ones concern the Dark Lady'.[23] Dubrow's observation (which deliberately resembles Malone's from 1790 in order to show how little approaches to the Sonnets have changed) still applies to many current critics and readers but is not a position shared by the co-editors of this volume. Our chronological approach no longer makes so simplistic a division of these poems possible.

Malone's influence has indeed been extensive, and over the last 250 years much ink has been spilt trying to convince us of the identities of real-life counterparts believed to exist in *Shakespeare's*

---

21 de Grazia, 'The Scandal of Shakespeare's Sonnets', p. 37.

22 *The Plays and Poems of William Shakespeare*, ed. Edmond Malone, 20 vols. (London: H. Baldwin, 1790), vol. XX, p. 191.

23 Heather Dubrow, '"Incertainties now crown themselves assur'd": The Politics of Shakespeare's Sonnets', *Shakespeare Quarterly*, 47 (1996), 291–305 (p. 291).

Sonnets. Colin Burrow considers this kind of biographical specu-
lation 'critically naïve' and mistaken in its tendency to relate *Shakespeare's Sonnets* to Shakespeare's life. It is partly because the poems
give the impression of being autobiographical in their 'modes of
address' that readers seek 'to marry these rhetorical features' to
Shakespeare's life story: 'once that marriage had occurred it was one
to which it was hard to admit impediments'.[24] These biographical
assumptions prevail not only in readings of *Shakespeare's Sonnets* but
also in some Shakespearian biographies, which continue to apply
readings of the sonnets to Shakespeare's life story. This kind of
biographical approach is simplistic and overrides the nuances and
complexities of some of the greatest poems ever written in English. Although from the 1980s sonnet criticism has demonstrated,
in the words of David Schalkwyk, a 'revulsion against biography',[25] the old critical and biographical memes (from Malone)
still remain. They are present whenever a critic refers to 'the first
126 sonnets' addressed to 'the Young Man' or 'Fair Youth', to 'the
Rival Poet' (in reference to Sonnets 78–86), and 'the Dark Lady'
(often in reference to Sonnets 127–54). It is time for readings and
studies of the Sonnets to leave behind these biographical tropes.
In contrast, our chronological approach enhances understanding
of Shakespeare as a developing writer of sonnets and challenges
the biographical assumptions and expectations that we as readers
might take with us. A chronological ordering frustrates attempts
to assume and impose a biographical narrative by (we hope) defa-
miliarising the poems and presenting them afresh.

Establishing chronologies is one outcome of our wanting to
understand as much as possible about Shakespeare's progression
and development as a writer. Chronologies of Shakespeare's works

24 Colin Burrow, 'Shakespeare's Sonnets as Event', in *The Sonnets: The State of Play*, ed.
Hannah Crawford, Elizabeth Scott-Baumann, and Clare Whitehead, The Arden
Shakespeare (London: Bloomsbury, 2017), 97–116 (pp. 100–1).
25 David Schalkwyk, '"She never told her love": Embodiment, Textuality, and Silence
in Shakespeare's Sonnets and Plays', *Shakespeare Quarterly*, 45 (1994), 381–407 (p.
398).

are difficult. Some of the plays can be dated confidently, others less so. This edition uses the scholarship which helped to construct the chronology of Shakespeare's plays and poems in *The New Oxford Shakespeare* (2016). Its methodology relies largely on study of the development of Shakespeare's vocabulary and his grammatical preferences in the sequence of his works (in so far as this can be established). It is, for instance, noticeable that Sonnet 73 includes the word 'sunset' which occurs elsewhere in the canon only in *Henry VI Part Three*, *Romeo and Juliet*, and *King John*: a sonnet published in 1609 was almost certainly written in the early to mid-1590s. Shakespeare's grammatical preferences can be helpful, too. He uses '-eth' rather than the '-es' verb ending much more regularly in plays usually dated before 1600. Work based on criteria such as these demonstrates that textual chronologies of this kind are always theories, hypotheses, and will no doubt continue to be tested and to evolve.

MacDonald P. Jackson has worked significantly on the dating of the Sonnets in the 1609 collection, showing that they seem to have been written over twenty-seven years, from 1582 to 1609. Based on the datability of some of them, the collection can be broken up into segments of chronological composition:

Sonne 1–60	Range: 1595–7 (probably revised 1600–9).
Sonnets 61–77	Range: 1593–1604; best guess 1594–5.
Sonnets 78–86	Range: 1596–1604; best guess 1598–1600.
Sonnets 87–103	Range: 1593–1604; best guess 1594–5.
Sonnets 104–26	Range: 1600–9; best guess 1600–4.
Sonnets 127–44, 146–54	Range: 1590–5.
Sonnet 145	1582?[26]

---

26 From Gary Taylor and Rory Loughnane, 'The Canon and Chronology of Shakespeare's Works', in *The New Oxford Shakespeare: Authorship Companion*, ed. Gary Taylor and Gabriel Egan (Oxford: Oxford University Press, 2017), 417–602 (p. 575).

Jackson is keen to qualify that the reality of when Shakespeare wrote particular sonnets or even stretches of sonnets is not as tidy as the above listing suggests. Shakespeare could have been revising any of the sonnets up until their publication in 1609.[27] These dated segments should not therefore be taken as clear-cut; they all contain poems which might be earlier or later than the identification of the segment suggests. But they do represent particular concentrations of rare and key words which are datable within our growing understanding of Shakespeare's wider artistic output. We anticipate this hypothesis will continue to evolve as the scholarship which attempts to date Shakespeare's linguistic practices becomes even more sophisticated. The current hypothesis posits that, of the 154 sonnets published in 1609, those that appear later in the collection (from Sonnet 127) are among the earliest composed; that the sonnets printed at the beginning of the collection (Sonnets 1–60) were composed at least five years later; and that Sonnets 104 to 126 are among the last that Shakespeare wrote. We cannot be certain when Shakespeare started to write sonnets. As we have shown (see pp. 4–6), our own ordering starts with the Oxford chronology but places Sonnets 154, 153, and 145 at the beginning because of the likelihood that they are the product of a young Shakespeare.

When the sonnets from the plays are added at their appropriate moments, Shakespeare emerges as a writer of sonnets from some time before 1582 up to 1613. A chronological ordering seeks to honour Shakespeare's bursts of creativity; his development as an artist, his skill in his use of the form for different purposes, his employment of it across different genres, and his engagement with the sonnet as a private, personal, intimate form of verse, and as one which could be heard in the public theatres. If he was writing sonnets over an almost thirty-year period, then we might imagine that

27 Other poets also revised their work. Michael Drayton reworked and augmented his sonnet sequence *Idea* (1594) over twenty-five years and published it as *Idea's Mirror* in 1619.

the Shakespeare of, say, 1613 was different from the Shakespeare of 1582. The chronological approach invites us to ask many questions, not least what kinds of personal and artistic development can we deduce across these poems, and how might the sonnets themselves relate to their implied historical context?

'Among His Private Friends'

Though many of Shakespeare's sonnets stand alone as personal utterances, others appear to be addressed to, or to concern, always unnamed individuals. Who were they? The first mention of Shakespeare as a writer of sonnets comes in Francis Meres's literary handbook *Palladis Tamia, or Wit's Treasury*, of 1598, where Meres writes of Shakespeare's 'sugared sonnets among his private friends'. This could refer to any number of sonnets, individually or collectively. The phrase 'sugared sonnets' had been used four years previously, by Richard Barnfield in his *The Affectionate Shepherd*, a collection of poems with strong Marlovian associations. Many of Barnfield's poems are unashamedly homoerotic, and it is conceivable that this is implied in Meres's epithet 'sugared' used along with 'private', meaning 'intimate'. It was common for poems to circulate in manuscript to a select readership. Sadly, Meres does not tell us who Shakespeare's 'private friends' were. In the same breath, he compares Shakespeare to 'honey-tongued' Ovid (because of his two narrative poems *Venus and Adonis* and *The Rape of Lucrece*, based on Ovidian sources). Meres's comments are the meeting place of a private and public Shakespeare: intimate (with his 'private' sonnets), rhetorical and self-consciously literary in his re-workings of Ovid. We do not know if any of those sonnets 'among his private friends' survived to be published in *Shakespeare's Sonnets*; perhaps some or all of them did. In any case, none of Shakespeare's 'private friends' are identifiable by the sonnets addressed to them.

But 121 of the sonnets do involve people, real, or (and remember these poems are from the quill of an expert dramatist) imaginary (see Table 2). There are a 'Lord of my love' (Sonnet 26, line 1); a male addressed as 'thy' described as being in his 'straying youth'

(Sonnet 41, line 10); a male addressed as 'you' who is a 'lovely youth' (Sonnet 54, line 13); a youthful male beauty described in the third person (Sonnet 63); a 'sweet boy' (sonnet 108, line 5); and a 'lovely boy' (Sonnet 126, line 1). Similarly, the terms by which we might seek to identify an addressee's gender are unstable and fluid. There is the female-appearing male 'master-mistress' (Sonnet 20, line 2); Sonnet 96 uses language evocative of both genders to describe the addressee who seems male because of Shakespeare's use of 'youth', 'wantonness', 'wolf', 'strength', and 'state' but has fingers like a 'queen' and, like a femme fatale, leads 'gazers [...] away'; Sonnet 97 compares its addressee's absence to 'widows' wombs' in a world of 'abundant issue'.

This volume consistently identifies the sex of a sonnet's address-ee, in part to draw attention to the different directions and kinds of love and desire in *Shakespeare's Sonnets*. Sometimes this can be con-fidently decided because of Shakespeare's use of personal pronouns ('he', 'she', 'him', or 'her'); sometimes it is less straightforward. Son-nets 1–17 form a discrete sequence of poems addressed to a male whom the poet is urging to beget children. Although the sex of the addressee is not revealed through the use of personal pronouns in all of these seventeen sonnets, their being addressed to a male is discernible through the kinds of language Shakespeare uses, for example, in Sonnet 13, the language of husbandry and fatherhood. Although Sonnet 5 is a meditation and does not mention an ad-dressee, it is syntactically related to its sequel, Sonnet 6, in which the addressee is clearly male. Sonnet 4 lacks personal pronouns and could, if read out of context, be the only one among the first seven-teen sonnets addressed to either a male or a female. Its expression is couched in the language of money, finance, commerce, and bequest, predominantly male-orientated activities in Shakespeare's time, but women transacted business, too, and also wrote wills.

But even when the sex of the addressee is not apparent through the use of personal pronouns, there is little doubt that the first seventeen sonnets, as printed in 1609, are addressed to a male. Shake-speare, writing in an extremely patriarchal culture, would not be trying to persuade a female to procreate. Whether those seventeen

Table 2: The Direction of *Shakespeare's Sonnets*

	Nos. in Q (chronologically ordered against each category)
Translations of a Greek epigram (2).	154, 153
Addressed to a male (14).	1, 3, 9, 10, 13, 15, 16, 20, 26 ('Lord of my love'), 41, 42, 54 ('beauteous and lovely youth'), 108 ('sweet boy'), 126 ('lovely boy')
Likely to be addressed to a male (13)	2, 4, 6, 7, 8, 11, 12, 14, 17, 34, 35, 36, 40
Addressed to a female (7)	135, 136, 139, 141, 142, 143, 151
Likely to be addressed to a female (3)	132, 140, 119
Could be addressed to either a male or a female (84)	128, 131, 133, 134, 147, 149, 152, 61, 62, 69, 70, 71, 72, 73, 74, 75, 76, 77, 87, 88, 89, 90, 91, 92, 93, 95, 96, 97, 98, 99, 102, 103, 18, 22, 24, 27, 28, 29, 30, 31, 32, 37, 38, 39, 43, 44, 45, 46, 47, 48, 49, 50, 51, 52, 53, 55, 56, 57, 58, 59, 78, 79, 80, 81, 82, 83, 84, 85, 86, 104, 106, 107, 109, 110, 111, 112, 113, 114, 115, 117, 118, 120, 122, 125.
Sonnet letters (2)	26 (accompanying a 'written embassage'), 77 (accompanies the gift of an almanack)
To Love (2)	137, 56 (56 could also be addressed to a male or female)
To Time (2)	19, 123
To the Muse (1)	100
To the poet's soul (1)	146
On a woman (3)	145, 127, 130
On a man (3)	63, 67, 68
On a relationship with a female (1)	138
On a relationship with a male (1)	33
On a relationship with a male and a female (1)	144 (see also 40-2 and 133-4)

Continued over

Table 2: *cont'd*

	Nos. in Q (chronologically ordered against each category)
On lust (1)	129
On love and eyesight (1)	148
On time (3)	64, 65, 60
On the world's wrongs (1)	66
On individual power over others (1)	94
On procreation (1)	5 (see also 1-17)
On poetry and truth (1)	21
On the lack of eloquence (1)	23
On the freedom of love (1)	25
On the nature of love (1)	116
On the sickness of love (1)	119
On being judged (1)	121
On the vulnerability of love (1)	124
On love and poetry (1)	105

121 sonnets are addressed to people (84 of which could be addressed to either a male or a female, and 2 of which are sonnet-letters); 6 sonnets are addressed to abstract concepts; 25 are meditations; 2 are translations of the same Greek epigram.

sonnets are all directed towards the same man, or to several men, or to men in general, is a different and unanswerable question. Certainly the intimacy among these sonnets varies. Sonnet 10 with its 'Make thee another self for love of me' (line 13) and Sonnet 13, in which the poet refers to the male addressee as 'dear my love' (line 13), are more intimate than, for example, Sonnets 8, 11, and 12, which read much more like professional acts of persuasion to procreate. In writing them, Shakespeare is in part borrowing terms and images from Desiderius Erasmus's (?1466–1536) 'Epistle to persuade a young man to marriage'.

Sometimes the mini-sequences within *Shakespeare's Sonnets* help us to determine the sex of the addressees. But this, too, is sometimes not straightforward. Sonnets 100 to 103 form a mini-sequence of four sonnets about the poetic muse. The first is addressed to the muse, the second to the muse about a male, the third and fourth are addressed to either a male or a female about the muse and the writing of poetry. The fact that one of those four sonnets is addressed to a male does not necessarily imply that the other three are.

Similarly, although Sonnets 139–42 are linked by the power of the addressee's looks to kill the poet, and by the poet's own sense of sinful loving, in two of the poems the sex of the addressee is not made clear. Sonnets 140 and 142, removed from their immediate mini-sequence, could be addressed to either a man or a woman. But the mini-sequence they form is more closely knit than that formed by Sonnets 100–3, and all four sonnets (139–42) seem to be addressed to a female, and possibly even the same one because of the continuation of dramatic and emotional experience across them.

If sonnets are syntactically rather than thematically related by a keyword indicative of a sequel or serialisation (for example, if a sonnet is followed by one which begins with 'So', 'Or', 'But', or 'Thus'), and if only one of the sonnets in the pair identifies the sex of the addressee, then this identification has been applied in this edition to the accompanying poem as well. When the sex of the addressee is genuinely indeterminate, we make this clear in the accompanying note.

Shakespeare was a master at projecting different tones of voice in the plays, and, whilst sonnet writing is a different genre and practice, readers find there a poetic scope and freedom to accommodate many different kinds of imagined speakers. Whilst *Shakespeare's Sonnets* (unlike the sonnets in the plays) were not written primarily for performance, they are rhetorically shaped and invite us to read them aloud. Presented alongside Shakespeare's dramatic sonnets from the plays, the gender, sex, and indeed sexuality of the poetic voice in *Shakespeare's Sonnets* seems to become much more open, playful, unstable. Whilst we might be likely to imagine the poetic voice as male, many of the sonnets can be convincingly voiced by a female. Sonnet 128, 'How oft, when thou, my music, music play'st', for example, usually read as an address by a man to a woman, may equally be imagined as being spoken by a woman watching her male lover play on a keyboard instrument. The poems themselves demonstrate a fluidity and openness of desire and identity (like the fluid desires depicted in *As You Like It*, or in *Twelfth Night, or What You Will*).

Whilst some critics have focused on reading *Shakespeare's Sonnets* through a gay lens,[28] relatively few have celebrated them as the seminal bisexual text of literature in English. Bisexuality attracts a lot of casual prejudice even in twenty-first-century culture, manifested, for example, by a common assumption that a bisexual person is probably really either gay or lesbian without wanting fully to admit it. When bisexuals look for literature about bisexuality, they often encounter a difficulty not faced by gay and lesbian people. In her bisexual reading of the 1609 sonnets, Marjorie Garber asks 'Why avoid the obvious? *Because* it is obvious? Or because a bisexual Shakespeare fits no one's erotic agenda?'[29] We hope that in consistently identifying the sex of the addressee, and especially by signalling when this cannot be determined, we have played a part in emphasising the bisexual quality of *Shakespeare's Sonnets*. The multiplicity of the Sonnets' sexual identities is matched by their gender fluidity – as dizzying and as complex as that bodied forth in Shakespeare's

---

28 See, for example, material included in Joseph Pequigney, *Such Is My Love: A Study of Shakespeare's Sonnets* (Chicago: University of Chicago Press, 1985); Bruce R. Smith, *Homosexual Desire in Shakespeare's England: A Cultural Poetics* (Chicago: University of Chicago Press, 1991); Jonathan Goldberg, *Sodometries: Renaissance Texts, Modern Sexualities* (Stanford: Stanford University Press, 1992); Stephen Orgel, 'Introduction', in *The Sonnets: Updated Edition*, ed. G. Blakemore Evans (Cambridge: Cambridge University Press, 1996; rev. 2006); Paul Hammond, *Figuring Sex between Men from Shakespeare to Rochester* (Oxford: Oxford University Press, 2002); *Shakesqueer*, ed. Madhavi Menon (Durham and London: Duke University Press, 2011); and *Queer Shakespeare: Desire and Sexuality*, ed. Goran Stanivukovic, The Arden Shakespeare (London: Bloomsbury, 2017).

29 Marjorie Garber, *Vice Versa: Bisexuality and the Eroticism of Everyday Life* (New York: Simon and Schuster, 1995), p. 515.

comedies. How far is the speaker of each poem taking upon him or herself binary, non-binary, or fluid gender portrayals?

An abiding, twentieth-century literary comparison which helps to illustrate and illuminate the complexity of sexuality and gender in *Shakespeare's Sonnets* is Virginia Woolf's playful, lyrical, elegiac *Orlando: A Biography* (1928). The poet Orlando wakes up one morning to discover that he has turned into a woman, and then transcends time from the sixteenth century to the present day, 'For she had a great variety of selves to call upon, far more than we have been able to find room for, since a biography is considered complete if it merely accounts for six or seven selves, whereas a person may well have as many thousands.'[30] The power of *Shakespeare's Sonnets* as poems lies in part within their multi-layered subjectivities. They plunge us into Shakespeare's real self and his imagined selves; his loved ones, friends, and acquaintances, and his talent for dramatic characterisation. If the sonnet is addressed to somebody, we might as we read it start to imagine the person to whom he is writing; or we might choose to turn it into a dramatic speech and bring characterisation to it (perhaps based on one of the plays); or we might read it as though Shakespeare were addressing it to us, imagining ourselves into the position of the addressee, the other person in the dialogue who reads, feels the range of Shakespeare's emotions, thinks, and then works out how to respond (creatively, critically, silently). We could, when we read *Shakespeare's Sonnets*, even take it upon ourselves to become Shakespeare's 'private friends'.

His Name Is Will

We believe that many of *Shakespeare's Sonnets* are deeply personal poems, written out of Shakespeare's own experience. This does not mean that we should seek to tell a coherent biographical narrative through them, nor should we impose one upon them. Thirty-three

30 Virginia Woolf, *Orlando: A Biography*, ed. Michael Whitworth (Oxford: Oxford University Press, 1992; repr. 2015), p. 179.

out of 154 sonnets are not addressed to a person; 25 of these are personal meditations (miniature soliloquies), and 6 are addressed to an abstract concept, for example to Time, or to Love; and 2 are translations (see Table 2). Biographical readings that misunderstand Shakespeare's collection as a unified sonnet sequence hunt for a single, deterministic narrative where, in fact, none exists. Indeed, though the sonnet form lends itself to a compressed narrative development across its fourteen lines, we do *Shakespeare's Sonnets* (1609) as a collection a disservice if we go to it expecting to find a story.[31]

They are personal poems in as much as they present themselves to us immediately and at varying levels of intimacy. They have Shakespeare's DNA running through them. Setting aside the classical names of Adonis and Helen (Sonnet 53) and Cupid and Dian (Sonnet 153), the only personal name mentioned in any of them is the poet's own: 'my name is Will' (Sonnet 136, line 14). Sonnets 22, 57, 89, 134, 135, and 143 also pun on Shakespeare's first name, reason enough to consider the collection as personally inflected – but to varying and of course ultimately unfathomable degrees.

Reading *Shakespeare's Sonnets* can intermittently seem like encountering miniaturised dispatches from life turned into poetry: the poet's relationships, inner turmoil, feelings of mortality, regret, self-loathing, guilt, but also his joys and gratitude. But rather than turning these elements into an historical, autobiographical narrative, *Shakespeare's Sonnets* can instead be read for traces of his personality, as though the poems were his emotional, psychological, and spiritual memoir, in part made up of his addresses to other people, in part his own soliloquies played out primarily for himself. In some of them he seems to take delight in his own ingenuity, the compactness of his own expression (for example Sonnets 39 and

---

31 Patrick Cheney interestingly suggests that 'Will' is the persona Shakespeare adopts for all of the Sonnets printed in 1609, rather as Sir Edmund Spenser uses the persona of Colin Clout for *The Shepheardes Calendar* (1579). But Spenser's name is not Colin. Cheney's assumption arises, too, from his reading the poems within the long-established biographical tropes. *Shakespeare, National Poet and Playwright* (Cambridge: Cambridge University Press, 2004), p. 215.

40), and only the toughest, most precise and demanding of minds could have written, for example, Sonnets 118 to 120. He wrote sonnets in Stratford-upon-Avon and London, and probably worked on them in his mind through his daily activities, as poets do, and as he commuted on horseback between the town and the city that divided up his life. Sonnets 50 and 51 are written from the perspective of someone riding a horse.

Many of them contain what might be regarded as personal allusions: 'the trophies of my lovers gone' (Sonnet 31, line 10); Sonnet 24 seems to refer to a portrait of the loved one which the poet's eye has copied in his heart (lines 1–2); Sonnet 23 refers to 'my books', which suggests private reading; and three sonnets refer to lameness or limping (Sonnets 37, 66, and 89), which might refer metaphorically to the lines of verse, or literally to the poet's own lameness. Some of the sonnets contain references to things or happenings the meaning of which has been lost to time, for example the 'peace' mentioned in Sonnet 107 which 'proclaims olive of endless age' (line 8). Nobody knows whether this refers to an actual political or personal moment (or, if so, when). Sonnet 125 begins 'Were't aught to me I bore the canopy', which might refer to an actual aristocratic or even royal procession, or one that took place in the context of stage production. Sonnets 78 to 86 refer to other poets writing about the loved one. Traditionally, these have been read as referring to 'a rival poet', but in fact only Sonnet 79 refers to one rival. Sonnet 83 refers to 'both your poets' (which could mean Shakespeare himself plus another, or two other poets), and Sonnet 86 mentions some secret confederacy of collaborators working with a rival poet in love, as well as one particular collaborator and advisor, 'that affable familiar ghost / Which nightly gulls him with intelligence' (lines 9–10). These references seem plausibly to refer to actual individuals who have been working against the poet in some way.

It is often said that there are no surviving examples of Shakespearian correspondence (apart from Richard Quiney's letter addressed to him in October 1598). But in fact two of the sonnets are letters by Shakespeare (in this resembling Helen's in *All's Well That Ends Well*, see p. 224). Sonnet 26 is the accompanying note for another 'written embassage' (line 3). Malone in his edition of 1790 cited Edward Capell's commentary on similarities between this sonnet and Shakespeare's dedication to the Earl of Southampton for his narrative poem, *The Rape of Lucrece* (1594). Sonnet 77 is another sonnet-letter, and one which accompanied a personal gift:

> The vacant leaves thy mind's imprint will bear,
> And of this book this learning mayst thou taste.
>
> (lines 2–3)

The 'book' to which the poet refers is usually thought to be a notebook. But Adam Barker identifies it as an almanac on the grounds that the gift already contains information ('learning') as well as blank pages ('vacant leaves'), as almanacs did. It was common practice to use the empty pages included in almanacs for memoranda, notes, and personal reflections.[32] Sonnet 122 does, however, mention a notebook, apparently containing memoranda, which the loved one has given to the poet ('Thy gift, thy tables', line 1). But the poet, it seems, has given the notebook away:

> Nor need I tallies thy dear love to score
> Therefore to give them from me I was bold.
>
> (Sonnet 122, lines 10–11)

In fact, Sonnet 122 marks the occasion of the poet explaining that notes from the loved one need not be kept because he or she is already etched into the poet's 'lasting memory' (line 2). Many of the sonnets – apart from these examples – can be read and thought of as similar to personal correspondence.

As readers we need to ask ourselves how far we imagine Shakespeare himself as the first-person voice in his sonnets. Poets fluctuate in how far they self-identify with their first-person subject – unless of course they are writing poetic drama or

---

32 Adam Barker, 'The Book with "Waste Blanks" referred to in Shakespeare's Sonnet 77 is an Almanac rather than an Empty Notebook as has previously been assumed', *Notes and Queries*, 66, 3 (September 2019), 429–30.

dramatic speeches. It has long been thought that Shakespeare, when writing sonnets, did indeed 'look into [his] heart and write'. Poets have been especially attentive to this quality of *Shakespeare's Sonnets*. William Wordsworth (1770–1850) powerfully admired Shakespeare for so doing in a sonnet which begins:

> Scorn not the Sonnet, Critic, you have frowned,
> Mindless of its just honours; with this key
> Shakespeare unlocked his heart.

Robert Browning (1812–89) refuted Wordsworth in his poem 'House' of 1876: 'Did Shakespeare? If so, the less Shakespeare he!'. Alfred, Lord Tennyson (1809–92) was inspired by *Shakespeare's Sonnets* and, over a period of seventeen years, wrote love lyrics in memory of his beloved friend Arthur Henry Hallam. He ordered them into a single collection of poems, *In Memoriam: A. H. H.* (1849), which sets out to show the development and progression of his grief and faith. In structuring it around a fictional, three-year period, Tennyson was probably inspired by Sonnet 104:

> Three winters cold
> Have from the forests shook three summers' pride;
> Three beauteous springs to yellow autumn turned.
>
> (lines 3–5)

The poems which form *In Memoriam* are at one and the same time deeply personal and literary, based on Tennyson's own experiences, his reading, and poetic inheritance. In one of the lyrics, he evokes the name of Shakespeare in order bravely to confess his love for his friend:

> I loved thee, Spirit, and love, nor can
> The soul of Shakespeare love thee more.
>
> (*In Memoriam*, 61, lines 11–12)

Wordsworth and Tennyson represent the many readers who, over the centuries, have sought a personal conversation with and within *Shakespeare's Sonnets* (1609).

Shakespeare made the sonnet form his own. He thought and felt through it; he brought an often astonishing compactness of articulation to its individual, disciplined lines; and to many, though by no means all of them, he brought his own strength of feeling and personality. Most of them seem to us to be costly, confessional poems, rather than merely literary exercises – but the imagination of a dramatist is always there. In being composed over at least twenty-seven years, *Shakespeare's Sonnets* (1609) is most likely to encompass many different occasions and people in his life, unidentifiable and anonymous moments which, because he was inspired to write about them in the ways he did, are obscured by but not lost to time.

*

It is our hope that in arranging all the sonnets of Shakespeare chronologically we have newly minted these poems and poetic extracts in a fresh and open context, furthering our understanding of what the sonnet form meant to Shakespeare, its difficulty, its individuality, its rhetorical and dramatic potential. This particular form of verse was an inspiration to Shakespeare for around three decades, and he used it to great effect and for a variety of purposes. His plays echo with his sonnets; his sonnets echo with his plays, and it is this interplay within his art that helps to make Shakespeare the supreme poet-dramatist. Sonnet writing forms a crucial part of his creative endeavour as well as being at the heart of Shakespeare's self-understanding. We hope the reader will be as fascinated as we are to read all the sonnets of Shakespeare in an approximate order of their composition, and without the over-deterministic biographical narratives of the past.

About This Volume

How Have We Decided What to Include?

In seeking to intersperse sonnets from Shakespeare's plays among the chronological re-ordering of *Shakespeare's Sonnets* (1609), we have had to establish principles of inclusion. This has not been straightforward.

Let us start by recognising Shakespeare's three variations of the form in the 1609 collection. Sonnet 145 is written in iambic tetrameter – four instead of five stresses to the line; Sonnet 99, with its fifteen lines, has an introductory opening line: 'The forward violet thus did I chide'; and Sonnet 126 (made up of six couplets) has only twelve lines. Its last line is followed in the quarto printing by two pairs of parentheses placed one above the other, italicised, spaced out to fill the length of the (apparently missing) lines, and indented:

> And her quietus is to render thee.
> (   )
> (   )

Throughout his plays, the units into which the regular Shakespearian sonnet naturally falls – three quatrains and a couplet – can be used independently as well as in combination.

We had to establish boundaries against the many instances of sestets, quatrains, and couplets which Shakespeare employs across his plays. A couplet often closes a scene:

> Hear it not, Duncan; for it is a knell
> That summons thee to heaven or to hell.
>
> (*Macbeth*, 2.2.333–4)

Sestets too can be used independently, as at the end of *Romeo and Juliet*:

> A glooming peace this morning with it brings.
> The sun for sorrow will not show his head,

Go hence, to have more talk of these sad things.
Some shall be pardoned, and some punishèd,
For never was a story of more woe
Than this of Juliet and her Romeo.

Shakespeare was especially adept at writing sestets. The verses which form *Venus and Adonis* provide 199 examples. Hortensio's coded note to Bianca in *The Taming of the Shrew* is cast as a sestet (3.2.71– 6): 'read the gamut of Hortensio' (3.2.70). There are the splendid stretches of dexterous and lyrical quatrains and couplets such as in Biron and the King of Navarre's dialogue (*Love's Labour's Lost*, 4.3.212–86); the playful exchanges between the Princess of France, her ladies-in-waiting, and Boyet (*Love's Labour's Lost*, 5.2.265–85); the dialogue between the King of Navarre and the Princess of France (*Love's Labour's Lost*, 5.2.338–61); and Biron's speech (*Love's Labour's Lost*, 5.2.384–415). Similarly, there are the continuation of Quince's Prologue in *A Midsummer Night's Dream* (5.1.126–50); Bottom's first speech as Pyramus (5.1.168–79); and Flute and Bottom's dialogue as Pyramus and Thisbe (5.1.187–202: sixteen lines made up of two quatrains and four couplets). This list of examples is, of course, far from complete. All of them represent the then fashionable sonnet-like sounds and elements with which Shakespeare was entertaining his audiences, and which serve to heighten the dialogue in these comic and mock-heroic moments. But they are not sonnet-enough for us to have included them as examples of the form put to dramatic use.

When Shakespeare uses quatrains and sestets in combination, and in a manner that relates them closely to the sonnet form, we have felt justified in including them in our collection as verse passages which may be regarded as dramatic sonnets embedded into the plays. We include five passages that are just ten lines long, and one which is eleven lines long, presenting them as foreshortened sonnets. These passages (described below) find a place in Shakespeare's wider sonnet output because of the way he employs the form to heighten a particular dramatic moment.

Valentine's love letter to Sylvia (which the Duke discovers, along with the rope-ladder concealed on Valentine's person) in *The Two Gentlemen of Verona* (3.1.140–50; p. 50, this volume) is included because of its subject matter and because, like the lords' sonnets in *Love's Labour's Lost*, it represents Shakespeare's depiction of a character trying to write a sonnet, which is not very good, and which turns out to be incomplete.

Another foreshortened sonnet occurs in the collaboratively authored *Edward III* (scene 2.322–3; p. 54). It is spoken by the King to Lodowick, his secretary, while Edward is seeking his help in writing a sonnet for the Countess of Salisbury, whom he hopes to seduce.

Shakespeare's use of a regular sonnet for a prologue to *Romeo and Juliet* has encouraged us to include Peter Quince's fretfully delivered and incompetently written ten-line Prologue to the play of *Pyramus and Thisbe* in *A Midsummer Night's Dream* (5.1.108–16; p. 187).

Beatrice's foreshortened sonnet in *Much Ado About Nothing* (p. 188) finds a place in our edition because it represents a moment of personal epiphany. She is reacting to having overheard that Benedick is in love with her and realises that she can love him back. Her foreshortened sonnet represents the only verse she speaks in the play – except just towards the end when she is talking with Benedick about love and recalling this same moment of hearing (5.4.71–83). Both she and Benedick have written love sonnets to each other, two sonnets which Shakespeare never needed to get around to writing since they are not read aloud but do appear on stage as props (5.4.85–90). Beatrice and Benedick read them silently. In performance, we can see their reactions to each other's poetry.

We include Orlando's abbreviated (ten-line) sonnet from *As You Like It* (3.2.1–10; p. 199) because it is a moment of pause during the writing of his own succession of poems in praise of Rosalind. He is running through the Forest of Ardenne, hanging them on the trees, publishing his love, and concludes with the couplet:

> Run, run, Orlando; carve on every tree
> The fair, the chaste, and unexpressive she.

> (3.2.9–10)

The goddess Diana's speech of instruction to Pericles (scene 21.225–35; p. 226) is a theophany, a heightened dramatic moment, and part of a staged dream. Shakespeare adopts a distinct poetic diction and verbal texture in the form of a foreshortened sonnet.

Cressida's fourteen-line speech is made up of seven rhyming couplets (*Troilus and Cressida*, 1.2.278–91; p. 223). In this it is analogous to Sonnet 126, made up of six rhyming couplets, where the pair of empty brackets suggests that it would have had a seventh had not Nature given up the loved one to Time. *In All's Well That Ends Well*, Helen speaks a similarly formed sonnet (1.1.212–25; p. 224).

We include one of the affectedly archaic speeches by the medieval poet John Gower, whom George Wilkins and Shakespeare body forth as a narrator in *Pericles* (p. 226). It also is formed of seven rhyming couplets, and in iambic tetrameter, like Sonnet 145. Even though this sonnet-speech is likely to have been written by George Wilkins, it is found in a play bearing Shakespeare's name, and on which he collaborated.

The god Jupiter's elongated sonnet-speech from *Cymbeline* (5.5.187–204; p. 228) has a visionary, dream-like function as a divine pronouncement which gives it comparable status to Diana's speech in *Pericles*. Jupiter, as father of the gods and the god of thunder, is given a specially amplified sonnet which ends with his delivering a prophetic text, with the help of his assistant ghosts, to the sleeping Posthumus.

The Epilogue to *All Is True* (*Henry VIII*), also made up of seven rhyming couplets, may be by Shakespeare's collaborator, John Fletcher, or might be co-written (p. 230).

In bringing together sonnets written on diverse occasions, alongside dramatic scripts, we have drawn attention in our notes to echoes of the plays in the sonnets and vice versa, the better to encourage a more integrated reading of the sonnets within Shakespeare's wider creative output. Shakespeare often employs theatrical metaphor in his sonnets (for example 'That this huge stage presenteth naught but shows', Sonnet 15, or 'As an unperfect actor on the stage', Sonnet 23). Several of them resemble speeches from plays (it is easy to imagine Sonnets 57 and 58 being spoken by Kate in *The Taming of the Shrew*, or Sonnet 121 being spoken by Iago in *Othello*). We might even think about the form as Shakespeare's dramatic sketchbook, a place where he could try out ideas, thoughts, and emotions that he then later amplified and bodied forth on stage.[1] On occasion, where we have felt this kind of creative connection between Shakespeare's characters and his sonnets to be especially compelling, we have drawn the reader's attention to it in our notes (for example, Sonnet 48: 'Dramatic analogy: Troilus to Cressida') and have highlighted where these occur in the Numerical Index of *Shakespeare's Sonnets* (1609).

The Layout of This Volume

The date range in which each sonnet is thought to have been composed appears in the top corner of the page on which it is printed. Our chronological re-ordering has provoked us to print *Shakespeare's Sonnets* without their original numbers above them (these are given in the footnotes on each page, and the 1609 ordering is readily reconstructable and consultable via the Numerical Index of *Shakespeare's Sonnets* (1609) and the Index of First Lines). Their numbered place in the 1609 quarto printing appears in our notes below each of them (for example: 'Q: No. 29').

The sonnets or dramatic extracts are set with their alternate lines indented, the better to help the reader follow the form of the poetry and see the patterns of rhyme.

Below each of the 154 sonnets from *Shakespeare's Sonnets* (1609), we offer a thumbnail sketch of the poem — an impression of its content, direction, and mood. Its number in the 1609 quarto, or play reference, follows, as well as information about whether it forms part of a pair or a mini-sequence of sonnets, and the nature of its addressee. Is it addressed to a male, or a female? Could it be addressed to either a male or a female?[2] Is it addressed to an abstract

---

1 See Paul Edmondson and Stanley Wells, *Shakespeare's Sonnets* (Oxford: Oxford University Press, 2004), pp. 101–4.

2 Six of the sonnets use the term 'friend' in ways that make the likelihood of a male addressee seem plausible (Sonnets 30, 50, 82, 104, 110, and 111). But, as Will Tosh reminds us, 'friend' was a capacious term and could be used by a male to a female, and in describing an intimate relationship (e.g. 'He hath got his friend with child', *Measure for Measure*, 1.4.29).

concept? Is it a meditation? For the sonnets from the plays, we include the conjectured date of composition and locate the speech within the dramatic situation and story.

Words or short phrases are glossed, and, especially, comparisons drawn between *Shakespeare's Sonnets* (1609) and the plays.

Towards the back of the volume, we offer literal paraphrases of all the sonnets and speeches. Our aim is to privilege accuracy of meaning over elegance of expression, and to convey the challenges of some of the sonnets' own distinctive awkwardnesses. Although it is impossible to convey the richness of a Shakespearian sonnet in prose, we hope we have been able to convey a sense of Shakespeare's feelings of joy, regret, self-loathing, playfulness, his (nearly always) longing for love (and sometimes lust) in absence, the shape of his thinking, and indeed the difficulty of these remarkable and often surreal poems. If the reader were to read through several paraphrases consecutively, then the variation, density, and sometimes contortion of Shakespeare's thought and feelings would quickly become apparent. Our paraphrases are not definitive and are probably best read aloud. Readers are encouraged to read against them and to produce their own.

A Note on the Text

The text of *Shakespeare's Sonnets* is based on that prepared by Stanley Wells for *The Oxford Shakespeare: The Complete Works*, with some minor revisions. A list of substantive changes made to the 1609 edition can be found on pp. 231–2. We are grateful to Oxford University Press for permission to use this text.

All quotations from Shakespeare's plays come from *The Oxford Shakespeare: The Complete Works*, edited by Stanley Wells, Gary Taylor, John Jowett, and William Montgomery (Oxford: Clarendon Press, 1986; repr. 1988; 2nd edn, 2005).

The chronology of Shakespeare's plays and sonnets is based mainly on *The New Oxford Shakespeare: The Complete Works*, edited by Gary Taylor, John Jowett, Terri Bourus, and Gabriel Egan (Oxford: Oxford University Press, 2016).

A Note on Abbreviations and Abstract Nouns

Unless otherwise stated, whenever 'Q' and *Shakespeare's Sonnets* are used, they refer to: *Shakespeare's Sonnets: Never before Imprinted* (London: G. Eld for Thomas Thorpe, 1609).

Many of the sonnets include abstract nouns (for example, Time, Love, Death, Desire, Nature, Winter) that are sometimes capitalised in the early printed texts, and in later editions, momentarily dramatising them as allegorical characters. This edition consistently modernises them to begin with a lower-case letter. The reader can then decide how far to assign dramatic prominence to them.

Some Suggestions for Further Reading

The study of *Shakespeare's Sonnets* can in part be achieved by consulting a variety of critical editions, for example: Stephen Booth (1977); John Kerrigan (The Penguin Shakespeare, 1986); G. Blakemore Evans (The Cambridge Shakespeare, 1996, with an introduction by Stephen Orgel, 2006); Katherine Duncan-Jones (The Arden Shakespeare, 1997; rev. 2010); Helen Vendler (1997); and Colin Burrow (The Oxford Shakespeare, 2002). Admirable and as useful as these editions are, they all either portray the traditional biographical tropes or use them as points of reference.

James Schiffer's *Shakespeare's Sonnets: Critical Essays* (1998) is a highly worthwhile overview and anthology of just over two centuries of criticism; our own *Shakespeare's Sonnets*, The Oxford Shakespeare Topics (2004) is a critical guide aimed at furthering the understanding and appreciation of the poems, and their afterlives. There is a fascinating reception history: Jane Kingsley-Smith, *The Afterlife of Shakespeare's Sonnets* (Cambridge University Press, 2019).

All the Sonnets of Shakespeare

Early Sonnets

❈

Pre-1582

The little love-god . . .

The little love-god lying once asleep
    Laid by his side his heart-inflaming brand,
Whilst many nymphs that vowed chaste life to keep
    Came tripping by; but in her maiden hand
The fairest votary took up that fire   5
    Which many legions of true hearts had warmed,
And so the general of hot desire
    Was sleeping by a virgin hand disarmed.
This brand she quenchèd in a cool well by,
    Which from love's fire took heat perpetual,   10
Growing a bath and healthful remedy
    For men diseased; but I, my mistress' thrall,
        Came there for cure; and this by that I prove:
        Love's fire heats water, water cools not love.

Q: No. 154. This narrative sonnet, and the following one (153), about how nymphs stole Cupid's torch, dipped it in a bath, and set fire to it so that it inflamed men's passions, are paraphrases of the same Greek epigram composed by Marianus Scholasticus in the fifth or sixth century, possibly based on or recalling a schoolboy exercise on Shakespeare's part.

1 **love-god** Cupid	7 **general ... desire** (Cupid)
2 **brand** torch (by implication, penis)	11 **Growing** becoming
	12 **thrall** slave
5 **votary** woman dedicated to chastity	13 **this** what I am about to say
	prove demonstrate
6 **many legions** a great number	

Cupid laid by his brand ...

Cupid laid by his brand and fell asleep.
   A maid of Dian's this advantage found,
And his love-kindling fire did quickly steep
   In a cold valley-fountain of that ground,
Which borrowed from this holy fire of love   5
   A dateless lively heat, still to endure,
And grew a seething bath which yet men prove
   Against strange maladies a sovereign cure.
But at my mistress' eye love's brand new fired,
   The boy for trial needs would touch my breast.   10
I, sick withal, the help of bath desired,
   And thither hied, a sad distempered guest,
      But found no cure; the bath for my help lies
      Where Cupid got new fire: my mistress' eyes.

Q: No. 153. This sonnet seems to be Shakespeare's later attempt to paraphrase the same Greek epigram by Marianus Scholasticus.

1, 9 **brand** torch (by implication, penis)
2 **Dian** goddess of chastity
  this advantage found took advantage of this
3 **his** its
6 **dateless** endless
  still continually, for ever
7 **grew** became
  seething boiling hot (to treat venereal disease)
  yet still
  prove find to be
8 **strange maladies** foreign diseases (such as syphilis, which spread from Europe)
9 **eye** (possibly implying her vagina)
12 **hied** travelled
  sad distempered sadly diseased
14 **eyes** Q prints 'eye', which some editors leave, proposing another bawdy allusion to 'vagina' (cf. line 9).

1582

Those lips that love's own hand ...

Those lips that love's own hand did make
   Breathed forth the sound that said 'I hate'
To me that languished for her sake;
   But when she saw my woeful state,
Straight in her heart did mercy come,   5
   Chiding that tongue that ever sweet
Was used in giving gentle doom,
   And taught it thus anew to greet:
'I hate' she altered with an end
   That followed it as gentle day   10
Doth follow night who, like a fiend,
   From heaven to hell is flown away.
      'I hate' from hate away she threw,
      And saved my life, saying 'not you'.

Her loving lips said 'I hate', but then she mercifully added 'not you'.

Q: No. 145. Exceptionally composed in iambic tetrameter (in lines of four metrical feet). Often thought to be Shakespeare's first poem, written when he was a teenager courting Anne Hathaway whose name is punned on in the couplet ('hate away' an alternative pronunciation of Hathaway; 'And' for Anne). A meditation about a woman.

1–3 **love's ... sake** (cf. *A Midsummer Night's Dream*, 2.2.35: 'Love and languish for his sake')
   love's Cupid's
3 **for her sake** because of her
5 **Straight** immediately
6–7 **Chiding ... doom** rebuking that tongue which, always sweet, was accustomed to pronounce a mild sentence
8 **thus anew to greet** to greet me in this new way
13 **hate away** punning on 'Hathaway'

1589–1595

❦

1589–1591

My thoughts do harbour . . .

DUKE (*reads*)
'My thoughts do harbour with my Silvia nightly,
    And slaves they are to me, that send them flying.
O, could their master come and go as lightly,
    Himself would lodge where, senseless, they are lying.
My herald thoughts in thy pure bosom rest them,   5
    While I, their king, that thither them importune,
Do curse the grace that with such grace hath blessed them,
    Because myself do want my servants' fortune.
        I curse myself for they are sent by me,
        That they should harbour where their lord should be.'   10

The Two Gentlemen of Verona, 3.1.140–9. The Duke of Milan reads aloud a love letter addressed to his daughter Silvia, which her wooer Valentine has been trying to conceal (with a rope-ladder) beneath his cloak.

1 **do harbour** dwell
3 **lightly** speedily, easily
4 **senseless** incapable of feeling
5 **herald thoughts** i.e. thoughts like
   heralds going in advance

6 **importune** impel
7 **grace … grace** fortune … favour
8 **want** lack

1590–1593

Sweet Cytherea ...

Sweet Cytherea, sitting by a brook
　With young Adonis, lovely, fresh, and green,
Did court the lad with many a lovely look,
　Such looks as none could look but beauty's queen.
She told him stories to delight his ear,　　　　　　　　　5
　She showed him favours to allure his eye;
To win his heart she touched him here and there –
　Touches so soft still conquer chastity.
But whether unripe years did want conceit,
　Or he refused to take her figured proffer,　　　　　　10
The tender nibbler would not touch the bait,
　But smile and jest at every gentle offer.
　　Then fell she on her back, fair queen and toward:
　　He rose and ran away – ah, fool too froward!

1599: The Passionate Pilgrim: No. 4. This and the next two sonnets, all closely related to Shakespeare's *Venus and Adonis* (1593), appeared in *The Passionate Pilgrim* of 1599. The volume is attributed to 'W. Shakespeare' on its title page and contains three extracts from *Love's Labour's Lost* and versions of Sonnets 138 and 144 along with fifteeen other poems. We print those sonnets (4, 6, 9) that cannot be certainly attributed to any other author. For the suggestion that they represent early sketches by Shakespeare for *Venus and Adonis*, see Introduction, pp. 6–7.

1　**Cytherea** Venus, named after the island Cythera near the sea from which she supposedly emerged
2　**Adonis** beautiful youth (cf. Sonnet 53.1.5)
　green inexperienced; callow
3　**lovely** amorous, loving

6　**favours** love tokens
8　**still** always
9　**want conceit** lack understanding
10　**figured proffer** i.e. implied or signalled offer of her body
13　**toward** yielding
14　**froward** gauche, awkward

1590–1593

Scarce had the sun . . .

Scarce had the sun dried up the dewy morn,
   And scarce the herd gone to the hedge for shade,
When Cytherea, all in love forlorn,
   A longing tarriance for Adonis made
Under an osier growing by a brook,   5
   A brook where Adon used to cool his spleen.
Hot was the day, she hotter, that did look
   For his approach that often there had been.
Anon he comes and throws his mantle by,
   And stood stark naked on the brook's green brim.   10
The sun looked on the world with glorious eye,
   Yet not so wistly as this queen on him.
     He, spying her, bounced in whereas he stood.
     'O Jove,' quoth she, 'why was not I a flood?'

1599: The Passionate Pilgrim: No. 6

3 **Cytherea** Venus
4 **tarriance** wait
5 **osier** willow
6 **spleen** hot and bothered state
9 **Anon** eventually

mantle cloak, robe
12 **wistly** longingly
13 **whereas he stood** on the spot
14 **flood** body of water

1590–1593

Fair was the morn . . .

Fair was the morn when the fair queen of love,
   [   ]
Paler for sorrow than her milk-white dove,
  For Adon's sake, a youngster proud and wild,
Her stand she takes upon a steep-up hill.   5
  Anon Adonis comes with horn and hounds.
She, seely queen, with more than love's good will
  Forbade the boy he should not pass those grounds.
'Once,' quoth she, 'did I see a fair sweet youth
  Here in these brakes deep-wounded with a boar,   10
Deep in the thigh, a spectacle of ruth.
  See in my thigh,' quoth she, 'here was the sore'.
    She showèd hers; he saw more wounds than one,
    And blushing fled, and left her all alone.

1599: The Passionate Pilgrim: No. 9

2 […] A line rhyming with 'wild'
is missing from the 1599 text, so
we conjecture our own: 'Didst
seek her love whilst weeping like a
child.'

3 **dove** Venus was traditionally
attended by doves
4 **wild** undisciplined
7 **seely** foolish, unfortunate
11 **ruth** pity

1590–1595

And let me have her likened . . .

And let me have her likened to the sun –
  Say she hath thrice more splendour than the sun,
That her perfections emulates the sun,
  That she breeds sweets as plenteous as the sun,
That she doth thaw cold winter like the sun,   5
  That she doth cheer fresh summer, like the sun,
That she doth dazzle gazers like the sun,
  And in this application to the sun
Bid her be free and general as the sun,
  Who smiles upon the basest weed that grows   10
  As lovingly as on the fragrant rose.

1592: *Edward III*, scene 2.322–3. King Edward is instructing his secretary, Lodowick, in the writing of a sonnet to the Countess of Salisbury (cf. Introduction, pp. 9–11).

3 **emulates** imitate
4 **sweets** delights
6 **cheer** encourage
  fresh blooming

8 **application** analogy, comparison
9 **free** generous
  general universally benevolent

1590–1595

In the old age . . .

In the old age black was not counted fair,
    Or if it were, it bore not beauty's name;
But now is black beauty's successive heir,
    And beauty slandered with a bastard shame:
For since each hand hath put on nature's power,   5
    Fairing the foul with art's false borrowed face,
Sweet beauty hath no name, no holy bower,
    But is profaned, if not lives in disgrace.
Therefore my mistress' eyes are raven-black,
    Her brow so suited, and they mourners seem   10
At such who, not born fair, no beauty lack,
    Sland'ring creation with a false esteem.
        Yet so they mourn, becoming of their woe,
        That every tongue says beauty should look so.

Although black used not to be considered beautiful, my mistress is now making it so, and better than any fair beauty enhanced by cosmetics.

Q: No. 127. A meditation about a mistress. Dramatic analogy: Biron on Rosaline's black features in *Love's Labour's Lost* (4.3.246–51); Silvius on Phoebe's black features in *As You Like It* (cf. Rosalind's observations at 3.5.45–9).

1 **old age** olden days   13 **becoming of** gracing, glamourising
10 **so suited** similarly dressed

1590–1595

How oft, when thou …

How oft, when thou, my music, music play'st
   Upon that blessèd wood whose motion sounds
With thy sweet fingers when thou gently sway'st
   The wiry concord that mine ear confounds,
Do I envy those jacks that nimble leap   5
   To kiss the tender inward of thy hand
Whilst my poor lips, which should that harvest reap,
   At the wood's boldness by thee blushing stand!
To be so tickled they would change their state
   And situation with those dancing chips   10
O'er whom thy fingers walk with gentle gait,
   Making dead wood more blessed than living lips.
     Since saucy jacks so happy are in this,
     Give them thy fingers, me thy lips to kiss.

Whenever I watch you play the keyboard, I wish my lips were the keys so
that I could kiss your hands.

Q: No. 128. The imagined speaker (male or female) watches the loved one
(male or female) playing a keyboard instrument.

2 **blessèd wood** wooden keys of the
  musical instrument blessed by the
  beloved's touch
  motion mechanism
3 **sway'st** governest
4 **confounds** amazes (with delight)

5 **jacks** keys
8 **by** beside
10 **chips** slivers of wood
13 **saucy jacks** punningly: the keys
  and 'impertinent fellows'

1590–1595

Th' expense of spirit . . .

Th' expense of spirit in a waste of shame
   Is lust in action; and till action, lust
Is perjured, murd'rous, bloody, full of blame,
   Savage, extreme, rude, cruel, not to trust,
Enjoyed no sooner but despisèd straight,   5
   Past reason hunted, and no sooner had
Past reason hated as a swallowed bait
   On purpose laid to make the taker mad;
Mad in pursuit and in possession so,
   Had, having, and in quest to have, extreme;   10
A bliss in proof and proved, a very woe;
   Before, a joy proposed; behind, a dream.
     All this the world well knows, yet none knows well
     To shun the heaven that leads men to this hell.

To be possessed by lust wastes vital energy which, being acted upon,
promises heaven but only leads to a hell of guilt.

Q: No. 129. An almost breathless meditation on the feelings and consequences of lust. Dramatic analogy: Angelo in *Measure for Measure*.

1 **spirit** vital energy; semen
  waste of shame shameful waste
  (with a pun on 'waist')
3 **perjured** dishonest
4 **rude** brutal
  to trust to be trusted

5 **straight** forthwith
6, 7 **Past reason** irrationally
11 **in proof** while being experienced
  very woe absolute source of grief
14 **hell** hellish guilt; vagina

1590–1595

My mistress' eyes . . .

My mistress' eyes are nothing like the sun;
   Coral is far more red than her lips' red.
If snow be white, why then her breasts are dun;
   If hairs be wires, black wires grow on her head.
I have seen roses damasked, red and white,   5
   But no such roses see I in her cheeks;
And in some perfumes is there more delight
   Than in the breath that from my mistress reeks.
I love to hear her speak, yet well I know
   That music hath a far more pleasing sound.   10
I grant I never saw a goddess go:
   My mistress when she walks treads on the ground.
     And yet, by heaven, I think my love as rare
     As any she belied with false compare.

My mistress is nothing like any of the false comparisons usually drawn in love poems, and is therefore more special than any woman about whom such false claims are made.

Q: No. 130. A meditation about a mistress. Dramatic analogy: Benedick on Beatrice in *Much Ado About Nothing*.

1 **My** (emphasised, as distinct from the objects of praise in Petrarchan love poetry)
  nothing not at all
3 **dun** dark grey
4 **wires** (a common term of comparison in Elizabethan love poems)

5 **damasked** dappled
8 **reeks** issues forth
11 **go** walk
14 **she** woman
  belied with misrepresented by
  compare comparison

1590–1595

Thou art as tyrannous . . .

Thou art as tyrannous so as thou art
    As those whose beauties proudly make them cruel,
For well thou know'st to my dear doting heart
    Thou art the fairest and most precious jewel.
Yet, in good faith, some say that thee behold   5
    Thy face hath not the power to make love groan.
To say they err I dare not be so bold,
    Although I swear it to myself alone;
And, to be sure that is not false I swear,
    A thousand groans but thinking on thy face,   10
One on another's neck do witness bear
    Thy black is fairest in my judgement's place.
      In nothing art thou black save in thy deeds,
      And thence this slander, as I think, proceeds.

You are proud and cruel and, although some say you are not that sexy,
I know you to be utterly so. Your physical blackness does not make you
unattractive, but your black deeds do.

Q: No. 131. Could be addressed to either a male or a female.

1–2 **so … cruel**, i.e. as those whose pride in their beauty makes them cruel
3 **dear** fondly, foolishly
9 **to be sure** as proof

that … swear that what I swear is not false
12 **black** blackness (of features or skin)

1590–1595

Thine eyes I love …

Thine eyes I love, and they, as pitying me –
   Knowing thy heart torment me with disdain –
Have put on black, and loving mourners be,
   Looking with pretty ruth upon my pain;
And truly, not the morning sun of heaven   5
   Better becomes the gray cheeks of the east,
Nor that full star that ushers in the even
   Doth half that glory to the sober west,
As those two mourning eyes become thy face.
   O, let it then as well beseem thy heart   10
To mourn for me, since mourning doth thee grace,
   And suit thy pity like in every part.
     Then will I swear beauty herself is black,
     And all they foul that thy complexion lack.

I love your pitying, black, mourning eyes, which set your beauty off, and show how beautiful black can be.

Q: No. 132. Probably addressed to a female because of 'pretty' (line 4), Beauty being personified as female, and 'black' being an attribute of a mistress in earlier sonnets (line 13). Dramatic analogy: Biron on Rosaline's black features in *Love's Labour's Lost* (4.3.246–51); Silvius on Phoebe's black features in *As You Like It* (cf. Rosalind's observations at 3.5.45–9).

2 **torment** to torment
4 **ruth** pity
6 **becomes** adorns
  cheeks clouds
7 **full star** Venus, the evening star
9 **mourning** (punning on 'morning')

10 **beseem** become, suit
11 **doth thee grace** suits, becomes you
12 **suit … like** dress your pity in the same way

1590–1595

Beshrew that heart . . .

Beshrew that heart that makes my heart to groan
    For that deep wound it gives my friend and me!
Is't not enough to torture me alone,
    But slave to slavery my sweet'st friend must be?
Me from myself thy cruel eye hath taken,   5
    And my next self thou harder hast engrossed.
Of him, myself, and thee I am forsaken —
    A torment thrice threefold thus to be crossed.
Prison my heart in thy steel bosom's ward,
    But then my friend's heart let my poor heart bail;   10
Whoe'er keeps me, let my heart be his guard;
    Thou canst not then use rigour in my jail.
      And yet thou wilt; for I, being pent in thee,
      Perforce am thine, and all that is in me.

You have completely trapped, monopolised, and imprisoned my friend
and me, and we cannot escape the thrall of your cruel heart and the hurt
it is causing.

Q: No. 133. This is the first in a pair of syntactically related sonnets (with
134) about a triangular relationship. Could be addressed to either a male
or a female.

1 **Beshrew** curse (a mild term)
2 **For** because of
  it (the first 'heart')
6 **next self** second self, closest
  friend
  harder hast engrossed hast more
  cruelly monopolised
7 **Of** by
8 **thrice threefold** nine times

9 **Prison** imprison
  ward prison cell
11 **keeps** guards
  his guard the friend's guardhouse,
  prison
12 **rigour** harshness
13 **pent** enthralled; imprisoned
14 **and** i.e. as is

1590–1595

So, now I have confessed . . .

So, now I have confessed that he is thine,
    And I myself am mortgaged to thy will,
Myself I'll forfeit, so that other mine
    Thou wilt restore to be my comfort still.
But thou wilt not, nor he will not be free,   5
    For thou art covetous, and he is kind.
He learned but surety-like to write for me
    Under that bond that him as fast doth bind.
The statute of thy beauty thou wilt take,
    Thou usurer that putt'st forth all to use,   10
And sue a friend came debtor for my sake;
    So him I lose through my unkind abuse.
      Him have I lost; thou hast both him and me;
      He pays the whole, and yet am I not free.

You will go to any lengths to keep my friend and me in your power: I have lost him to your thrall, and remain in your debt.

Q: No. 134. This is the second in a pair of syntactically related sonnets (with 133) about a triangular relationship. This sonnet could be addressed to either a male or a female and is possibly connected to 22, 57, 89, 135, 136, and 143 because of the allusion to the poet's name, Will (line 2).

1 **now** now that
2 **mortgaged ... will** legally bound to obey you
    will desire (possibly alluding to Will)
3 **so that** provided that, in order that
5 **will not** does not wish to
7 **surety-like** as a guarantor
    write for endorse on my behalf

9 **statute** full amount secured under the bond
10 **putt'st ... use** dost invest everything
    to use at interest, for sexual activity
11 **came** who came
12 **my unkind abuse** your unkind treatment of me

1590–1595

Whoever hath her wish...

Whoever hath her wish, thou hast thy will,
  And will to boot, and will in overplus.
More than enough am I that vex thee still,
  To thy sweet will making addition thus.
Wilt thou, whose will is large and spacious,   5
  Not once vouchsafe to hide my will in thine?
Shall will in others seem right gracious,
  And in my will no fair acceptance shine?
The sea, all water, yet receives rain still,
  And in abundance addeth to his store;   10
So thou, being rich in will, add to thy will
  One will of mine to make thy large will more.
    Let no unkind no fair beseechers kill;
    Think all but one, and me in that one will.

You have everything you can possibly desire in me, and I long to satisfy
you.

Q: No. 135. This is the first in a pair of syntactically related sonnets (with
136), and addressed to a woman. Linked with 136, and possibly connected
to 22, 57, 89, 134, and 143 because of the pun on the poet's name: Will.

1 **will** sexual desire; wish; male and
  female sexual organs (e.g. like
  the modern 'willy'); punning on
  Shakespeare's first name, William
2 **to boot** in addition
5 **will** vagina, sexual desire

6 **will** penis, sexual desire
9 **still** continually
10 **his** its
13 **unkind ... kill** unkindness of
  yours kill any of your attractive
  wooers

1590—1595

If thy soul check thee ...

If thy soul check thee that I come so near,
  Swear to thy blind soul that I was thy Will,
And will, thy soul knows, is admitted there;
  Thus far for love my love-suit, sweet, fulfil.
Will will fulfil the treasure of thy love,   5
  Ay, fill it full with wills, and my will one.
In things of great receipt with ease we prove
  Among a number one is reckoned none.
Then in the number let me pass untold,
  Though in thy store's account I one must be;   10
For nothing hold me, so it please thee hold
  That nothing me a something, sweet, to thee.
    Make but my name thy love, and love that still,
    And then thou lov'st me for my name is Will.

My name, my desire, and my penis want to fill you entirely.

Q: No. 136. This is the second in a pair of syntactically related sonnets (with 135), and therefore addressed to a woman. Possibly connected to 22, 57, 89, 134, and 143 because of the pun on the poet's name: Will.

1 **check** rebuke
  near near your conscience (as in the previous sonnet); physically close to you
2 **blind** ignorant
4 **fulfil** grant
5 **fulfil the treasure** fill the treasury
6 **my will** (the sense 'my sexual organ', 'my willy' comes to prevail)
7 **receipt** capacity
8 **one ... none** proverbially 'one is no number'

9 **in the number** among the number (of your suitors)
10 **untold** uncounted
  account (punning on 'cunt')
11–12 **For ... me** (also implying 'hold me to your vagina and your vagina to me')
12 **a something ... thee** (also implying 'a penis which is pleasing to you')
13 **still** continually

1590–1595

Thou blind fool love . . .

Thou blind fool love, what dost thou to mine eyes
    That they behold and see not what they see?
They know what beauty is, see where it lies,
    Yet what the best is take the worst to be.
If eyes corrupt by over-partial looks   5
    Be anchored in the bay where all men ride,
Why of eyes' falsehood hast thou forgèd hooks
    Whereto the judgement of my heart is tied?
Why should my heart think that a several plot
    Which my heart knows the wide world's common place?   10
Or mine eyes, seeing this, say this is not,
    To put fair truth upon so foul a face?
      In things right true my heart and eyes have erred,
      And to this false plague are they now transferred.

Love is blind and makes me see things falsely, even convincing me that I am in love with a promiscuous woman.

Q: No. 137. This sonnet is addressed to Cupid and is probably about a female object of desire ('the bay where all men ride', line 6).

1 **blind fool** (Cupid was proverbially blind)
2 **and see not** and yet see not, misinterpret
5 **corrupt** corrupted, misled **over-partial** prejudiced, doting
6 **Be ... ride** harbour where all men may cast their anchors (and have sex, 'ride')
7 **of eyes' falsehood** from the false judgement of my eyes

9 **that ... plot** that to be a private property
10 **common place** common land, open to all
11 **Or** or why should
12 **face** appearance
14 **false ... transferred** are now shifted into a plague of seeing things falsely

1590–1595

When my love swears . . . (early version)

When my love swears that she is made of truth
  I do believe her though I know she lies,
That she might think me some untutored youth
  Unskilful in the world's false forgeries.
Thus vainly thinking that she thinks me young,   5
  Although I know my years be past the best,
I, smiling, credit her false-speaking tongue,
  Outfacing faults in love with love's ill rest.
But wherefore says my love that she is young,
  And wherefore say not I that I am old?   10
O, love's best habit's in a soothing tongue,
  And age in love loves not to have years told.
    Therefore I'll lie with love, and love with me,
    Since that our faults in love thus smothered be.

This sonnet first appeared in *The Passionate Pilgrim* of 1599, an early or corrupt version of what would later be printed as Sonnet 138, in 1609. The differences between them are collated below.

4 **Unskilful** undiscerning, ignorant]
  1599; Unlearnèd 1609
  false forgeries false and
  deliberately deceptive accounts]
  false subtleties 1609
6 **years**] days 1609
7 **I, smiling**] Simply I 1609
8 **Outfacing faults in love with
  love's ill rest**] On both sides thus is
  simple truth suppressed 1609
  Outfacing defying
  ill rest uneasy complacency

9 **my love that she is young**] she
  not she is unjust 1609
11 **habit's in a soothing tongue**]
  habit is in seeming trust 1609
13 **Therefore I'll lie with love
  and love with me**] Therefore I lie
  with her and she with me 1609
  love i.e. my love (punning on
  love)
14 **Since that our faults in love thus
  smothered be**] And in our faults
  by lies we flattered be 1609

1590–1595

When my love swears … (later version)

When my love swears that she is made of truth
  I do believe her though I know she lies,
That she might think me some untutored youth
  Unlearnèd in the world's false subtleties.
Thus vainly thinking that she thinks me young,   5
  Although she knows my days are past the best,
Simply I credit her false-speaking tongue;
  On both sides thus is simple truth suppressed.
But wherefore says she not she is unjust,
  And wherefore say not I that I am old?   10
O, love's best habit is in seeming trust,
  And age in love loves not to have years told.
    Therefore I lie with her, and she with me,
    And in our faults by lies we flattered be.

My loved one and I both know we are lying to each other, she about her faithfulness, I about my age, but our lies help our relationship to function.

Q: No. 138. A meditation about a relationship. A version of this sonnet appeared in *The Passionate Pilgrim* of 1599. Dramatic analogy: Antony about Cleopatra.

1 **made of truth** totally loyal
3 **That** with the result that
  untutored unsophisticated
4 **false subtleties** vain deceits
5 **vainly thinking** falsely seeming to
  think

7 **Simply** in assumed folly
  credit (seem to) believe
9 **unjust** unfaithful
11 **habit … trust** demeanour lies in
  the appearance of fidelity
13 **lie** tell untruths; sleep

1590–1595

O, call not me . . .

O, call not me to justify the wrong
  That thy unkindness lays upon my heart.
Wound me not with thine eye but with thy tongue;
  Use power with power, and slay me not by art.
Tell me thou lov'st elsewhere, but in my sight,   5
  Dear heart, forbear to glance thine eye aside.
What need'st thou wound with cunning when thy might
  Is more than my o'erpressed defence can bide?
Let me excuse thee: 'Ah, my love well knows
  Her pretty looks have been mine enemies,   10
And therefore from my face she turns my foes
  That they elsewhere might dart their injuries.'
    Yet do not so; but since I am near slain,
    Kill me outright with looks, and rid my pain.

You are hurting me, there is no excuse for it, and you are causing me such pain that I would rather you kill me with your awful behaviour.

Q: No. 139. This sonnet is addressed to a female, and begins a sequence of four sonnets (with 140, 141, and 142) about the power of a loved one's eyes. Dramatic analogy: Silvius to Phoebe in *As You Like It* (who says to him 'And if mine eyes can wound, now let them kill thee', 3.5.16).

1 **justify** excuse
3 **with thine eye** i.e. by looking elsewhere
4 **with power** i.e. directly
  art deceit
7 **What** why
8 **o'erpressed** overtaxed
  bide withstand
11 **my foes** (her eyes)
14 **rid** rid me of, put an end to

1590–1595

Be wise as thou art cruel …

Be wise as thou art cruel; do not press
  My tongue-tied patience with too much disdain,
Lest sorrow lend me words, and words express
  The manner of my pity-wanting pain.
If I might teach thee wit, better it were,   5
  Though not to love, yet, love, to tell me so –
As testy sick men when their deaths be near
  No news but health from their physicians know.
For if I should despair I should grow mad,
  And in my madness might speak ill of thee.   10
Now this ill-wresting world is grown so bad
  Mad slanderers by mad ears believèd be.
    That I may not be so, nor thou belied,
    Bear thine eyes straight, though thy proud heart go wide.

Even though you are cruel, you would be wise to pretend that you love me,
otherwise I will go mad.

Q: No. 140. Probably addressed to a female because it is one of a sequence
of four related sonnets (with 139, 141, and 142). Dramatic analogy: Hamlet
to Ophelia; Ophelia to Hamlet.

4 **pity-wanting** unpitied
5 **wit** wisdom
6 **Though … so** even if you don't
  love, nevertheless, love, to tell me
  you do
7 **testy** fretful
8 **know** hear

11 **ill-wresting** unfavourably
  misinterpreting
13 **belied** be slandered
14 **Bear … straight** look as if you are
  being honest
  wide astray

1590–1595

In faith, I do not love thee …

In faith, I do not love thee with mine eyes,
    For they in thee a thousand errors note;
But 'tis my heart that loves what they despise,
    Who in despite of view is pleased to dote.
Nor are mine ears with thy tongue's tune delighted,   5
    Nor tender feeling to base touches prone;
Nor taste nor smell desire to be invited
    To any sensual feast with thee alone;
But my five wits nor my five senses can
    Dissuade one foolish heart from serving thee,   10
Who leaves unswayed the likeness of a man,
    Thy proud heart's slave and vassal-wretch to be.
      Only my plague thus far I count my gain:
      That she that makes me sin awards me pain.

Neither my intellect nor my five senses are attracted to you, but you have enslaved my heart and make me suffer.

Q: No. 141. Addressed to a woman, and one of a sequence of four sonnets (with 139, 140, and 142). Dramatic analogy: Orlando to Ganymede (who is Rosalind in disguise) in *As You Like It*.

4 **Who** which (my heart)
  in … view in spite of what it sees
9 **five wits** intellectual faculties (common sense, imagination, fancy, judgement, memory)
  five senses (called upon in lines 1, 5, 6, and 7)

11 **Who** which (the heart, devoted to serving you)
  unswayed without a commander
  likeness mere semblance
12 **vassal-wretch** contemptible hanger-on

1590–1595

Love is my sin ...

Love is my sin, and thy dear virtue hate,
   Hate of my sin grounded on sinful loving.
O, but with mine compare thou thine own state,
   And thou shalt find it merits not reproving;
Or if it do, not from those lips of thine   5
   That have profaned their scarlet ornaments
And sealed false bonds of love as oft as mine,
   Robbed others' beds' revenues of their rents.
Be it lawful I love thee as thou lov'st those
   Whom thine eyes woo as mine importune thee.   10
Root pity in thy heart, that when it grows
   Thy pity may deserve to pitied be.
     If thou dost seek to have what thou dost hide,
     By self example mayst thou be denied!

My love for you is a sin, but you are in no position to judge me because you are just as bad in the way you turn your attention to others. Pity me, and by doing so win the pity of others.

Q: No. 142. Addressed to a female because it is one of a sequence of four sonnets (with 139, 140, and 141), and follows on from 141.

2 **grounded on** built upon
3 **mine** my (state)
4 **it** my state
6 **scarlet ornaments** (also occurs in *Edward III*, scene 2.176)
7 **sealed** (as 'scarlet' wax is used to seal documents, or 'bonds')
8 **revenues** (accented on the second syllable)
9 **Be it lawful** let it be thought lawful that
10 **importune** implore

1590–1595

Lo, as a care-full housewife . . .

Lo, as a care-full housewife runs to catch
   One of her feathered creatures broke away,
Sets down her babe and makes all swift dispatch
   In pursuit of the thing she would have stay,
Whilst her neglected child holds her in chase,   5
   Cries to catch her whose busy care is bent
To follow that which flies before her face,
   Not prizing her poor infant's discontent:
So runn'st thou after that which flies from thee,
   Whilst I, thy babe, chase thee afar behind;   10
But if thou catch thy hope, turn back to me
   And play the mother's part: kiss me, be kind.
     So will I pray that thou mayst have thy will
     If thou turn back and my loud crying still.

You make me feel like a suddenly neglected baby pursuing its mother while you run after things beyond your reach. Turn back to me, and stop my crying.

Q: No. 143. Addressed to a female. Possibly connected to 22, 57, 89, 134, 135, and 136 because of the pun on the poet's name, Will (line 13).

5 **holds ... chase** runs after her
6 **bent** directed
8 **prizing** caring about
13 **will** used punningly as in earlier sonnets
14 **still** pacify

1590–1595

Two loves I have (early version) . . .

Two loves I have, of comfort and despair,
　That like two spirits do suggest me still.
My better angel is a man right fair,
　My worser spirit a woman coloured ill.
To win me soon to hell my female evil 　　　　　　　5
　Tempteth my better angel from my side,
And would corrupt my saint to be a devil,
　Wooing his purity with her fair pride;
And whether that my angel be turned fiend,
　Suspect I may, yet not directly tell; 　　　　　　　10
For being both to me, both to each friend,
　I guess one angel in another's hell.
　　The truth I shall not know, but live in doubt
　　Till my bad angel fire my good one out.

This sonnet first appeared in *The Passionate Pilgrim* of 1599, an early or corrupt version of what would later be printed as Sonnet 144 in 1609. The differences between them are collated below.

When compared to the 1609 version, this is a slightly less tough-edged account of the poet's 'two loves'. It uses the possessive 'my' (lines 3 and 4), calls the woman's pride (her 'lust') 'fair' rather than 'foul' (line 8), and seeks a greater certainty in its outcome by naming 'the truth' (line 13).

2 **That**] Which (1609)
3 **My**] The (1609)
4 **My**] The (1609)
8 **fair**] foul (1609)

11 **For**] But (1609)
　to] from (1609)
13 **The truth I shall not know**] Yet
　this shall I ne'er know (1609)

1590–1595

Two loves I have (later version) ...

Two loves I have, of comfort and despair,
    Which like two spirits do suggest me still.
The better angel is a man right fair,
    The worser spirit a woman coloured ill.
To win me soon to hell my female evil   5
    Tempteth my better angel from my side,
And would corrupt my saint to be a devil,
    Wooing his purity with her foul pride;
And whether that my angel be turned fiend
    Suspect I may, yet not directly tell;   10
But being both from me, both to each friend,
    I guess one angel in another's hell.
      Yet this shall I ne'er know, but live in doubt
      Till my bad angel fire my good one out.

The man and woman whom I love are like good and bad angels, and I suspect her of infecting him.

Q: No. 144. A meditation about a male and a female for whom the poet feels contrasting love.

2 **suggest** tempt
  still continually
4 **coloured ill** of unpleasing colour, dark (and in appearance); also morally corrupt
5, 12 **hell** punning on the slang sense 'vagina'
8 **foul** ugly

pride sexual desire, lust
11 **from** away from
  each each other
13 **doubt** suspicion
14 **fire ... out** expels; infects with venereal disease
  good one i.e. good angel

1590–1595

Poor soul . . .

Poor soul, the centre of my sinful earth,
   [   ] these rebel powers that thee array;
Why dost thou pine within and suffer dearth,
   Painting thy outward walls so costly gay?
Why so large cost, having so short a lease,   5
   Dost thou upon thy fading mansion spend?
Shall worms, inheritors of this excess,
   Eat up thy charge? Is this thy body's end?
Then, soul, live thou upon thy servant's loss,
   And let that pine to aggravate thy store.   10
Buy terms divine in selling hours of dross;
   Within be fed, without be rich no more.
      So shalt thou feed on death, that feeds on men,
      And death once dead, there's no more dying then.

Poor soul: do not waste any more time trying to help my deteriorating body. Look inwardly and eternally, and kill death.

Q: No. 146. An address to the poet's soul, and a meditation on mortality.

2 [ ] The first edition repeats 'my sinful earth'. Many guesses as to what Shakespeare wrote include 'Rebuke', 'Fooled by', and 'Spoiled by.'
   rebel powers rebellious passions
   array surround; adorn; line up for battle
3 **pine** dwindle (also line 10)
   dearth famine
4 **Painting** decorating
   outward walls (body)
   costly gay extravagantly
6 **fading** (because mortal)

mansion dwelling, body
8 **thy charge** your expenditure; what has been entrusted to you
   thy body's end (cf. *The Tragedy of King Lear*, 5.3.238: 'Is this the promised end?')
9 **thy servant's** my body's
10 **aggravate** increase
   store wealth
11 **terms divine** i.e. eternal life
12 **without** externally
   rich showy

1590–1595

My love is as a fever . . .

My love is as a fever, longing still
　For that which longer nurseth the disease,
Feeding on that which doth preserve the ill,
　Th' uncertain sickly appetite to please.
My reason, the physician to my love,　　　　　　　　　　5
　Angry that his prescriptions are not kept,
Hath left me, and I desperate now approve
　Desire is death, which physic did except.
Past cure I am, now reason is past care,
　And frantic-mad with evermore unrest.　　　　　　　　10
My thoughts and my discourse as madmen's are,
　At random from the truth vainly expressed;
　　For I have sworn thee fair, and thought thee bright,
　　Who art as black as hell, as dark as night.

I am sick from loving you, but want to remain so, even though I know it
is fatal and is driving me mad.

Q: No. 147. Could be addressed to either a male or a female.

1　**still** continually
2　**nurseth** nourishes, prolongs
3　**preserve the ill** prolong the
　　sickness
7　**approve** learn by experience (that)
8　**physic** medicine, treatment

　　did except refused
9　**past care** beyond treatment
10　**evermore unrest** perpetual
　　sleeplessness
12　**vainly** uselessly, foolishly

1590—1595

O me, what eyes ...

O me, what eyes hath love put in my head,
    Which have no correspondence with true sight!
Or if they have, where is my judgement fled,
    That censures falsely what they see aright?
If that be fair whereon my false eyes dote,   5
    What means the world to say it is not so?
If it be not, then love doth well denote
    Love's eye is not so true as all men's. No,
How can it, O, how can love's eye be true,
    That is so vexed with watching and with tears?   10
No marvel then though I mistake my view:
    The sun itself sees not till heaven clears.
        O cunning love, with tears thou keep'st me blind
        Lest eyes, well seeing, thy foul faults should find!

Being in love means that I cannot see properly, lack judgement, and am
blind to love's faults.

Q: No. 148. A meditation on how love makes one see. Dramatic analogy:
Titania on realising she has been in love with Bottom in *A Midsummer
Night's Dream*.

4 **censures falsely** misjudges,
   misinterprets
7 **denote** demonstrate

10 **watching** staying awake
11 **mistake my view** see amiss

1590–1595

Canst thou, O cruel . . .

Canst thou, O cruel, say I love thee not
   When I against myself with thee partake?
Do I not think on thee when I forgot
   Am of myself, all-tyrant, for thy sake?
Who hateth thee that I do call my friend?   5
   On whom frown'st thou that I do fawn upon?
Nay, if thou lour'st on me, do I not spend
   Revenge upon myself with present moan?
What merit do I in myself respect
   That is so proud thy service to despise,   10
When all my best doth worship thy defect,
   Commanded by the motion of thine eyes?
     But, love, hate on; for now I know thy mind.
     Those that can see thou lov'st, and I am blind.

My love for you means that I even take your side against myself, so you
might as well hate me because love has made me blind.

Q: No. 149. Could be addressed to either a male or a female. This is the
first in a pair (with 150) of syntactically related sonnets.

2 **partake** take part, side
3 **forgot** forgotten
4 **all-tyrant** total tyrant (or referring
   to himself)
6 **fawn upon** delight, revel in
7 **lour'st** look unfavourably
8 **present moan** instant censure

9 **respect** value
11 **best** best qualities
   defect faults
13 **But, love, hate on** cf. Beatrice,
   'And, Benedict, love on', *Much Ado*
   About Nothing (3.1.111).
14 **blind** (with love)

1590–1595

O, from what power. . .

O, from what power hast thou this powerful might
    With insufficiency my heart to sway,
To make me give the lie to my true sight
    And swear that brightness doth not grace the day?
Whence hast thou this becoming of things ill,   5
    That in the very refuse of thy deeds
There is such strength and warrantise of skill
    That in my mind thy worst all best exceeds?
Who taught thee how to make me love thee more
    The more I hear and see just cause of hate?   10
O, though I love what others do abhor,
    With others thou shouldst not abhor my state.
        If thy unworthiness raised love in me,
        More worthy I to be beloved of thee.

You have some special power because I love you in spite of your unworthiness and even though others loathe you.

Q: No. 150. Could be addressed to either a male or a female. This is the second in a pair (with 149) of syntactically related sonnets.

2 **With insufficiency** by your shortcomings
3 **give the lie to** deny
6 **very refuse** most contemptible
7 **warrantise** guarantee

skill good workmanship
11 and 12 **abhor** loathe, regard with disgust (with a pun on 'whore')
13 **raised** excited (with a sexual allusion to an erection)

1590–1595

Love is too young . . .

Love is too young to know what conscience is,
 Yet who knows not conscience is born of love?
Then, gentle cheater, urge not my amiss,
 Lest guilty of my faults thy sweet self prove.
For, thou betraying me, I do betray   5
 My nobler part to my gross body's treason.
My soul doth tell my body that he may
 Triumph in love; flesh stays no farther reason,
But rising at thy name doth point out thee
 As his triumphant prize. Proud of this pride,   10
He is contented thy poor drudge to be,
 To stand in thy affairs, fall by thy side.
  No want of conscience hold it that I call
  Her 'love' for whose dear love I rise and fall.

Do not hold it against me that my love for you is also powerfully sexual.

Q: No. 151. A meditation on love and sex, addressed to a woman.

1 **Love** (the boy Cupid)
 conscience a sense of right and
 wrong (also carnal knowledge)
3 **cheater** deceiver
 urge press, insist on, hold to
 amiss faults
4 **prove** turn out to be
6 **nobler part** (i.e. soul)
8 **flesh** (specifically my penis)
 stays waits for
9 **rising** springing to attention;
 growing erect

10 **Proud ... pride** proud of this
 erection
12 **stand in** wait on; stand erect
 affairs service (pun on sexual
 affairs)
 fall follow; droop
13 **conscience** (possibly alluding to
 the French 'con', for 'cunt')
14 **I** (a) the speaker; (b) the speaker's
 penis

1590–1595

In loving thee . . .

In loving thee thou know'st I am forsworn,
    But thou art twice forsworn to me love swearing:
In act thy bed-vow broke, and new faith torn
    In vowing new hate after new love bearing.
But why of two oaths' breach do I accuse thee   5
    When I break twenty? I am perjured most,
For all my vows are oaths but to misuse thee,
    And all my honest faith in thee is lost.
For I have sworn deep oaths of thy deep kindness,
    Oaths of thy love, thy truth, thy constancy,   10
And to enlighten thee gave eyes to blindness,
    Or made them swear against the thing they see.
        For I have sworn thee fair – more perjured eye
        To swear against the truth so foul a lie.

We have both broken vows in order to make love, but I more than you
because I promised myself to betray you, and promised myself you would
be loyal.

Q: No. 152. Could be addressed to either a male or a female.

1 **forsworn** unfaithful (to someone else)	**bearing** possessing
3 **act** your (sexual) actions	7 **misuse** deceive
bed-vow vow to your husband (or lover)	11 **enlighten** make bright
faith torn commitment betrayed	13 **perjured** falsely swearing
4 **hate** (presumably towards a previous lover)	**eye** (punning on 'I')

1594–1595

※

1594

But if that I am I . . .

ANTIPHOLUS OF SYRACUSE
But if that I am I, then well I know
  Your weeping sister is no wife of mine,
Nor to her bed no homage do I owe.
  Far more, far more, to you do I decline.

O, train me not, sweet mermaid, with thy note   5
  To drown me in thy sister's flood of tears.
Sing, siren, for thyself, and I will dote.
  Spread o'er the silver waves thy golden hairs,

And as a bed I'll take them, and there lie,
  And in that glorious supposition think   10
He gains by death that hath such means to die.
  Let love, being light, be drownèd if she sink.

LUCIANA
What, are you mad, that you do reason so?

ANTIPHOLUS OF SYRACUSE
Not mad, but mated – how, I do not know.

1594: *The Comedy of Errors*, 3.2.41–54. Antipholus of Syracuse is mistaken by
his identical twin's sister-in-law.

4 **decline** incline
5 **train** entice, lure
  note singing
7 **dote** dote on you, capitulate

10 **supposition** delusion
14 **mated** confused, punning on
  the senses of 'astounded' and
  'partnered'.

1594–1595

Study me how to please ...

BIRON
Study me how to please the eye indeed
   By fixing it upon a fairer eye,
Who dazzling so, that eye shall be his heed,
   And give him light that it was blinded by.
Study is like the heavens' glorious sun,   5
   That will not be deep searched with saucy looks.
Small have continual plodders ever won
   Save base authority from others' books.
These earthly godfathers of heaven's lights,
   That give a name to every fixèd star,   10
Have no more profit of their shining nights
   Than those that walk and wot not what they are.
     Too much to know is to know naught but fame,
     And every godfather can give a name.

1594–5: *Love's Labour's Lost*, 1.1.80–9. Lord Biron responds to the course of study to which he and his friends intend to subject themselves during their exaggerated and unreasonable three-year fast.

1 **Study** teach
3 **Who dazzling so** which, being thus dazzled
  his heed a guide to him, a lodestar
6 **saucy** cheeky, presumptuous

9 **godfathers ... lights** astronomers
11 **of** from
12 **wot** know
13 **fame** hearsay, second-hand facts

1594–1595

Ay, that there is …

KING

Ay, that there is. Our court, you know, is haunted
  With a refinèd traveller of Spain,
A man in all the world's new fashion planted,
  That hath a mint of phrases in his brain.
One whom the music of his own vain tongue   5
  Doth ravish like enchanting harmony;
A man of complements, whom right and wrong
  Have chose as umpire of their mutiny.
This child of fancy, that Armado hight,
  For interim to our studies shall relate   10
In high-borne words the worth of many a knight
  From tawny Spain lost in the world's debate.
How you delight, my lords, I know not, I;
  But, I protest, I love to hear him lie,
  And I will use him for my minstrelsy.

1594–5: *Love's Labour's Lost*, 1.1.159–74. A reply to Lord Biron's 'But is there no quick recreation granted?' This otherwise regular sonnet of the King of Navarre's ends with a triplet, rather than a couplet – appropriate for his description of the fantastic braggart Don Armado.

2 **refinèd … Spain** (Don Armado)
4 **phrases** fashionable sayings
7 **complements** accomplishments
8 **mutiny** disputes
9 **child of fancy** fantastical being
  hight is called

10 **For interim** as an interlude
12 **tawny** sunburnt
  debate disputes, also warfare
15 **minstrelsy** entertainment

1594–1595

If love make me forsworn …

NATHANIEL *(reads)*

'If love make me forsworn, how shall I swear to love?
    Ah, never faith could hold, if not to beauty vowed.
Though to myself forsworn, to thee I'll faithful prove.
    Those thoughts to me were oaks, to thee like osiers bowed.
Study his bias leaves, and makes his book thine eyes,   5
    Where all those pleasures live that art would comprehend.
If knowledge be the mark, to know thee shall suffice.
    Well learnèd is that tongue that well can thee commend;
All ignorant that soul that sees thee without wonder;
    Which is to me some praise that I thy parts admire.   10
Thy eye Jove's lightning bears, thy voice his dreadful thunder,
    Which, not to anger bent, is music and sweet fire.
        Celestial as thou art, O pardon, love, this wrong,
        That singeth heaven's praise with such an earthly tongue.'

1594–5: *Love's Labour's Lost*, 4.2.106–19. Lord Biron's incorrectly delivered sonnet letter to Rosaline, one of the Princess of France's ladies-in-waiting, is read by the curate, Sir Nathaniel. Written in iambic hexameter, rather than the usual iambic pentameter.

The minor differences between this version and that printed in *The Passionate Pilgrim* (1599) are collated below.

2 **Ah**] O (1599)
   faith could hold could devotion remain constant
3 **faithful**] constant (1599)
4 **were**] like (1599)
   osiers willow trees (flexible)
5 **Study … leaves** the student goes astray
6 **art would comprehend** study would seek to understand

   would] can (1599)
7 **mark** aim
10 **parts** features, good qualities
11 **Thy**] Thine (1599)
12 **not … bent** when it is not directed by anger
13 **pardon … wrong**] do not love that wrong (1599)
14 **That singeth**] to sing (1599)

1594–1595

So sweet a kiss . . .

KING (*reads*)
'So sweet a kiss the golden sun gives not
   To those fresh morning drops upon the rose
As thy eyebeams when their fresh rays have smote
   The night of dew that on my cheeks down flows.
Nor shines the silver moon one-half so bright   5
   Through the transparent bosom of the deep
As doth thy face through tears of mine give light.
   Thou shin'st in every tear that I do weep.
No drop but as a coach doth carry thee,
   So ridest thou triumphing in my woe.   10
Do but behold the tears that swell in me
   And they thy glory through my grief will show.
But do not love thyself; then thou wilt keep
   My tears for glasses, and still make me weep.
      O Queen of queens, how far dost thou excel,   15
      No thought can think nor tongue of mortal tell.'

1594–5: *Love's Labour's Lost*, 4.3.24–39. The King of Navarre reads aloud the unintentionally parodic and extended sonnet that he has written to the Princess of France. It has an extra couplet and is burlesque in tone.

3 **smote** smitten
4 **night of dew** nightly dew, the night's complement of tears

6 **deep** ocean
14 **for glasses** for looking-glasses
   still continually

1594–1595

Did not the heavenly rhetoric . . .

LONGUEVILLE (*reads*)
'Did not the heavenly rhetoric of thine eye,
  'Gainst whom the world cannot hold argument,
Persuade my heart to this false perjury?
  Vows for thee broke deserve not punishment.
A woman I forswore, but I will prove,   5
  Thou being a goddess, I forswore not thee.
My vow was earthly, thou a heavenly love.
  Thy grace being gained cures all disgrace in me.
Vows are but breath, and breath a vapour is.
  Then thou, fair sun, which on my earth dost shine,   10
Exhal'st this vapour-vow; in thee it is.
  If broken then, it is no fault of mine.
    If by me broke, what fool is not so wise
    To lose an oath to win a paradise?'

1594–5: *Love's Labour's Lost*, 4.3.57–70. Lord Longueville reads aloud the sonnet he has written to Maria, one of the Princess of France's ladies-in-waiting.

The minor differences between this version and that printed in *The Passionate Pilgrim* (1599) are collated below (see note, p. 85).

2 **whom** which
  cannot] could not (1599)
3 **this false perjury** (he has taken a vow of celibacy)
9 **Vows are but**] My vow was (1599)

10 **which on my earth dost**] that on this earth doth (1599)
11 **Exhal'st**] drawest up; Exhale (1599)
14 **lose**] break (1599)

1594–1595

O, never will I trust …

BIRON

O, never will I trust to speeches penned,
   Nor to the motion of a schoolboy's tongue,
Nor never come in visor to my friend,
   Nor woo in rhyme, like a blind harper's song.
Taffeta phrases, silken terms precise,   5
   Three-piled hyperboles, spruce affectation,
Figures pedantical – these summer-flies
   Have blown me full of maggot ostentation.
I do forswear them, and I here protest,
   By this white glove – how white the hand, God knows! –   10
Henceforth my wooing mind shall be expressed
   In russet yeas, and honest kersey noes.
     And to begin, wench, so God help me, law!
     My love to thee is sound, sans crack or flaw.

1594–5: *Love's Labour's Lost*, 5.2.401–15. This sonnet forms part of Biron's speech to his beloved Rosaline in which he promises to speak more plainly.

3 **in visor** masked
4 **harper** harp-player, minstrel
5 **Taffeta** rich, silk fabric (i.e. overblown language)
8 **maggot ostentation** (the image is one of being riddled with pretentious and highly rhetorical expressions: all vanity for decay)

12 **russet** rustic, homely
    kersey plain, ordinary
13 **law!** look!
14 **sans** without (itself an affected usage)

1594–1595

Two households . . .

CHORUS

Two households, both alike in dignity
    In fair Verona, where we lay our scene,
From ancient grudge break to new mutiny,
    Where civil blood makes civil hands unclean.
From forth the fatal loins of these two foes   5
    A pair of star-crossed lovers take their life,
Whose misadventured piteous overthrows
    Doth with their death bury their parents' strife.
The fearful passage of their death-marked love
    And the continuance of their parents' rage –   10
Which but their children's end, naught could remove –
    Is now the two-hours' traffic of our stage;
        The which if you with patient ears attend,
        What here shall miss, our toil shall strive to mend.

1594–5: *Romeo and Juliet*, Prologue

3 **grudge** resentment
4 **civil hands unclean** blood spilt
in civic dispute stains civilised
hands

6 **star-crossed** ill-fated
9 **passage** course
11 **but** except for
14 **our** (the actors')

1594–1595

If I profane . . .

ROMEO   If I profane with my unworthiest hand
       This holy shrine, the gentler sin is this:
       My lips, two blushing pilgrims, ready stand
       To smooth that rough touch with a tender kiss.
JULIET   Good pilgrim, you do wrong your hand too much,   5
       Which mannerly devotion shows in this.
       For saints have hands that pilgrims' hands do touch,
       And palm to palm is holy palmers' kiss.
ROMEO   Have not saints lips, and holy palmers, too?
JULIET   Ay, pilgrim, lips that they must use in prayer.   10
ROMEO   O then, dear saint, let lips do what hands do:
       They pray; grant thou, lest faith turn to despair.
JULIET   Saints do not move, though grant for prayers' sake.
ROMEO   Then move not while my prayer's effect I take.
                He kisses her
       Thus from my lips, by thine my sin is purged.   15
JULIET   Then have my lips the sin that they have took.
ROMEO   Sin from my lips? O trespass sweetly urged!
       Give me my sin again.
                He kisses her
JULIET   You kiss by th' book.

1594–5: *Romeo and Juliet*, 1.5.92–109. This passage, made up of a sonnet followed by the first four lines of an uncompleted second sonnet, portrays
the first meeting between Romeo and Juliet.

2 **shrine** Juliet is imagined as a
  statue of a saint
5 **pilgrim** (who approaches a 'shrine')
6 **mannerly** well-mannered
8 **palm to palm** i.e. not lips to lips

palmers' pilgrims'
12 **pray** (to kiss you)
17 **trespass** sin
19 **by th' book** according to the rules;
  in an exemplary manner

1594–1595

Now old desire . . .

CHORUS
Now old desire doth in his deathbed lie,
  And young affection gapes to be his heir.
That fair for which love groaned for and would die,
  With tender Juliet matched, is now not fair.
Now Romeo is beloved and loves again,   5
  Alike bewitchèd by the charm of looks;
But to his foe supposed he must complain,
  And she steal love's sweet bait from fearful hooks.
Being held a foe, he may not have access
  To breathe such vows as lovers use to swear,   10
And she as much in love, her means much less
  To meet her new belovèd anywhere.
  But passion lends them power, time means, to meet,
  Temp'ring extremities with extreme sweet.

1594–5: *Romeo and Juliet*, 2.0. The introduction to Act Two.

1 **old desire** (Romeo's love for Rosaline)
2 **gapes** longs (as with open mouth)
3 **fair** beauty (Rosaline, Romeo's previous object of affection)
4 **matched** pitted against
5 **again** in return

7 **his foe supposed** imagined enemy (because Juliet is a Capulet)
11 **means** opportunity
14 **Temp'ring extremities** modifying extreme hardships
   sweet sweetness, pleasure

1594–1595

Is it thy will ...

Is it thy will thy image should keep open
  My heavy eyelids to the weary night?
Dost thou desire my slumbers should be broken
  While shadows like to thee do mock my sight?
Is it thy spirit that thou send'st from thee   5
  So far from home into my deeds to pry,
To find out shames and idle hours in me,
  The scope and tenor of thy jealousy?
O no; thy love, though much, is not so great.
  It is my love that keeps mine eye awake,   10
Mine own true love that doth my rest defeat,
  To play the watchman ever for thy sake.
    For thee watch I whilst thou dost wake elsewhere,
    From me far off, with others all too near.

I am awake all night thinking of you, but that's because of my love for
you, rather than yours for me. You're probably off enjoying yourself with
others.

Q: No. 61. Could be addressed to either a male or a female.

4 **shadows** images; actors; ghosts
5 **spirit** ghost-like presence
7 **shames** shameful deeds
  idle wasted
8 **scope and tenor** focus and
  purpose

12 **watchman** constable who patrols
  the streets at night
13 **watch** stay awake

1594–1595

Sin of self-love . . .

Sin of self-love possesseth all mine eye,
  And all my soul, and all my every part;
And for this sin there is no remedy,
  It is so grounded inward in my heart.
Methinks no face so gracious is as mine,   5
  No shape so true, no truth of such account,
And for myself mine own worth do define
  As I all other in all worths surmount.
But when my glass shows me myself indeed,
  Beated and chapped with tanned antiquity,   10
Mine own self-love quite contrary I read;
  Self so self-loving were iniquity.
    'Tis thee, my self, that for myself I praise,
    Painting my age with beauty of thy days.

I am full of self-love, but realise that this is only because you love me.

Q: No. 62. Could refer to either a male or a female. Dramatic analogy: Malvolio in *Twelfth Night, or What You Will*.

1 **Sin** wrongdoing (against God)
2 **part** limbs and feelings
5 **Methinks** it seems to me
6 **No … true** no other body as well formed
    truth (i.e. appearance of truth)
    account value
7 **do** I do
    define frame (with appreciation)
8 **other** others

9 **glass** looking-glass, mirror
10 **Beated and chapped** weather-beaten and wrinkled
    tanned antiquity skin made leathery with age
12 **were iniquity** would be wickedness
13 **thee, my self** you, my other self
14 **Painting** describing; covering up with make-up (also poetry)

1594–1595

Against my love . . .

Against my love shall be as I am now,
   With time's injurious hand crushed and o'erworn;
When hours have drained his blood and filled his brow
   With lines and wrinkles; when his youthful morn
Hath travelled on to age's steepy night,   5
   And all those beauties whereof now he's king
Are vanishing, or vanished out of sight,
   Stealing away the treasure of his spring:
For such a time do I now fortify
   Against confounding age's cruel knife,   10
That he shall never cut from memory
   My sweet love's beauty, though my lover's life.
     His beauty shall in these black lines be seen,
     And they shall live, and he in them still green.

I am preparing myself against my loved one being ruined by time and age.
He will live on in my verse and be ever youthful.

Q: No. 63. A meditation about a male loved one.

1 **Against** ready for when	**steepy** steep; precipitous; deep
love beloved person	(like the sun setting)
2 **time's injurious hand** (cf. *Troilus*	8 **Stealing** furtively hiding
and Cressida, 4.5.41: 'Injurious Time')	**spring** i.e. youth
o'erworn worn away	9 **For** in readiness
3 **blood** spirit; vigour	**fortify** construct a defence
brow countenance; appearance	10 **confounding** destructive
5 **travelled** journeyed; worked	14 **green** youthful; innocent
(travailed)	

1594–1595

When I have seen . . .

When I have seen by time's fell hand defaced
  The rich proud cost of outworn buried age;
When sometime-lofty towers I see down razed,
  And brass eternal slave to mortal rage;
When I have seen the hungry ocean gain   5
  Advantage on the kingdom of the shore,
And the firm soil win of the wat'ry main,
  Increasing store with loss and loss with store;
When I have seen such interchange of state,
  Or state itself confounded to decay,   10
Ruin hath taught me thus to ruminate:
  That time will come and take my love away.
    This thought is as a death, which cannot choose
    But weep to have that which it fears to lose.

When I see that everything decays, I realise I will lose my loved one, and this makes me weep.

Q: No. 64. The first of two sonnets (with 65) without an addressee, but which are about a loved one (male or female).

1 **fell** cruel
2 **rich proud cost** lavish, showy expense
  outworn buried age a worn away and vanished era
4 **mortal rage** death's destruction
7 **win of** a prize gained by

9 **interchange of state** exchange of territory
10 **state** stability, commonwealth, grandeur
  confounded ruined
11 **ruminate** ponder
14 **to have** at having

1594–1595

Since brass, nor stone . . .

Since brass, nor stone, nor earth, nor boundless sea,
　But sad mortality o'ersways their power,
How with this rage shall beauty hold a plea,
　Whose action is no stronger than a flower?
O how shall summer's honey breath hold out　　　　　　5
　Against the wrackful siege of battering days
When rocks impregnable are not so stout,
　Nor gates of steel so strong, but time decays?
O fearful meditation! Where, alack,
　Shall time's best jewel from time's chest lie hid,　　　10
Or what strong hand can hold his swift foot back,
　Or who his spoil of beauty can forbid?
　　O none, unless this miracle have might:
　　That in black ink my love may still shine bright.

Nothing can survive the destruction wrought by time, but my poetry, and in that my love will remain ever beautiful.

Q: No. 65. The second of two sonnets (with 64) without an addressee, but which are about a loved one (male or female).

2 **o'ersways** overrules	10 **from … hid** escape from being
3 **rage** destruction (by death)	gathered up into time's treasure-chest
hold uphold (as in a law suit)	11 and 12 **his** time's
6 **wrackful** wrecking	12 **spoil** ruin; stolen treasure

1594—1595

Tired with all these . . .

Tired with all these, for restful death I cry:
    As, to behold desert a beggar born,
And needy nothing trimmed in jollity,
    And purest faith unhappily forsworn,
And gilded honour shamefully misplaced,   5
    And maiden virtue rudely strumpeted,
And right perfection wrongfully disgraced,
    And strength by limping sway disablèd,
And art made tongue-tied by authority,
    And folly, doctor-like, controlling skill,   10
And simple truth miscalled simplicity,
    And captive good attending captain ill.
        Tired with all these, from these would I be gone,
        Save that to die I leave my love alone.

I am so sick and tired of things as they are, that I am looking forward to death — except that in dying I would leave my loved one alone.

Q: No. 66. A meditation about all that's wrong with the world, which refers to a male or a female loved one.

1 **these** all that is about to be mentioned	7 **disgraced** disparaged
2 **desert ... born** merit born into beggary	8 **limping sway** poor leadership
3 **jollity** finery	9 **art** learning (literature and science)
4 **unhappily forsworn** wretchedly, maliciously abandoned, betrayed	**made ... authority** silenced, censored, stifled
5 **gilded** apparently splendid	10 **controlling** directing
6 **rudely** violently	12 **attending** serving, following behind

1594–1595

Ah, wherefore with infection ...

Ah, wherefore with infection should he live
   And with his presence grace impiety,
That sin by him advantage should achieve
   And lace itself with his society?
Why should false painting imitate his cheek,   5
   And steal dead seeming of his living hue?
Why should poor beauty indirectly seek
   Roses of shadow, since his rose is true?
Why should he live now nature bankrupt is,
   Beggared of blood to blush through lively veins,   10
For she hath no exchequer now but his,
   And proud of many, lives upon his gains?
      O, him she stores to show what wealth she had
      In days long since, before these last so bad.

My loved one is too good for this world, more beautiful and truer than any art. He exceeds even nature herself.

Q: No. 67. The first of two meditations (with 68) about a male.

1 **infection** moral contamination in the world
2 **grace** adorn
  impiety unholiness
4 **lace** decorate (with embroidery)
5 **false painting** insincere poetry; poor visual representation (in art or make-up)
7 **poor** inferior
8 **Roses of shadow** fake roses (rouged cheeks; in art; in poetry)
  his rose is true (i.e. he is faithful)
10 **Beggared** deprived
11 and 13 **she** nature
  exchequer treasury
12 **gains** the interest he earns

1594–1595

Thus is his cheek …

Thus is his cheek the map of days outworn,
   When beauty lived and died as flowers do now,
Before these bastard signs of fair were borne
   Or durst inhabit on a living brow;
Before the golden tresses of the dead,   5
   The right of sepulchres, were shorn away
To live a second life on second head;
   Ere beauty's dead fleece made another gay.
In him those holy antique hours are seen
   Without all ornament, itself and true,   10
Making no summer of another's green,
   Robbing no old to dress his beauty new;
      And him as for a map doth nature store,
      To show false art what beauty was of yore.

My loved one's face encapsulates all natural beauty, harking back to a sacred time before people started to rely on false adornment.

Q: No. 68. The second of two meditations (with 67) about a male.

1 **map** epitome; guide
days outworn time past
3 **bastard … fair** fake tokens of beauty
borne worn (like clothes); also 'born'
4 **durst inhabit** dared to be seen
5 **tresses** hair
5–8 **Before … gay** (cf. *The Merchant of Venice*, 3.2.92–96: 'golden locks / Which makes such wanton gambols with the wind / Upon supposèd fairness, often known / To be the dowry of a second head,

/ The skull that bred them in the sepulchre.')
6 **The … sepulchres** which should be buried
shorn away shaved
7 **To … head** i.e. made into a wig for the living
9 **holy antique hours** sacred, olden days
12 **old** former fashions
14 **what beauty was** what beauty used to look like; how much beauty there used to be; what used to constitute beauty

1594–1595

Those parts of thee …

Those parts of thee that the world's eye doth view
    Want nothing that the thought of hearts can mend.
All tongues, the voice of souls, give thee that due,
    Utt'ring bare truth even so as foes commend.
Thy outward thus with outward praise is crowned,   5
    But those same tongues that give thee so thine own
In other accents do this praise confound
    By seeing farther than the eye hath shown.
They look into the beauty of thy mind,
    And that in guess they measure by thy deeds.   10
Then, churls, their thoughts – although their eyes were kind –
    To thy fair flower add the rank smell of weeds.
      But why thy odour matcheth not thy show,
      The soil is this: that thou dost common grow.

Everyone praises your physical beauty, but when they look more closely, they find something amiss. And that's because you are cheapening yourself.

Q: No. 69. The first of two sonnets (with 70) addressed to either a male or a female.

1 **parts** aspects (both physical and personal characteristics)
2 **Want** lack
  mend improve
3 **All tongues … due** (cf. *Coriolanus*, 2.1.202: 'All tongues speak of him')
4 **bare** simple; obvious
7 **confound** spoil; ruin

10 **And … guess** and by doing that and guessing
  measure weigh up; judge
11 **churls** ungracious people
13 **odour** smell (inward personality)
  show appearance (behaviour)
14 **soil** answer (base fact of the matter)
  common vulgar, cheap

1594–1595

That thou art blamed . . .

That thou art blamed shall not be thy defect,
    For slander's mark was ever yet the fair.
The ornament of beauty is suspect,
    A crow that flies in heaven's sweetest air.
So thou be good, slander doth but approve   5
    Thy worth the greater, being wooed of time;
For canker vice the sweetest buds doth love,
    And thou present'st a pure unstainèd prime.
Thou hast passed by the ambush of young days
    Either not assailed, or victor being charged;   10
Yet this thy praise cannot be so thy praise
    To tie up envy, evermore enlarged.
      If some suspect of ill masked not thy show,
      Then thou alone kingdoms of hearts shouldst owe.

You cannot help being blamed or slandered because you are beautiful, but your beauty might easily become infected, and your reputation suspect. If it weren't for this, you would be the most captivating of all lovers.

Q: No. 70. The second of two sonnets (with 69) addressed to either a male or a female.

2 **mark** target
3 **suspect** suspicion
4 **A crow** like a bird of ill omen
5 **So** as long as
  approve prove
6 **being wooed of time** time being on your side
7 **canker vice** bad practices, like an infecting worm
8 **unstainèd prime** unblemished spring (youth)
9 **passed by** avoided
10 **charged** attacked; blamed
12 **To** as to
  evermore enlarged ever-increasing
13 **show** reputation
14 **owe** own

1594–1595

No longer mourn for me . . .

No longer mourn for me when I am dead
  Than you shall hear the surly sullen bell
Give warning to the world that I am fled
  From this vile world with vilest worms to dwell.
Nay, if you read this line, remember not 5
  The hand that writ it; for I love you so
That I in your sweet thoughts would be forgot
  If thinking on me then should make you woe.
O, if, I say, you look upon this verse
  When I perhaps compounded am with clay, 10
Do not so much as my poor name rehearse,
  But let your love even with my life decay,
    Lest the wise world should look into your moan
    And mock you with me after I am gone.

Let your mourning for me be short. I would rather you forget me, even when you read my poem, than be unhappy, for which you might be mocked.

Q: No. 71. The first of two related sonnets (with 72) addressed to either a male or a female. Dramatic analogy: Feste's song 'Come away, come away death' in *Twelfth Night, or What You Will* (2.4.50–65).

2 **sullen** solemn
4 **vile** wretched, contemptible
6 **so** in such a way
8 **make** cause
10 **compounded** mixed, mingled
11 **rehearse** repeat, speak over

12 **life** body as well as reputation
13 **look into** investigate, question
  moan grieving
14 **mock** deride you for loving me (as they used to deride me)

1594–1595

O, lest the world . . .

O, lest the world should task you to recite
    What merit lived in me that you should love,
After my death, dear love, forget me quite;
    For you in me can nothing worthy prove –
Unless you would devise some virtuous lie   5
    To do more for me than mine own desert,
And hang more praise upon deceasèd I
    Than niggard truth would willingly impart.
O, lest your true love may seem false in this,
    That you for love speak well of me untrue,   10
My name be buried where my body is,
    And live no more to shame nor me nor you;
       For I am shamed by that which I bring forth,
       And so should you, to love things nothing worth.

Just forget me when I am dead, because you might shame yourself and me by saying things that make your love seem false. My poetry is not worth loving either.

Q: No. 72. The second of two sonnets (with 71) addressed to either a male or a female.

1 **recite** tell (perhaps an 'official' version learnt by rote)
4 **prove** find; demonstrate (even set forth legally)
6 **mine own desert** I deserve (or that I already have)
8 **niggard** miserly

9 **false** dishonest (as well as inconstant)
10 **untrue** untruly
13 **that … forth** i.e. my poetic composition (this and other of my sonnets)
14 **should you** you ought to be ashamed

1594–1595

That time of year . . .

That time of year thou mayst in me behold
    When yellow leaves, or none, or few, do hang
Upon those boughs which shake against the cold,
    Bare ruined choirs where late the sweet birds sang.
In me thou seest the twilight of such day   5
    As after sunset fadeth in the west,
Which by and by black night doth take away,
    Death's second self, that seals up all in rest.
In me thou seest the glowing of such fire
    That on the ashes of his youth doth lie   10
As the death-bed whereon it must expire,
    Consumed with that which it was nourished by.
        This thou perceiv'st, which makes thy love more strong,
        To love that well which thou must leave ere long.

I am in the winter and sunset of my life, an old, fading fire. But seeing me like this might make your love for me even stronger.

Q: No. 73. The first of two syntactically related sonnets (with 74) addressed to either a male or a female.

3 **those boughs** my bodily frame, my limbs
4 **choirs** chancels (and branches of trees, that look like ruined chancels); also 'quires', the gathering of pages in a book
   late of late, recently
   sweet birds choir boys (as well as the birds now departed because of autumn); also the musicality of my poetic words (about you)
8 **Death's second self** night, an agent of death
12 **Consumed … by** choked by the fuel that made it (now ash)
14 **that** me (the poet) and everything about me, as well as life itself

1594–1595

But be contented . . .

But be contented when that fell arrest
 Without all bail shall carry me away.
My life hath in this line some interest,
 Which for memorial still with thee shall stay.
When thou reviewest this, thou dost review   5
 The very part was consecrate to thee.
The earth can have but earth, which is his due;
 My spirit is thine, the better part of me.
So then thou hast but lost the dregs of life,
 The prey of worms, my body being dead,   10
The coward conquest of a wretch's knife,
 Too base of thee to be rememberèd.
  The worth of that is that which it contains,
  And that is this, and this with thee remains.

Death can only take away my body; my spirit remains in this poem.

Q: No. 74. The continuation of two sonnets (with 73) addressed to either a male or a female.

1 **fell** cruel, deadly
2 **bail** security for a prisoner pending a trial (death allows no such bail)
3 **this line** the poem you are reading
5 **reviewest** re-read
6 **part was** aspect of me which was

consecrate devoted, dedicated (religiously)
11 **coward … knife** (death operates like a coward and strikes dishonourably)
13 **that** my spirit
14 **this** this sonnet

1594–1595

So are you to my thoughts . . .

So are you to my thoughts as food to life,
  Or as sweet-seasoned showers are to the ground;
And for the peace of you I hold such strife
  As 'twixt a miser and his wealth is found:
Now proud as an enjoyer, and anon   5
  Doubting the filching age will steal his treasure;
Now counting best to be with you alone,
  Then bettered that the world may see my pleasure;
Sometime all full with feasting on your sight,
  And by and by clean starvèd for a look;   10
Possessing or pursuing no delight
  Save what is had or must from you be took.
    Thus do I pine and surfeit day by day,
    Or gluttoning on all, or all away.

You are so essential to my life that I am as possessive of you as a miser is
of his money.

Q: No. 75. Could be addressed to a male or a female. Dramatic analogy:
Lorenzo to Jessica in *The Merchant of Venice*; Helena to Demetrius in *A Midsummer Night's Dream*; Helen to Bertram in *All's Well That Ends Well*.

3 **peace of you** tranquillity you
  bring with you
  hold such strife encounter the
  kind of conflict
5 **enjoyer** one who glories in
  possessing
6 **filching** thieving

7 **counting** thinking it; reckoning
  the worth
8 **bettered** preferring
10 **clean** entirely
14 **Or** either
  all away without anything

1594–1595

Why is my verse . . .

Why is my verse so barren of new pride,
　So far from variation or quick change?
Why, with the time, do I not glance aside
　To new-found methods and to compounds strange?
Why write I still all one, ever the same,　　　　　　　　　5
　And keep invention in a noted weed,
That every word doth almost tell my name,
　Showing their birth and where they did proceed?
O know, sweet love, I always write of you,
　And you and love are still my argument;　　　　　　　10
So all my best is dressing old words new,
　Spending again what is already spent;
　　For as the sun is daily new and old,
　　So is my love, still telling what is told.

I do not seek to write decorated or fashionable poetry because you and love are all I write about, and that's why my verse tries to present the same words and ideas in different ways.

Q: No. 76. Could be addressed to either a male or a female.

1 **pride** decoration
2 **quick change** lively difference
3 **with the time** as would be
　fashionable
4 **compounds** compound words
6 **noted weed** familiar form of
　clothing

8 **where** from whence
12 **Spending … spent** giving vent to
　that which is constantly being used
　up

1594–1595

Thy glass will show thee ...

Thy glass will show thee how thy beauties wear,
　Thy dial how thy precious minutes waste,
The vacant leaves thy mind's imprint will bear,
　And of this book this learning mayst thou taste:
The wrinkles which thy glass will truly show 　　　　　　5
　Of mouthèd graves will give thee memory;
Thou by thy dial's shady stealth mayst know
　Time's thievish progress to eternity;
Look what thy memory cannot contain
　Commit to these waste blanks, and thou shalt find 　　10
Those children nursed, delivered from thy brain,
　To take a new acquaintance of thy mind.
　　These offices so oft as thou wilt look
　　Shall profit thee and much enrich thy book.

Time is passing, so here's an almanac which you can learn from and in which you can record your thoughts.

Q: No. 77. Could be addressed to a male or a female. Like Sonnet 26, this is an example of Shakespeare's personal, verse correspondence. This one accompanies the gift of a book (an almanac, see 'Introduction', pp. 34–5).

1 **glass** looking-glass, mirror
　wear are enduring (i.e. fading)
2 **Thy ... waste** (cf. *Richard, Duke of York* (*3 Henry VI*), 2.5.24–5: 'To carve out dials quaintly, point by point, / Thereby to see the minutes how they run')
　dial time-piece (or sundial)
3 **vacant leaves** blank pages
　mind's imprint thoughts in writing (published or handwritten); memories
4 **this book** (i.e. the almanac being gifted)

6 **mouthèd** gaping
　give thee memory remind you
7 **shady stealth** imperceptible movement
9 **Look what** whatever
10 **blanks** blank pages (of the almanac, for personal notes)
11 **delivered** born
13 **offices** practices, duties, functions (i.e. those mentioned in lines 5–11)
14 **thy book** my gift of an almanac to you

1594–1595

Farewell — thou art too dear...

Farewell — thou art too dear for my possessing,
  And like enough thou know'st thy estimate.
The charter of thy worth gives thee releasing;
  My bonds in thee are all determinate.
For how do I hold thee but by thy granting,   5
  And for that riches where is my deserving?
The cause of this fair gift in me is wanting,
  And so my patent back again is swerving.
Thyself thou gav'st, thy own worth then not knowing,
  Or me to whom thou gav'st it else mistaking;   10
So thy great gift, upon misprision growing,
  Comes home again, on better judgement making.
    Thus have I had thee as a dream doth flatter:
    In sleep a king, but waking no such matter.

Farewell, you are too precious for me to keep, and I was mistaken in your love.

Q: No. 87. Could be addressed to either a male or a female.

1 **dear** precious; expensive
2 **thy estimate** what you are worth
3 **charter** legal (royal) privilege
  releasing freedom; dispensation
  (from love)
4 **bonds** ties in love
  determinate ended
5 **granting** giving me permission

6 **riches** treasure
8 **patent ... swerving** privileges in
  love (granted by you) are reverting
  back to you
10 **mistaking** misjudging
11 **misprision** misunderstanding
12 **Comes home again** returns to
  you

1594–1595

When thou shalt be disposed . . .

When thou shalt be disposed to set me light
    And place my merit in the eye of scorn,
Upon thy side against myself I'll fight,
    And prove thee virtuous though thou art forsworn.
With mine own weakness being best acquainted,   5
    Upon thy part I can set down a story
Of faults concealed wherein I am attainted,
    That thou in losing me shall win much glory;
And I by this will be a gainer too;
    For bending all my loving thoughts on thee,   10
The injuries that to myself I do,
    Doing thee vantage, double vantage me.
      Such is my love, to thee I so belong,
      That for thy right myself will bear all wrong.

However you treat me, I am on your side. I will even help you to get rid of me, and carry all the hurt you are causing me.

Q: No. 88. Could be addressed to either a male or a female.

1 **set me light** undervalue me
2 **eye of scorn** public ridicule
4 **forsworn** lying
6 **story** account
7 **attainted** guilty
8 **losing** (Q's 'loosing': also setting free)

10 **bending** turning
11 **The injuries … do** (cf. *The Tragedy of King Lear*, 2.2.475: 'The injuries that they themselves procure')
14 **right** advantage; virtue; privilege

1594–1595

Say that thou didst forsake me . . .

Say that thou didst forsake me for some fault,
  And I will comment upon that offence;
Speak of my lameness, and I straight will halt,
  Against thy reasons making no defence.
Thou canst not, love, disgrace me half so ill,   5
  To set a form upon desirèd change,
As I'll myself disgrace, knowing thy will.
  I will acquaintance strangle and look strange,
Be absent from thy walks, and in my tongue
  Thy sweet belovèd name no more shall dwell,   10
Lest I, too much profane, should do it wrong,
  And haply of our old acquaintance tell.
    For thee, against myself I'll vow debate;
    For I must ne'er love him whom thou dost hate.

If you wanted to leave and blame me, I would do all I could to help you feel good about it, because I love you.

Q: No. 89. The first of two syntactically related sonnets (with 90) which could be addressed to either a male or a female. Possibly connected to 22, 57, 134, 135, 136, and 143 because of the pun on the poet's name, Will (line 7).

1 **Say** let's suppose
3 **lameness** disability (physical; emotional; in writing poetry)
  straight will halt will immediately affect a limp
6 **To** than to
  set ... upon define

7 **will** desire; power (also a pun on the poet's first name)
8 **acquaintance strangle** choke all sense of familiarity
  strange indifferent
12 **haply** by chance
13 **debate** strife

1594–1595

Then hate me when thou wilt . . .

Then hate me when thou wilt, if ever, now,
   Now while the world is bent my deeds to cross,
Join with the spite of fortune, make me bow,
   And do not drop in for an after-loss.
Ah do not, when my heart hath 'scaped this sorrow,   5
   Come in the rearward of a conquered woe;
Give not a windy night a rainy morrow
   To linger out a purposed overthrow.
If thou wilt leave me, do not leave me last,
   When other petty griefs have done their spite,   10
But in the onset come; so shall I taste
   At first the very worst of fortune's might,
     And other strains of woe, which now seem woe,
     Compared with loss of thee will not seem so.

If you are going to leave me, do it quickly.

Q: No. 90. The second of two related sonnets (with 89) which could be addressed to either a male or a female.

2 **bent** determined
  cross oppose; thwart
3 **bow** behave like a servant (and like an actor at the end of a performance)
4 **drop in** swoop down upon me (like a bird of prey)

after-loss another, later thwarting
5 **'scaped** escaped
6 **in the rearward** from the rearguard; from behind
8 **purposed** already intended
13 **strains** stresses; kinds

1594–1595

Some glory in their birth ...

Some glory in their birth, some in their skill,
   Some in their wealth, some in their body's force,
Some in their garments (though new-fangled ill),
   Some in their hawks and hounds, some in their horse,
And every humour hath his adjunct pleasure   5
   Wherein it finds a joy above the rest.
But these particulars are not my measure;
   All these I better in one general best.
Thy love is better than high birth to me,
   Richer than wealth, prouder than garments' cost,   10
Of more delight than hawks or horses be,
   And having thee of all men's pride I boast,
     Wretchèd in this alone: that thou mayst take
     All this away, and me most wretchèd make.

Everyone has something they deeply enjoy: for me it's your love.

Q: No. 91. This is the first of three syntactically related sonnets (with 92 and 93) which could be addressed to either a male or a female. Dramatic analogy: Othello to Desdemona.

1 **glory** take pride

3 **new-fangled ill** cheaply made but fashionable

4 **horse** (also horses)

5 **humour** taste; temperament; pursuit

7 **my measure** the things for which I am known; that make me happy; the topic of my verse

9 **is better than** exceeds

1594–1595

But do thy worst . . .

But do thy worst to steal thyself away,
    For term of life thou art assurèd mine,
And life no longer than thy love will stay,
    For it depends upon that love of thine.
Then need I not to fear the worst of wrongs   5
    When in the least of them my life hath end.
I see a better state to me belongs
    Than that which on thy humour doth depend.
Thou canst not vex me with inconstant mind,
    Since that my life on thy revolt doth lie.   10
O, what a happy title do I find –
    Happy to have thy love, happy to die!
        But what's so blessèd fair that fears no blot?
        Thou mayst be false, and yet I know it not.

I am not afraid of you leaving me because it would end my life.

Q: No. 92. This is the second of three syntactically related sonnets (with
91 and 93) which could be addressed to either a male or a female. Dramatic analogy: Othello to Desdemona.

3 **life** my life
6 **least of them** slightest wrong you
  might commit against me
7 **state** condition
8 **humour** temperament

11 **title** possession (legal ownership
  of property)
13 **fair** fortunate
  blot taint; drawback

1594–1595

So shall I live . . .

So shall I live supposing thou art true
    Like a deceivèd husband; so love's face
May still seem love to me, though altered new –
    Thy looks with me, thy heart in other place.
For there can live no hatred in thine eye,   5
    Therefore in that I cannot know thy change.
In many's looks the false heart's history
    Is writ in moods and frowns and wrinkles strange;
But heaven in thy creation did decree
    That in thy face sweet love should ever dwell;   10
Whate'er thy thoughts or thy heart's workings be,
    Thy looks should nothing thence but sweetness tell.
      How like Eve's apple doth thy beauty grow
      If thy sweet virtue answer not thy show!

Since you always appear beautiful and loving, I always assume you are being faithful to me, though you may not be.

Q: No. 93. This is the third of three syntactically related sonnets (with 91 and 92) which could be addressed to either a male or a female.

1 **So** therefore
2 **so** as a result of this
   face appearance
4 **looks** glances
   heart affection
5 **For** since

7 **many's** many people's
8 **wrinkles strange** insincere looks
13 **Eve's apple** The forbidden fruit that brought about the fall of humankind.

1594–1595

They that have power…

They that have power to hurt and will do none,
    That do not do the thing they most do show,
Who moving others are themselves as stone,
    Unmovèd, cold, and to temptation slow –
They rightly do inherit heaven's graces,   5
    And husband nature's riches from expense;
They are the lords and owners of their faces,
    Others but stewards of their excellence.
The summer's flower is to the summer sweet
    Though to itself it only live and die,   10
But if that flower with base infection meet
    The basest weed outbraves his dignity;
        For sweetest things turn sourest by their deeds:
        Lilies that fester smell far worse than weeds.

Some apparently admirable people have a natural power over others and over themselves, but this might eventually turn nasty.

Q: No. 94. A meditation in the third person, an essay in miniature.

1 **that have power** (also occurs in *Edward III*, scene 2.553)
  none no hurt
2 **they … show** they seem most likely to do
3 **as stone** unemotional
5 **rightly** indeed; by right
6 **husband** manage prudently
  expense wastefulness
8 **stewards** hired managers

their (could refer to either the 'lords and owners' or the 'Others', 'stewards')
12 **basest weed** (also occurs in *Edward III*, scene 2.331)
  outbraves surpasses
  his its (the summer's flower)
  dignity fine outward appearance
14 **Lilies … weeds** (also occurs in *Edward III*, scene 2.619)

1594–1595

How sweet and lovely . . .

How sweet and lovely dost thou make the shame
　Which, like a canker in the fragrant rose,
Doth spot the beauty of thy budding name!
　O, in what sweets dost thou thy sins enclose!
That tongue that tells the story of thy days,　　　　　5
　Making lascivious comments on thy sport,
Cannot dispraise, but in a kind of praise,
　Naming thy name, blesses an ill report.
O, what a mansion have those vices got
　Which for their habitation chose out thee,　　　　　10
Where Beauty's veil doth cover every blot
　And all things turns to fair that eyes can see!
　　Take heed, dear heart, of this large privilege:
　　The hardest knife ill used doth lose his edge.

You look beautiful and your name has a good reputation, which you use
powerfully to hide your misdemeanours, but it is a power you should use
with caution.

Q: No. 95. Could be addressed to either a male or a female.

2 **canker** canker-worm
　fragrant rose (also occurs in
　Edward III, scene 2.332)
3 **budding** flowering (reputational)
4 **sweets** pleasant appearances (and
　behaviour)
6 **lascivious** lewd

sport fooling around (romantic
　and sexual life)
9 **mansion** dwelling (the lover's self
　and body)
11 **blot** disgrace (moral misdemeanour)
13 **privilege** freedom
14 **his** its

1594–1595

Some say thy fault is youth . . .

Some say thy fault is youth, some wantonness;
  Some say thy grace is youth and gentle sport.
Both grace and faults are loved of more and less;
  Thou mak'st faults graces that to thee resort.
As on the finger of a thronèd queen   5
  The basest jewel will be well esteemed,
So are those errors that in thee are seen
  To truths translated and for true things deemed.
How many lambs might the stern wolf betray
  If like a lamb he could his looks translate!   10
How many gazers mightst thou lead away
  If thou wouldst use the strength of all thy state!
    But do not so: I love thee in such sort
    As, thou being mine, mine is thy good report.

You could deceive many people because you even turn your faults into admired blessings, but I hope you don't because of my love for you.

Q: No. 96. Could be addressed to either a male or a female.

1	**wantonness** lawlessness; caprice; lechery	9	stern cruel
2	**sport** playfulness; romantic and sexual encounters	10	like into the appearance of
		11	gazers admirers
3	**of … less** by all social ranks (high and low)	12	state commanding power (also way of being)
4	**to thee resort** come your way	13–14	This couplet also ends Sonnet 36.
8	translated transformed		

How like a winter ...

How like a winter hath my absence been
   From thee, the pleasure of the fleeting year!
What freezings have I felt, what dark days seen,
   What old December's bareness everywhere!
And yet this time removed was summer's time,   5
   The teeming autumn big with rich increase,
Bearing the wanton burden of the prime
   Like widowed wombs after their lords' decease.
Yet this abundant issue seemed to me
   But hope of orphans and unfathered fruit,   10
For summer and his pleasures wait on thee,
   And thou away, the very birds are mute;
     Or if they sing, 'tis with so dull a cheer
     That leaves look pale, dreading the winter's near.

Being away from you feels like winter, and even though it is summer and autumn, the best of the year is always where you are.

Q: No. 97. The first of three related sonnets (with 98 and 99) about absence. Could be addressed to either a male or a female.

1 **absence** (physical and emotional)	7 **Bearing** storing; delivering
2 **fleeting** swift-changing; changeable, fickle	**wanton ... prime** the state of pregnancy from a carefree, passionate spring
5 **removed** away (from you)	
6 **teeming** fruitful; fertile	10 **unfathered** illegitimate
big pregnant	11 **wait** attend
increase procreation	13 **cheer** mood

1594–1595

From you have I been absent . . .

From you have I been absent in the spring
   When proud-pied April, dressed in all his trim,
Hath put a spirit of youth in everything,
   That heavy Saturn laughed and leapt with him.
Yet nor the lays of birds nor the sweet smell   5
   Of different flowers in odour and in hue
Could make me any summer's story tell,
   Or from their proud lap pluck them where they grew;
Nor did I wonder at the lily's white,
   Nor praise the deep vermilion in the rose.   10
They were but sweet, but figures of delight
   Drawn after you, you pattern of all those;
      Yet seemed it winter still, and, you away,
      As with your shadow I with these did play.

Away from you in the spring, I was reminded of you everywhere I looked, but it still felt like winter.

Q: No. 98. The second of three related sonnets (with 97 and 99) about absence. Could be addressed to either a male or a female.

2 **proud-pied** splendidly varied in colour
4 **Saturn** the god of melancholy
5 **lays** songs
6 **hue** colour
8 **proud lap** i.e. the earth (cf. *Richard II*, 5.2.47: 'the green lap of the new-come spring')

10 **vermilion** deep red
11 **figures** likenesses
12 **Drawn** pictured
   pattern model; precedent
14 **shadow** semblance; copy; spirit

1594–1595

The forward violet ...

The forward violet thus did I chide:
  'Sweet thief, whence didst thou steal thy sweet that smells,
If not from my love's breath? The purple pride
  Which on thy soft cheek for complexion dwells
In my love's veins thou hast too grossly dyed.'   5
  The lily I condemnèd for thy hand,
And buds of marjoram had stol'n thy hair;
  The roses fearfully on thorns did stand,
One blushing shame, another white despair;
  A third, nor red nor white, had stol'n of both,   10
And to his robb'ry had annexed thy breath;
  But for his theft in pride of all his growth
A vengeful canker ate him up to death.
    More flowers I noted, yet I none could see
    But sweet or colour it had stol'n from thee.

You are present in many flowers, but only because they have stolen their scent and colour from you.

Q: No. 99. The third of three related sonnets (with 97 and 98) about absence. Could be addressed to either a male or a female. This sonnet has an extra, introductory line, and is about theft.

1 **forward** lively; presumptuous
2 **Sweet** attractive
  thy sweet your pleasing scent
3 **pride** splendour
5 **grossly** obviously
6 **condemnèd** discredited
  thy hand for stealing the whiteness
of your hand
7 **marjoram** a sweet-smelling herb
  with blonde-looking buds
8 **fearfully** timorously, nervously
11 **annexed** added
13 **canker** canker-worm
15 **sweet** scent

1594–1595

Where art thou, muse . . .

Where art thou, muse, that thou forget'st so long
  To speak of that which gives thee all thy might?
Spend'st thou thy fury on some worthless song,
  Dark'ning thy power to lend base subjects light?
Return, forgetful muse, and straight redeem   5
  In gentle numbers time so idly spent;
Sing to the ear that doth thy lays esteem
  And gives thy pen both skill and argument.
Rise, resty muse, my love's sweet face survey
  If time have any wrinkle graven there.   10
If any, be a satire to decay
  And make time's spoils despisèd everywhere.
    Give my love fame faster than time wastes life;
    So, thou prevenest his scythe and crookèd knife.

Come back to me, muse, and help me to conquer time by inspiring me to
set forth the beauty of my loved one in poetry.

Q: No. 100. The first of four sonnets (with 101, 102, and 103) about the
poetic muse and poetic writing. Addressed to the muse and could be
about a male or a female.

3 **fury** poetic inspiration, energy
4 **Dark'ning** sullying
  lend give
5–6 **redeem … spent** (cf. *1 Henry IV*,
  1.2.213–14, 'Redeeming time when
  men least think I will.')
6 **gentle** honourable; refined
  numbers lines of poetry

idly frivolously
7 **lays** songs
8 **argument** subject matter
9 **resty** lazy
11 **be** let it become
12 **spoils** acts of plundering
14 **prevenest** anticipates; outstrippest

1594–1595

O truant muse . . .

O truant muse, what shall be thy amends
  For thy neglect of truth in beauty dyed?
Both truth and beauty on my love depends;
  So dost thou too, and therein dignified.
Make answer, muse. Wilt thou not haply say   5
  'Truth needs no colour with his colour fixed,
Beauty no pencil beauty's truth to lay,
  But best is best if never intermixed'?
Because he needs no praise wilt thou be dumb?
  Excuse not silence so, for't lies in thee   10
To make him much outlive a gilded tomb,
  And to be praised of ages yet to be.
    Then do thy office, muse; I teach thee how
    To make him seem long hence as he shows now.

I know why you are playing truant with me, my muse, because my loved one already embodies all truth and beauty. But I need you to help me preserve his beauty by inspiring me to write about it.

Q: No. 101. The second of four sonnets (with 100, 102, and 103) about the poetic muse and poetic writing. Addressed to the muse about a male.

1 **amends** compensation
2 **dyed** suffused
3 **my love** my own feelings of love; my lover
5 **haply** perhaps
6 **his** truth's
7 **pencil** paint-brush (also writing equipment)

lay apply
8 **intermixed** cross-bred
9 **he** i.e. the person about whom the poet wants to write
13 **office** duty
14 **long hence** in the future
  shows appears

1594–1595

My love is strengthened . . .

My love is strengthened, though more weak in seeming.
   I love not less, though less the show appear.
That love is merchandized whose rich esteeming
   The owner's tongue doth publish everywhere.
Our love was new and then but in the spring   5
   When I was wont to greet it with my lays,
As Philomel in summer's front doth sing,
   And stops his pipe in growth of riper days –
Not that the summer is less pleasant now
   Than when her mournful hymns did hush the night,   10
But that wild music burdens every bough,
   And sweets grown common lose their dear delight.
      Therefore like her I sometime hold my tongue,
      Because I would not dull you with my song.

Although I am not writing about you as often as I used to, my love is stronger. I just do not want it to lose its natural sincerity.

Q: No. 102. The third of four sonnets (with 100, 101, and 103) about the poetic muse and poetic writing. A confession about the writing of poetry, which could be addressed to either a male or a female.

3 **merchandized** commercialised
  esteeming value; reputation
4 **owner's tongue** i.e. the poet's pen
6 **lays** verses
7 **Philomel** In Ovid's *Metamorphoses* she is raped by her brother-in-law King Tereus, who also cuts out her tongue. She then turns into a nightingale.
  front commencement
8 **pipe** 'his' (as in Q) singing throat; Shakespeare's nightingale is male

(identified here with his own persona as a poet), and female (lines 10 and 12).
11 **wild** natural; uncontrolled; common
  burdens weighs down (also act as a chorus, refrain)
12 **sweets** lovers, sweethearts; pleasantries
13 **her** Philomel, the nightingale
14 **dull** take the edge off; bore

1594–1595

Alack, what poverty . . .

Alack, what poverty my muse brings forth
    That, having such a scope to show her pride,
The argument all bare is of more worth
    Than when it hath my added praise beside!
O blame me not if I no more can write!   5
    Look in your glass and there appears a face
That overgoes my blunt invention quite,
    Dulling my lines and doing me disgrace.
Were it not sinful then, striving to mend,
    To mar the subject that before was well?   10
For to no other pass my verses tend
    Than of your graces and your gifts to tell;
        And more, much more, than in my verse can sit
        Your own glass shows you when you look in it.

My muse is poor, and I cannot write anything better than your actual appearance when you look into a mirror.

Q: No. 103. The fourth of four sonnets (with 100, 101, and 102) about the poetic muse and poetic writing, addressed to either a male or a female.

2 **scope** range of possibility (i.e. the person to whom the poem is addressed)
3 **all bare** with no poetic ornament
6 **glass** mirror
7 **overgoes** supersedes; overwhelms
blunt invention unsophisticated poetic powers
8 **Dulling** taking the edge off
9 **striving to mend** (cf. *King Lear*, 1.4.326 'Striving to better, oft we mar what's well.')
10 **subject** i.e. of the poetry: the addressee
11 **pass** goal; purpose

1595–1597

❧

1595–1597

From fairest creatures . . .

From fairest creatures we desire increase,
    That thereby beauty's rose might never die,
But as the riper should by time decease,
    His tender heir might bear his memory;
But thou, contracted to thine own bright eyes,   5
    Feed'st thy light's flame with self-substantial fuel,
Making a famine where abundance lies,
    Thyself thy foe, to thy sweet self too cruel.
Thou that art now the world's fresh ornament
    And only herald to the gaudy spring   10
Within thine own bud buriest thy content,
    And, tender churl, mak'st waste in niggarding.
        Pity the world, or else this glutton be:
        To eat the world's due, by the grave and thee.

Beauty should procreate; you are too self-absorbed to do so, but you should.

Q: No. 1. Sonnets 1–17 are about procreation. Addressed to a male.

1 **creatures** created beings (not just humans)
increase procreation
2 **beauty's rose** the best bloom of beauty (evoking Medieval courtly poetry)
3 **riper** older beauties
decease die; cease to be beautiful
4 **tender** young; considerate
bear carry; give birth to
5 **contracted** betrothed
6 **self-substantial fuel** self-supporting energy

8 **Thyself thy foe** What you are doing now makes you an enemy to yourself
10 **only** chief
gaudy joyful
11 **bud** beauty's promise (possibly alludes to tip of a penis)
content possible children; happiness
12 **tender** delicate, gentle
waste expenditure
niggarding hoarding up, being miserly

1595–1597

When forty winters . . .

When forty winters shall besiege thy brow
  And dig deep trenches in thy beauty's field,
Thy youth's proud livery, so gazed on now,
  Will be a tattered weed, of small worth held.
Then being asked where all thy beauty lies,   5
  Where all the treasure of thy lusty days,
To say within thine own deep-sunken eyes
  Were an all-eating shame and thriftless praise.
How much more praise deserved thy beauty's use
  If thou couldst answer 'This fair child of mine   10
Shall sum my count, and make my old excuse',
  Proving his beauty by succession thine.
    This were to be new made when thou art old,
    And see thy blood warm when thou feel'st it cold.

When you become old, you should be able to show that you have a successor to your beauty – but only if you beget a child.

Q: No. 2. Sonnets 1–17 are about procreation. Probably addressed to a male ('youth's proud livery', line 3).

2 **trenches** wrinkles (with age)
  field agricultural plot (i.e.
  intended for productivity);
  battlefield
3 **livery** uniform (of a soldier or
  servant)
4 **weed** item of clothing; unwanted
  plant (from 'beauty's field')
6 **lusty** vigorous; pleasant; sex-full
8 **thriftless** worthless
9 **use** investment; sexual activity
11 **sum** present the balance of
12 **his** i.e. the child's

1595–1597

Look in thy glass . . .

Look in thy glass, and tell the face thou viewest
  Now is the time that face should form another,
Whose fresh repair if now thou not renewest
  Thou dost beguile the world, unbless some mother.
For where is she so fair whose uneared womb   5
  Disdains the tillage of thy husbandry?
Or who is he so fond will be the tomb
  Of his self-love to stop posterity?
Thou art thy mother's glass, and she in thee
  Calls back the lovely April of her prime;   10
So thou through windows of thine age shalt see,
  Despite of wrinkles, this thy golden time.
    But if thou live remembered not to be,
    Die single, and thine image dies with thee.

It is time for you to save both your looks and your prime of life by having a child.

Q: No. 3. Sonnets 1–17 are about procreation. Addressed to a male ('thy husbandry', line 6).

1 **glass** mirror
3 **repair** condition
4 **beguile** cheat (with charm); bewitch
  unbless deprive
  mother future mother; also the addressee's own mother (by not producing a grandchild)
5 **uneared** unploughed (because unseeded)
6 **tillage** cultivation
  husbandry farming; thrift; sexual and domestic duties
7 **so fond will** so foolish (and infatuated) that he will
8 **stop posterity** put an end to breeding
9 **glass** double; reflection
10 **prime** flourishing; spring
11 **windows** the eyes
  age old age
13 **remembered . . . be** not to be remade in the form of another

1595–1597

Unthrifty loveliness ...

Unthrifty loveliness, why dost thou spend
  Upon thyself thy beauty's legacy?
Nature's bequest gives nothing, but doth lend,
  And being frank, she lends to those are free.
Then, beauteous niggard, why dost thou abuse   5
  The bounteous largess given thee to give?
Profitless usurer, why dost thou use
  So great a sum of sums yet canst not live?
For having traffic with thyself alone,
  Thou of thyself thy sweet self dost deceive.   10
Then how when nature calls thee to be gone:
  What acceptable audit canst thou leave?
    Thy unused beauty must be tombed with thee,
    Which usèd, lives th' executor to be.

You should invest your beauty rather than keeping it all for yourself.

Q: No. 4. Sonnets 1–17 are about procreation. This one is most likely to be addressed to a male.

1 **Unthrifty** unprofitable; prodigal
  spend waste (also ejaculate)
4 **frank** generous
  free (i.e. and easy); generous; wanton; sexually liberal
5 **niggard** miser
7 **Profitless usurer** a money-lender who makes no money

8 **live** thrive (by procreating)
9 **traffic ... alone** trade and (sexual) commerce (i.e. masturbation)
10 **deceive** defraud
12 **audit** reckoning
14 **usèd** invested
  lives ... be would live on in your executor (i.e. son and heir)

1595–1597

Those hours that with gentle work …

Those hours that with gentle work did frame
   The lovely gaze where every eye doth dwell
Will play the tyrants to the very same,
   And that unfair which fairly doth excel;
For never-resting time leads summer on   5
   To hideous winter, and confounds him there,
Sap checked with frost, and lusty leaves quite gone,
   Beauty o'er-snowed, and bareness everywhere.
Then were not summer's distillation left
   A liquid prisoner pent in walls of glass,   10
Beauty's effect with beauty were bereft,
   Nor it nor no remembrance what it was.
      But flowers distilled, though they with winter meet,
      Lose but their show; their substance still lives sweet.

Nature made and will destroy beauty but can be defied by preserving the essence of beauty.

Q: No. 5. Sonnets 1–17 are about procreation. This is the first in a pair of syntactically related sonnets (with 6). This one is a meditation without an addressee.

1 **gentle work** careful craftsmanship
2 **The lovely gaze** (both observing and being observed)
4 **unfair** make unbeautiful
8 **bareness** empty bleakness; barrenness (like a woman who can't have children)
9 **distillation** essence (i.e. scent; goodness)
10 **pent** shut up, confined
11 **bereft** deprived; lost
14 **substance** essence
   sweet fragrant

1595–1597

Then let not winter's raggèd hand . . .

Then let not winter's raggèd hand deface
   In thee thy summer ere thou be distilled.
Make sweet some vial, treasure thou some place
   With beauty's treasure ere it be self-killed.
That use is not forbidden usury   5
   Which happies those that pay the willing loan:
That's for thyself to breed another thee,
   Or ten times happier, be it ten for one;
Ten times thyself were happier than thou art,
   If ten of thine ten times refigured thee.   10
Then what could death do if thou shouldst depart,
   Leaving thee living in posterity?
     Be not self-willed, for thou art much too fair
     To be death's conquest and make worms thine heir.

Invest in the future and defy death by having ten children and one hundred grandchildren.

Q: No. 6. Sonnets 1–17 are about procreation. This is the second in a pair of syntactically related sonnets (with 5). Most likely addressed to a male.

1 **deface** spoil (also take away your lovely face)
4 **self-killed** murdered by you because of your self-absorption
5 **forbidden** i.e. forbidden to practise
6 **happies** makes happy
pay ... loan pay back the interest owed on a loan (i.e. by the begetting of children)
9 **Ten times thyself** ten of yourself in ten children
10 **If ... thee** And imagine if your ten children had ten children of their own (i.e. one hundred grandchildren)
12 **Leaving thee living** Since you would remain alive (in the one hundred and ten children)
13 **self-willed** obstinate; self-obsessed; self-desiring; self-bequesting

1595–1597

Lo, in the orient . . .

Lo, in the orient when the gracious light
    Lifts up his burning head, each under eye
Doth homage to his new-appearing sight,
    Serving with looks his sacred majesty,
And having climbed the steep-up heavenly hill,   5
    Resembling strong youth in his middle age,
Yet mortal looks adore his beauty still,
    Attending on his golden pilgrimage.
But when from highmost pitch, with weary car,
    Like feeble age he reeleth from the day,   10
The eyes, 'fore duteous, now converted are
    From his low tract, and look another way.
      So thou, thyself outgoing in thy noon,
      Unlooked on diest unless thou get a son.

Just as the adored sun sinks daily away once it is beyond its noon, so will you, after your middle age, unless you beget a son.

Q: No. 7. Sonnets 1–17 are about procreation. Probably addressed to a male because of its emphasis on begetting a son (line 14).

1	**orient** east (i.e. the dawn)		human life
	light sun	9	**pitch** peak
2	**under eye** eye on earth looking up		**car** chariot
	(also each self, each 'I')	11	**converted** turned away
6	**middle age** noon	12	**tract** continuance
7	**mortal** human	14	**son** i.e. and another 'sun'
8	**pilgrimage** i.e. of the sun and of		

1595–1597

Music to hear ...

Music to hear, why hear'st thou music sadly?
  Sweets with sweets war not, joy delights in joy.
Why lov'st thou that which thou receiv'st not gladly,
  Or else receiv'st with pleasure thine annoy?
If the true concord of well-tunèd sounds   5
  By unions married do offend thine ear,
They do but sweetly chide thee, who confounds
  In singleness the parts that thou shouldst bear.
Mark how one string, sweet husband to another,
  Strikes each in each by mutual ordering,   10
Resembling sire and child and happy mother,
  Who all in one one pleasing note do sing;
    Whose speechless song, being many, seeming one,
    Sings this to thee: 'Thou single wilt prove none.'

Take your part in the musical harmonies of family life, rather than playing
your own, solo tune.

Q: No. 8. Sonnets 1–17 are about procreation. Probably addressed to a
male because of 'sweet husband' (line 9).

2 **sweets** delights; sweethearts	9 **husband** i.e. sustainer
4 **annoy** trouble, vexation	10 **Strikes ... ordering** The image
5 **concord** harmony, tunefulness	evokes a keyboard instrument,
6 **unions** unisons	possibly a lute, whose strings are
7 **sweetly** charmingly	being struck.
chide rebuke	13 **Whose** i.e. the strings'
confounds ruins	
8 **parts ... bear** notes you should be	
playing	

1595–1597

Is it for fear...

Is it for fear to wet a widow's eye
   That thou consum'st thyself in single life?
Ah, if thou issueless shalt hap to die,
   The world will wail thee like a makeless wife.
The world will be thy widow, and still weep   5
   That thou no form of thee hast left behind,
When every private widow well may keep
   By children's eyes her husband's shape in mind.
Look what an unthrift in the world doth spend
   Shifts but his place, for still the world enjoys it;   10
But beauty's waste hath in the world an end,
   And kept unused, the user so destroys it.
     No love toward others in that bosom sits
     That on himself such murd'rous shame commits.

You are killing your own beauty by not marrying and having children.

Q: No. 9. Sonnets 1–17 are about procreation. This is the first in a pair of syntactically related sonnets (with 10). To a male (because of the making of widows).

3 **hap** happen
4 **makeless** mateless
5 **still** continually
7 **private** particular, personal (i.e. widows other than the world's)
8 **shape** appearance
9 **Look what** whatever

unthrift prodigal
spend waste (i.e. money as well as during sex)
10 **Shifts but his** only provides for its **enjoys** indulges
12 **user** owner of the beauty (i.e. the addressee)

1595–1597

For shame deny . . .

For shame deny that thou bear'st love to any,
   Who for thyself art so unprovident.
Grant, if thou wilt, thou art beloved of many,
   But that thou none lov'st is most evident;
For thou art so possessed with murd'rous hate   5
   That 'gainst thyself thou stick'st not to conspire,
Seeking that beauteous roof to ruinate
   Which to repair should be thy chief desire.
O, change thy thought, that I may change my mind!
   Shall hate be fairer lodged than gentle love?   10
Be as thy presence is, gracious and kind,
   Or to thyself at least kind-hearted prove.
     Make thee another self for love of me,
     That beauty still may live in thine or thee.

Love yourself and others more by starting a family, and love me by begetting a child of your own, and preserving your beauty.

Q: No. 10. Sonnets 1–17 are about procreation. This sonnet is a sequel (and therefore to a male) and starts by repeating the 'shame' with which Sonnet 9 ends (Sonnet 9, line 14; Sonnet 10, line 1).

2 **unprovident** unproviding
5 **possessed** consumed
6 **'gainst** even against
  stick'st … conspire don't hesitate to plot

7 **roof** body; the potential home of a family
  ruinate make ruinous
11 **presence** appearance; personality
  kind humane

1595–1597

As fast as thou shalt wane . . .

As fast as thou shalt wane, so fast thou grow'st
  In one of thine from that which thou departest,
And that fresh blood which youngly thou bestow'st
  Thou mayst call thine when thou from youth convertest.
Herein lives wisdom, beauty, and increase;   5
  Without this, folly, age, and cold decay.
If all were minded so, the times should cease,
  And threescore year would make the world away.
Let those whom nature hath not made for store,
  Harsh, featureless, and rude, barrenly perish.   10
Look whom she best endowed she gave the more,
  Which bounteous gift thou shouldst in bounty cherish.
    She carved thee for her seal, and meant thereby
    Thou shouldst print more, not let that copy die.

Youth could be yours again in a child; children give comfort and keep the world going; and nature gave you natural gifts in order to replicate them.

Q: No. 11. Sonnets 1–17 are about procreation. Probably addressed to a male because of the metaphor of impression and printing (lines 13–14).

1 **wane** diminish (with age)
2 **that … departest** (your youth)
3 **youngly** in your youth
4 **convertest** turn away
8 **threescore year** sixty years
9 **store** breeding; future resourcing
10 **rude** rough, wild
11 **Look whom** whomever

12 **thou … cherish** you should make the most of by being bountiful (i.e. by begetting children)
13 **seal** authoritative, wax impression (on a letter or document)
14 **copy** i.e. the version in which nature formed you

1595–1597

When I do count the clock . . .

When I do count the clock that tells the time,
  And see the brave day sunk in hideous night;
When I behold the violet past prime,
  And sable curls ensilvered o'er with white;
When lofty trees I see barren of leaves,   5
  Which erst from heat did canopy the herd,
And summer's green all girded up in sheaves
  Borne on the bier with white and bristly beard:
Then of thy beauty do I question make
  That thou among the wastes of time must go,   10
Since sweets and beauties do themselves forsake,
  And die as fast as they see others grow;
    And nothing 'gainst time's scythe can make defence
    Save breed to brave him when he takes thee hence.

Everything dies, so the only way to survive is to have children.

Q: No. 12. Sonnets 1–17 are about procreation. Probably to a male because of the image of creating a defence (line 13) and 'breed' (line 14).

2 **brave** splendid
  hideous terrifying; terrible
3 **past prime** beyond its best (after spring)
4 **sable** black
6 **erst** before; previously
8 **bier** harvest wagon; carrier for a coffin

beard bristles on the heads of grain (and corpses)
10 **wastes** desolate spaces
11 **sweets** delights; lovers, sweethearts
14 **breed** procreation

1595–1597

O that you were yourself …

O that you were yourself! But, love, you are
   No longer yours than you yourself here live.
Against this coming end you should prepare,
   And your sweet semblance to some other give.
So should that beauty which you hold in lease   5
   Find no determination; then you were
Yourself again after your self's decease,
   When your sweet issue your sweet form should bear.
Who lets so fair a house fall to decay,
   Which husbandry in honour might uphold   10
Against the stormy gusts of winter's day,
   And barren rage of death's eternal cold?
      O, none but unthrifts, dear my love, you know.
      You had a father; let your son say so.

To bequeath your good looks to your own child would keep you alive, and
be an act of good husbandry for yourself.

Q: No. 13. Sonnets 1–17 are about procreation. To a male because of the
language of husbandry (lines 9–10), and fatherhood (line 14).

1 **were** had full possession of
2 **you … live** the time you are alive
3 **Against** in defence of
4 **sweet semblance** good looks
6 **determination** expiry of a legal
  agreement (i.e. the lease of the
  addressee's beauty)

8 **issue** child
  bear carry (also give birth to – in
  a grandchild)
9 **fair** handsome, beautiful
13 **unthrifts** prodigals, wastrels

1595–1597

Not from the stars . . .

Not from the stars do I my judgement pluck,
  And yet methinks I have astronomy;
But not to tell of good or evil luck,
  Of plagues, of dearths, or seasons' quality.
Nor can I fortune to brief minutes tell,   5
  'Pointing to each his thunder, rain, and wind,
Or say with princes if it shall go well
  By oft predict that I in heaven find;
But from thine eyes my knowledge I derive,
  And, constant stars, in them I read such art   10
As truth and beauty shall together thrive
  If from thyself to store thou wouldst convert.
    Or else of thee this I prognosticate:
    Thy end is truth's and beauty's doom and date.

I am no fortune-teller, but I know that you need to procreate the truth and beauty I see in your eyes, or else truth and beauty will die out with you.

Q: No. 14. Sonnets 1–17 are about procreation. Probably to a male because of 'If from thyself to store' (line 12).

1 **judgement** knowledge
2 **astronomy** (i.e. and astrology)
5 **fortune** the future
  to brief minutes within a few minutes (i.e. closely)
6 **'Pointing** i.e. appointing (also point: to mark down accurately)
8 **oft predict** frequent predictions

9 **But … derive** (cf. *Love's Labour's Lost*, 4.3.326: 'From women's eyes this doctrine I derive')
12 **to store** towards breeding and providing for the future
  convert turn to
13 **prognosticate** predict
14 **doom and date** last judgement and end

1595–1597

When I consider ...

When I consider every thing that grows
Holds in perfection but a little moment,
That this huge stage presenteth naught but shows
Whereon the stars in secret influence comment;
When I perceive that men as plants increase,   5
Cheerèd and checked even by the selfsame sky,
Vaunt in their youthful sap, at height decrease,
And wear their brave state out of memory:
Then the conceit of this inconstant stay
Sets you most rich in youth before my sight,   10
Where wasteful time debateth with decay
To change your day of youth to sullied night;
And all in war with time for love of you,
As he takes from you, I engraft you new.

All life is temporal, changing, and mortal, and I war with time over your
love and preservation by giving you new life with my writing.

Q: No. 15. Sonnets 1–17 are about procreation. This is the first in a pair
of syntactically related sonnets (with 16, which is to a male).

2 **Holds** preserves; survives; benefits
3 **huge stage** i.e. the world in the universe
   shows temporary appearances (like plays)
   huge ... shows (cf. *As You Like It*, 2.7.139: 'All the world's a stage')
4 **influence** the ethereal fluid which astrologers believed stars produced in order to govern human events
6 **Cheerèd** urged on
   checked restrained
   sky (also course of the stars)

7 **Vaunt** exult
   at height in older age; at their zenith
8 **brave** splendid
9 **conceit** fanciful imagining; conception
   stay existence
10 **Sets** places
12 **sullied night** polluted darkness
14 **he** time
   engraft insert new growth into (as gardeners do for old trees, and also by writing)

1595–1597

But wherefore do not you ...

But wherefore do not you a mightier way
  Make war upon this bloody tyrant, time,
And fortify yourself in your decay
  With means more blessèd than my barren rhyme?
Now stand you on the top of happy hours,   5
  And many maiden gardens yet unset
With virtuous wish would bear your living flowers,
  Much liker than your painted counterfeit.
So should the lines of life that life repair
  Which this time's pencil or my pupil pen   10
Neither in inward worth nor outward fair
  Can make you live yourself in eyes of men.
    To give away yourself keeps yourself still,
    And you must live drawn by your own sweet skill.

Having children is a stronger way of defying time than the writing of poetry.

Q: No. 16. Sonnets 1–17 are about procreation. This is the second in a pair of syntactically related sonnets (with 15). Addressed to a male (because of 'maiden gardens', line 6).

4 **barren** infertile; fruitless
5 **Now ... hours** you are now in your prime, capable of your full potential
6 **maiden gardens** virginities; young virgins
  unset unseeded; unfurnished with plants
8 **Much liker** more like you
9 **that life** i.e. your life (the addressee's)

repair renew
12 **live yourself** i.e. see yourself alive (in your child)
13 **give away** i.e. by procreating
14 **must** will be able to
  drawn figured; reproduced
  sweet skill i.e. the act of love-making, sex

1595–1597

Who will believe my verse . . .

Who will believe my verse in time to come
    If it were filled with your most high deserts?
Though yet, heaven knows, it is but as a tomb
    Which hides your life, and shows not half your parts.
If I could write the beauty of your eyes   5
    And in fresh numbers number all your graces,
The age to come would say 'This poet lies;
    Such heavenly touches ne'er touched earthly faces.'
So should my papers, yellowed with their age,
    Be scorned, like old men of less truth than tongue,   10
And your true rights be termed a poet's rage
    And stretchèd metre of an antique song.
      But were some child of yours alive that time,
      You should live twice: in it, and in my rhyme.

My poetry alone cannot convey your many wonders, and might be mistrusted, so have a child as well.

Q: No. 17. Sonnets 1–17 are about procreation. Could be addressed to either a male or a female.

2 **deserts** worths, merits
4 **parts** attributes
6 **numbers** poetic metres
   number enumerate (and make into verse)

11 **rage** outburst; frenzy; folly
12 **stretchèd** exaggerated; indulgent
   antique old-fashioned (also fantastical, bizarre)

1595–1597

Shall I compare thee . . .

Shall I compare thee to a summer's day?
　Thou art more lovely and more temperate.
Rough winds do shake the darling buds of May,
　And summer's lease hath all too short a date.
Sometime too hot the eye of heaven shines,　　　　　5
　And often is his gold complexion dimmed,
And every fair from fair sometime declines,
　By chance or nature's changing course untrimmed;
But thy eternal summer shall not fade
　Nor lose possession of that fair thou ow'st,　　　　10
Nor shall death brag thou wander'st in his shade
　When in eternal lines to time thou grow'st.
　　　So long as men can breathe or eyes can see,
　　　So long lives this, and this gives life to thee.

My poetry turns you into an eternal summer in which you will be forever
beautiful.

Q: No. 18. Could be addressed to either a male or a female.

2 **temperate** moderate, equable
4 **lease** time agreed for a tenancy
5 **eye of heaven** sun
7 **fair from fair** beautiful creature
　from beauty
8 **changing course** movement
　through the seasons and weather
　(i.e. of life)

untrimmed stripped bare of
ornament
10 **ow'st** ownest
11 **wander'st** wanderest
14 **this** the sonnet you are reading

1595–1597

Devouring time . . .

Devouring time, blunt thou the lion's paws,
  And make the earth devour her own sweet brood;
Pluck the keen teeth from the fierce tiger's jaws,
  And burn the long-lived phoenix in her blood.
Make glad and sorry seasons as thou fleet'st,   5
  And do whate'er thou wilt, swift-footed time,
To the wide world and all her fading sweets.
  But I forbid thee one most heinous crime:
O, carve not with thy hours my love's fair brow,
  Nor draw no lines there with thine antique pen.   10
Him in thy course untainted do allow
  For beauty's pattern to succeeding men.
    Yet do thy worst, old time; despite thy wrong
    My love shall in my verse ever live young.

Time: you destroy everything, but I forbid you to spoil my loved one's beauty. But, even if you do, he will always be young because of my poetry.

Q: No. 19. To time, about a male. Dramatic analogy: an invocation by King Lear.

2 **sweet brood** fair offspring
4 **phoenix** mythical, eternal bird which dies in fire every six hundred years and comes to life again **in her blood** in her fullness of vigour
5 **fleet'st** fliest

7 **fading** mortal
  sweets beautiful things
10 **antique** well-worn
11 **course** passage
  untainted unblemished; and (possibly) not hit in jousting, with time's lance

1595–1597

A woman's face …

A woman's face with nature's own hand painted
   Hast thou, the master-mistress of my passion;
A woman's gentle heart, but not acquainted
   With shifting change as is false women's fashion;
An eye more bright than theirs, less false in rolling,   5
   Gilding the object whereupon it gazeth;
A man in hue, all hues in his controlling,
   Which steals men's eyes and women's souls amazeth.
And for a woman wert thou first created,
   Till nature as she wrought thee fell a-doting,   10
And by addition me of thee defeated
   By adding one thing to my purpose nothing.
   But since she pricked thee out for women's pleasure,
   Mine be thy love and thy love's use their treasure.

You look like both a man and a woman, and everyone is attracted to you.
I can love you, but your love-making is really for women.

Q: No. 20. The first of two syntactically related sonnets (with 21). To a
male. Dramatic analogy: Orsino to Cesario (who is Viola in disguise) in
Twelfth Night, or What You Will.

1 **with … hand** naturally
  painted made-up; depicted
2 **master-mistress** man-woman;
  male-and-female-looking subject;
  and (possibly) patron and sexual
  partner (cf. *Twelfth Night, or What*
  You Will, 5.1.122–3: Orsino to Viola,
  disguised as the androgynous
  Cesario, 'You shall from this time
  be / Your master's mistress.')
  passion overpowering emotions;
  suffering
5 **rolling** flirtatious glances

6 **Gilding** superficially enriching
7 **hue** figure, form
  controlling enthralment
8 **amazeth** overwhelms,
  dumbfounds
9 **for** as
10 **a-doting** besotted
11 **And … defeated** and by adding
  something to you made you not
  for me
12 **one thing** i.e. a penis (cf. *Twelfth*
  Night, or What You Will, 3.4.293–4:
  Viola, 'a little thing would make

me tell them how much I lack of a man.')

nothing of no use

13 **pricked thee out** selected you; decked you out; sketched you; gave you a penis (a 'prick')

14 **Mine be** It is my pleasure to be, to have

thy love's use your body; the activities, profits of your love

1595–1597

So is it not with me . . .

So is it not with me as with that muse
    Stirred by a painted beauty to his verse,
Who heaven itself for ornament doth use,
    And every fair with his fair doth rehearse,
Making a couplement of proud compare   5
    With sun and moon, with earth, and sea's rich gems,
With April's first-born flowers, and all things rare
    That heaven's air in this huge rondure hems.
O let me, true in love, but truly write,
    And then believe me my love is as fair   10
As any mother's child, though not so bright
    As those gold candles fixed in heaven's air.
      Let them say more that like of hearsay well;
      I will not praise that purpose not to sell.

I am not inspired by anyone who is overly-made-up, and will not apply such tricks of painting to my poetry: my loved one is simply beautiful.

Q: No. 21. The second of two syntactically related sonnets (with 20). A meditation on being honest in poetry when writing about the loved one (who could be either male or female, but probably male because of its pairing with the previous sonnet).

1 **muse** i.e. poet
2 **Stirred** inspired
  painted beauty overly-made-up subject (male or female)
3 **for ornament** as poetic imagery
4 **rehearse** compare

5 **couplement** link
8 **rondure** sphere
  hems encloses
12 **gold candles** stars
14 **purpose not** do not intend

1595–1597

My glass shall not persuade . . .

My glass shall not persuade me I am old
　　So long as youth and thou are of one date;
But when in thee time's furrows I behold,
　　Then look I death my days should expiate.
For all that beauty that doth cover thee　　　　　　　5
　　Is but the seemly raiment of my heart,
Which in thy breast doth live, as thine in me;
　　How can I then be elder than thou art?
O therefore, love, be of thyself so wary
　　As I, not for myself, but for thee will,　　　　　10
Bearing thy heart, which I will keep so chary
　　As tender nurse her babe from faring ill.
　　　　Presume not on thy heart when mine is slain:
　　　　Thou gav'st me thine not to give back again.

You keep me young, and we share the same beauty and heart. We will take care of ourselves, but part of your heart will die when I do.

Q: No. 22. Could be addressed to either a male or a female. Puns on the poet's first name, Will (line 10; cf. 57, 89, 134, 135, 136, and 143).

1 **glass** looking-glass, mirror
2 **one date** the same age
3 **furrows** strips of ploughed land (i.e. wrinkles)
4 **look** expect
　expiate bring peace to, end
6 **seemly raiment** appropriate clothing
9 **be … wary** be as careful of yourself
11 **Bearing** carrying
　keep look after
　chary carefully, tenderly
13 **Presume not on** do not expect to recover

1595–1597

As an unperfect actor ...

As an unperfect actor on the stage
  Who with his fear is put besides his part,
Or some fierce thing replete with too much rage
  Whose strength's abundance weakens his own heart,
So I, for fear of trust, forget to say   5
  The perfect ceremony of love's rite,
And in mine own love's strength seem to decay,
  O'er-charged with burden of mine own love's might.
O let my books be then the eloquence
  And dumb presagers of my speaking breast,   10
Who plead for love, and look for recompense
  More than that tongue that more hath more expressed.
    O learn to read what silent love hath writ;
    To hear with eyes belongs to love's fine wit.

Sometimes I lose the ability to express my love, but realise it is there – in the silence of what I have already written.

Q: No. 23. A meditation about a lack of eloquence, which suggests an addressee (lines 13–14, who could be male or female), but which could also be a soliloquy.

1 **unperfect** not word-perfect
2 **with his fear** by his stage-fright
  is put besides forgets
3 **replete with** full of
5 **fear of trust** lack of confidence
  forget forget how
6 **perfect ... rite** exact words
  appropriate to a lover

8 **O'er-charged ... burden**
  overburdened with
9 **books** notebooks, writings
10 **dumb presagers** silent presenters
12 **More ... expressed** expressed
  more often or more fully
14 **fine** acute

1595–1597

Mine eye hath played the painter...

Mine eye hath played the painter, and hath stelled
　Thy beauty's form in table of my heart.
My body is the frame wherein 'tis held,
　And perspective it is best painter's art;
For through the painter must you see his skill　　　　5
　To find where your true image pictured lies,
Which in my bosom's shop is hanging still,
　That hath his windows glazèd with thine eyes.
Now see what good turns eyes for eyes have done:
　Mine eyes have drawn thy shape, and thine for me　　10
Are windows to my breast, wherethrough the sun
　Delights to peep, to gaze therein on thee.
　　Yet eyes this cunning want to grace their art:
　　They draw but what they see, know not the heart.

My eyes paint your beauty, and you can see through them and find your
true likeness in my heart. But my eyes lack the ability to paint your innermost being.

Q: No. 24. Could be addressed to either a male or a female.

1 **stelled** portrayed, engraved	8 **his** its
2 **in table of** (the) tablet, panel	**glazèd** fitted with glass
4 **perspective** seen from the right angle	13 **cunning want** lack this skill
7 **shop** workshop	**grace** enhance

1595–1597

Let those who are in favour …

Let those who are in favour with their stars
   Of public honour and proud titles boast,
Whilst I, whom fortune of such triumph bars,
   Unlooked-for joy in that I honour most.
Great princes' favourites their fair leaves spread   5
   But as the marigold at the sun's eye,
And in themselves their pride lies burièd,
   For at a frown they in their glory die.
The painful warrior famousèd for might,
   After a thousand victories once foiled   10
Is from the book of honour razèd quite,
   And all the rest forgot for which he toiled.
     Then happy I, that love and am beloved
     Where I may not remove nor be removed.

I can love more joyfully and freely than princes or famous soldiers, and I am resilient in that love.

Q: No. 25. A meditation on the freedom to love irrespective of social rank. The subject of this love could be male or female.

4 **Unlooked-for** unexpectedly
  that that which (his love)
5 **their … spread** i.e. flourish
6 **But as** only like
  marigold (which opens only painfully when the sun shines)

7 **pride** splendour, glory
9 **painful** painstaking
10 **foiled** overcome
12 **the rest** i.e. his 'thousand victories'
14 **remove** shift; be unfaithful
  removed alienated

1595–1597

Lord of my love …

Lord of my love, to whom in vassalage
   Thy merit hath my duty strongly knit,
To thee I send this written embassage
   To witness duty, not to show my wit;
Duty so great which wit so poor as mine   5
   May make seem bare in wanting words to show it,
But that I hope some good conceit of thine
   In thy soul's thought, all naked, will bestow it,
Till whatsoever star that guides my moving
   Points on me graciously with fair aspect,   10
And puts apparel on my tattered loving
   To show me worthy of thy sweet respect.
      Then may I dare to boast how I do love thee;
      Till then, not show my head where thou mayst prove me.

Lord of my love I write this out of respect for you, rather than to demonstrate my skill, and hope you will look kindly on my bare ability and efforts – then I shall be able to boast about my love for you.

Q. No. 26. Addressed to a male ('Lord', line 1), and an example (like 77) of Shakespeare's own, personal, verse correspondence. It may have accompanied another 'written embassage'.

1 **vassalage** servitude
3 **embassage** message (i.e. the sonnet itself or something accompanying it, such as a dedication to another work)
4 **wit** skill

6 **wanting** lacking
7 **good conceit** favourable opinion, sympathetic understanding
8 **all naked** although 'bare'
14 **prove me** put me to the test

1595–1597

Weary with toil . . .

Weary with toil I haste me to my bed,
   The dear repose for limbs with travail tired;
But then begins a journey in my head
   To work my mind when body's work's expired;
For then my thoughts, from far where I abide,   5
   Intend a zealous pilgrimage to thee,
And keep my drooping eyelids open wide,
   Looking on darkness which the blind do see:
Save that my soul's imaginary sight
   Presents thy shadow to my sightless view,   10
Which like a jewel hung in ghastly night
   Makes black night beauteous and her old face new.
     Lo, thus by day my limbs, by night my mind,
     For thee, and for myself, no quiet find.

I cannot sleep, even though I go to bed exhausted, because my mind sees you in the darkness.

Q: No. 27. Could be addressed to either a male or a female. This is the first in a pair of related sonnets (with 28) about sleeplessness.

2 **travail** work (also pun on 'travel')
6 **Intend** set out upon
8 **which** i.e. such as
9 **imaginary** imaginative, image-
   forming
10 **shadow** image
11 **ghastly** terrifying

1595–1597

How can I then return ...

How can I then return in happy plight,
   That am debarred the benefit of rest,
When day's oppression is not eased by night,
   But day by night and night by day oppressed,
And each, though enemies to either's reign,   5
   Do in consent shake hands to torture me,
The one by toil, the other to complain
   How far I toil, still farther off from thee?
I tell the day to please him thou art bright,
   And do'st him grace when clouds do blot the heaven;   10
So flatter I the swart-complexioned night:
   'When sparkling stars twire not, thou gild'st the even.'
     But day doth daily draw my sorrows longer,
     And night doth nightly make grief's strength seem stronger.

I do not sleep, and, when I work, I think how far away I am from you. I try to make the best of it, but I am sad during the day, and grieve at night.

Q: No. 28. The second in a pair of related sonnets (with 27) about sleeplessness. Could be addressed to either a male or a female.

1 **plight** state
3 **day's oppression** the oppression endured during daytime
6 **shake hands** agree, conspire
7 **to complain** by causing me to complain

11 **So flatter I** in a similar way do I please
   swart dark
12 **twire** peep

1595–1597

When, in disgrace . . .

When, in disgrace with fortune and men's eyes,
    I all alone beweep my outcast state,
And trouble deaf heaven with my bootless cries,
    And look upon myself and curse my fate,
Wishing me like to one more rich in hope,   5
    Featured like him, like him with friends possessed,
Desiring this man's art and that man's scope,
    With what I most enjoy contented least:
Yet in these thoughts myself almost despising,
    Haply I think on thee, and then my state,   10
Like to the lark at break of day arising
    From sullen earth, sings hymns at heaven's gate;
      For thy sweet love remembered such wealth brings
      That then I scorn to change my state with kings'.

When I am feeling out of favour with the world, I happen to think of you and am so transported to heaven that my happiness is greater than kings'.

Q: No. 29. Could be addressed to either a male or a female. Dramatic analogy: Romeo in banishment.

1 **disgrace** disfavour
2 **state** condition
3 **bootless** unavailing
6 **like him, like him** like one man, then like another
7 **art** skill
  scope range
8 **enjoy** take pleasure in, possess

10 **Haply** by chance (with a pun on 'happily')
  state inner spirit
11–12 **Like... gate** (cf. *Cymbeline*, 2.319: 'Hark, hark, the lark at heaven [*sic*] gate sings')
12 **sullen** dark
14 **state** condition (and 'throne')

1595–1597

When to the sessions . . .

When to the sessions of sweet silent thought
  I summon up remembrance of things past,
I sigh the lack of many a thing I sought,
  And with old woes new wail my dear time's waste.
Then can I drown an eye unused to flow   5
  For precious friends hid in death's dateless night,
And weep afresh love's long-since-cancelled woe,
  And moan th' expense of many a vanished sight.
Then can I grieve at grievances foregone,
  And heavily from woe to woe tell o'er   10
The sad account of fore-bemoanèd moan,
  Which I new pay as if not paid before.
    But if the while I think on thee, dear friend,
    All losses are restored, and sorrows end.

When I call to mind the past, I grieve; but when I think of you, my sense of loss and my grief end.

Q: No. 30. The first in a pair of related sonnets (with 31) which recall absent friends and lovers. Could be addressed to either a male or a female. Dramatic analogy: Antonio about Bassanio in *The Merchant of Venice*.

1 **sessions** (court) sittings	9 **grievances foregone** past sorrows
3 **sigh** regret, beweep	10 **heavily** sadly
6 **dateless** endless	**tell o'er** recount; sum up
7 **long-since-cancelled woe** debt of grief that I paid off long ago	11 **account** tale, financial record
8 **expense** loss	**fore-bemoanèd moan** griefs that I have already lamented

1595–1597

Thy bosom is endearèd. . .

Thy bosom is endearèd with all hearts
   Which I by lacking have supposèd dead,
And there reigns love, and all love's loving parts,
   And all those friends which I thought burièd.
How many a holy and obsequious tear   5
   Hath dear religious love stol'n from mine eye
As interest of the dead, which now appear
   But things removed that hidden in thee lie!
Thou art the grave where buried love doth live,
   Hung with the trophies of my lovers gone,   10
Who all their parts of me to thee did give:
   That due of many now is thine alone.
     Their images I loved I view in thee,
     And thou, all they, hast all the all of me.

All of the friends and lovers who I thought were dead are living in the memory of your heart.

Q: No. 31. The second in a pair of related sonnets (with 30) which recall absent friends and lovers. Could be addressed to either a male or a female.

1 **endearèd with** made precious by
2 **Which** (the poet's past lovers)
5 **obsequious** dutifully mourning
6 **religious** dedicated
7 **interest of** dues to
8 **removed** absent
10 **trophies** relics

11 **parts of** shares in
12 **That … many** with the result that what was due to many
13 **Their … loved** the images of those whom I loved
14 **all they** made up of all of them

1595–1597

If thou survive . . .

If thou survive my well-contented day
  When that churl death my bones with dust shall cover,
And shalt by fortune once more resurvey
  These poor rude lines of thy deceasèd lover,
Compare them with the bett'ring of the time,   5
  And though they be outstripped by every pen,
Reserve them for my love, not for their rhyme
  Exceeded by the height of happier men.
O then vouchsafe me but this loving thought:
  'Had my friend's muse grown with this growing age,   10
A dearer birth than this his love had brought
  To march in ranks of better equipage;
    But since he died, and poets better prove,
    Theirs for their style I'll read, his for his love.'

If you survive me, look on this poem and realise that, though it is not as good as others' work, it is very loving.

Q: No. 32. Could be addressed to either a male or a female.

3 **fortune** chance	10 **grown with** developed
4 **rude** unpolished	commensurately with
5 **bett'ring** improved writing	11 **dearer** more valuable
6 **outstripped** surpassed	**had** would have
7 **Reserve** preserve	12 **ranks … equipage** the ranks of
for for the sake of	better equipped poets
8 **height** skill	13 **better prove** turn out to be better
happier more fortunate, more able	

1595–1597

Full many a glorious morning . . .

Full many a glorious morning have I seen
   Flatter the mountain tops with sovereign eye,
Kissing with golden face the meadows green,
   Gilding pale streams with heavenly alchemy;
Anon permit the basest clouds to ride   5
   With ugly rack on his celestial face,
And from the forlorn world his visage hide,
   Stealing unseen to west with this disgrace.
Even so my sun one early morn did shine
   With all-triumphant splendour on my brow;   10
But out, alack, he was but one hour mine;
   The region cloud hath masked him from me now.
     Yet him for this my love no whit disdaineth:
     Suns of the world may stain when heaven's sun staineth.

The morning sun makes everything look splendid, but then dark clouds appear: that is how I feel about the light of my life.

Q: No. 33. A meditation on a relationship which is growing cool, and about a male ('suns' line 14 punning on 'sons', i.e. male loved ones). This is the first in a series of four closely connected sonnets (with 34, 35, and 36) about making mistakes in love, which along with 34 and 35 uses weather imagery. Sonnet 33 functions as an introduction to the short sequence.

2 **sovereign** kingly, glorious
4 **Gilding … alchemy** (cf. *King John*, 3.1.3–4: 'the glorious sun / Stays in his course and plays the alchemist')
   heavenly alchemy the sun's ability to turn things into gold
5 **basest** darkest
5–7 **Anon … hide** (cf. *1 Henry IV*, 1.2.194–6: 'the sun, / Who doth permit the base contagious clouds / To smother up his beauty from the world')
6 **ugly rack** disfiguring mass
11 **out, alack** alas
   he that sun
12 **region** i.e. high
   him that sun (also line 13)
13 **no whit** not at all
   disdaineth despises
14 **stain** grow dim

1595–1597

Why didst thou promise ...

Why didst thou promise such a beauteous day
   And make me travel forth without my cloak,
To let base clouds o'ertake me in my way,
   Hiding thy brav'ry in their rotten smoke?
'Tis not enough that through the cloud thou break   5
   To dry the rain on my storm-beaten face,
For no man well of such a salve can speak
   That heals the wound and cures not the disgrace.
Nor can thy shame give physic to my grief;
   Though thou repent, yet I have still the loss.   10
Th' offender's sorrow lends but weak relief
   To him that bears the strong offence's cross.
     Ah, but those tears are pearl which thy love sheds,
     And they are rich, and ransom all ill deeds.

You have let me suffer and your trying to rescue the situation, and being repentant, does not help. But your tears do.

Q: No. 34. This is the second in a series of four closely connected sonnets (with 33, 35, and 36) about making mistakes in love, which, along with 33 and 35, uses weather imagery. Probably addressed to a male (because of its connection to 33).

1 **thou** (the sun, the beloved)	8 **disgrace** disfigurement, scar
3 **To** only to	9 **shame** repentance
4 **brav'ry** splendour	12 **cross** affliction
rotten smoke foul vapours	14 **ransom** atone for
7 **salve** remedy	

1595–1597

No more be grieved . . .

No more be grieved at that which thou hast done:
  Roses have thorns, and silver fountains mud.
Clouds and eclipses stain both moon and sun,
  And loathsome canker lives in sweetest bud.
All men make faults, and even I in this,   5
  Authorizing thy trespass with compare,
Myself corrupting salving thy amiss,
  Excusing thy sins more than thy sins are;
For to thy sensual fault I bring in sense –
  Thy adverse party is thy advocate –   10
And 'gainst myself a lawful plea commence.
  Such civil war is in my love and hate
    That I an accessory needs must be
    To that sweet thief which sourly robs from me.

Do not be upset: everyone makes mistakes, and so do I by making more excuses than your actual misdeeds require.

Q: No. 35. This is the third in a series of four closely connected sonnets (with 33, 34, and 36) about making mistakes in love which, along with 33 and 34, uses weather imagery. Probably addressed to a male (because of its connection to 33).

3 **stain** dim
4 **canker** canker-worm
5 **make** commit
7 **salving** palliating
  amiss misdeed

9 **sensual** of the senses, physical
  sense reason
10 **adverse party** opponent (the poet himself)
13 **accessory** accomplice

1595–1597

Let me confess . . .

Let me confess that we two must be twain
　Although our undivided loves are one;
So shall those blots that do with me remain
　Without thy help by me be borne alone.
In our two loves there is but one respect,　　　　　5
　Though in our lives a separable spite
Which, though it alter not love's sole effect,
　Yet doth it steal sweet hours from love's delight.
I may not evermore acknowledge thee
　Lest my bewailèd guilt should do thee shame,　　10
Nor thou with public kindness honour me
　Unless thou take that honour from thy name.
　　But do not so. I love thee in such sort
　　As, thou being mine, mine is thy good report.

We should accept that we must love apart and not acknowledge each other in public in case that shames us.

Q: No. 36. This is the fourth in a series of four closely connected sonnets (with 33, 34, and 35), in which the poet seeks to acknowledge a distancing in the relationship with the loved one. Probably addressed to a male (because of its connections to the previous three sonnets).

1 **confess** admit
　twain parted
3 **blots** offences
4 **borne** carried
5 **respect** focus of attention
6 **separable spite** vexatious
　separation

7 **sole** single-minded
10 **bewailèd guilt** lamented sense of
　doing wrong
13–14 **But ... report** This couplet
　also ends Sonnet 96.
14 **As** as that

1595–1597

As a decrepit father ...

As a decrepit father takes delight
    To see his active child do deeds of youth,
So I, made lame by fortune's dearest spite,
    Take all my comfort of thy worth and truth;
For whether beauty, birth, or wealth, or wit,   5
    Or any of these all, or all, or more,
Entitled in thy parts do crownèd sit,
    I make my love engrafted to this store.
So then I am not lame, poor, nor despised,
    Whilst that this shadow doth such substance give   10
That I in thy abundance am sufficed
    And by a part of all thy glory live.
        Look what is best, that best I wish in thee;
        This wish I have, then ten times happy me.

I am like an old father who delights to see your flourishing youth: I share in your good qualities and want what is best for you.

Q: No. 37. Could be addressed to either a male or a female.

3 **made lame** handicapped (literally, or figuratively: cf. Sonnet 89 line 3 and *The History of King Lear*, scene 20.213: 'A most poor man made lame by fortune's blows.')
    dearest spite direst cruelty
4 **of** from

5 **wit** intelligence
7 **thy parts** your good qualities (also 'this store', line 8)
10 **shadow** image, idea
13 **Look what** whatever
14 **This ... have** i.e. if I have

1595–1597

How can my muse …

How can my muse want subject to invent
   While thou dost breathe, that pour'st into my verse
Thine own sweet argument, too excellent
   For every vulgar paper to rehearse?
O, give thyself the thanks if aught in me   5
   Worthy perusal stand against thy sight;
For who's so dumb that cannot write to thee,
   When thou thyself dost give invention light?
Be thou the tenth muse, ten times more in worth
   Than those old nine which rhymers invocate,   10
And he that calls on thee, let him bring forth
   Eternal numbers to outlive long date.
     If my slight muse do please these curious days,
     The pain be mine, but thine shall be the praise.

You are the source of all poetic inspiration, and anyone who invokes you
as the tenth muse will be able to write immortal verses about you.

Q: No. 38. Could be addressed to either a male or a female.

3 **argument** theme
4 **vulgar paper** commonplace piece
  of writing
  rehearse set forth
6 **stand … sight** withstands your
  scrutiny
7 **dumb** inarticulate; stuck for words
  write to address
8 **give invention light** inspire
  composition

9 **tenth** i.e. beyond the normal nine
10 **rhymers invocate** mere rhymesters
  call upon
12 **Eternal numbers** immortal verses
  outlive long date live for ever
13 **curious** critical
14 **pain** labour, effort

1595–1597

O, how thy worth …

O, how thy worth with manners may I sing
    When thou art all the better part of me?
What can mine own praise to mine own self bring,
    And what is't but mine own when I praise thee?
Even for this let us divided live,   5
    And our dear love lose name of single one,
That by this separation I may give
    That due to thee which thou deserv'st alone.
O absence, what a torment wouldst thou prove
    Were it not thy sour leisure gave sweet leave   10
To entertain the time with thoughts of love,
    Which time and thoughts so sweetly doth deceive,
        And that thou teachest how to make one twain
        By praising him here who doth hence remain!

We are too interconnected for me to praise you on your own terms. Let us separate, and the absence, though bitter, will be filled with loving thoughts, and praise.

Q: No. 39. Could be addressed to either a male or a female.

1 **manners** due modesty
  sing celebrate
3 **mine own self** (myself or the addressee)
5 **for** because of
6 **name … one** the reputation of unity

10 **sour** bitter
11 **entertain** while away
14 **him** i.e. the poet
  here in this poem

1595–1597

Take all my loves . . .

Take all my loves, my love, yea, take them all:
  What hast thou then more than thou hadst before?
No love, my love, that thou mayst true love call –
  All mine was thine before thou hadst this more.
Then if for my love thou my love receivest,   5
  I cannot blame thee for my love thou usest;
But yet be blamed if thou this self deceivest
  By wilful taste of what thyself refusest.
I do forgive thy robb'ry, gentle thief,
  Although thou steal thee all my poverty;   10
And yet love knows it is a greater grief
  To bear love's wrong than hate's known injury.
    Lascivious grace, in whom all ill well shows,
    Kill me with spites, yet we must not be foes.

Why don't you just take away all the love I have? I forgive you, but love's
deception is worse than straightforward hatred.

Q: No. 40. This sonnet could be addressed to either a male or a female,
but it seems to be connected to the next two (41 and 42) and is probably
addressed to a man who has taken away the poet's female loved one. Dramatic analogy: Antony to Cleopatra.

1 **all my loves** 'all my lovers' and 'all
my feelings of love for you'
4 **mine** my love for you
6 **for … usest** in that you use
(sexually) my beloved
8 **wilful taste** lustful use

thyself your true, better self (?)
9 **gentle thief** (paradoxically) noble
robber
10 **all my poverty** what little I own
12 **wrong** deception
14 **spites** outrages

1595–1597

Those pretty wrongs . . .

Those pretty wrongs that liberty commits
    When I am sometime absent from thy heart
Thy beauty and thy years full well befits,
    For still temptation follows where thou art.
Gentle thou art, and therefore to be won;   5
    Beauteous thou art, therefore to be assailed;
And when a woman woos, what woman's son
    Will sourly leave her till he have prevailed?
Ay me, but yet thou mightst my seat forbear,
    And chide thy beauty and thy straying youth   10
Who lead thee in their riot even there
    Where thou art forced to break a two-fold troth:
      Hers, by thy beauty tempting her to thee,
      Thine, by thy beauty being false to me.

Of course you go astray a little: you are beautiful and well-born. But stay away from my patch, even if that means breaking two vows: tempting her, and being unfaithful to me.

Q: No. 41. The second of three sonnets (with 40 and 42), addressed to a male who has taken away the poet's female loved one.

1 **pretty** engaging little
2 **sometime** from time to time
4 **still** always
5 **Gentle** well-born; tender
6 **to be assailed** liable to be seduced
8 **sourly** cruelly
9 **my seat forbear** leave my rightful place (my loved one) alone (cf.

Othello, 2.1.294–5: 'I do suspect the lusty Moor / Hath leapt into my seat')
10 **chide** rebuke
11 **riot** debauchery
12 **two-fold troth** double pledge (to her and to me)

1595–1597

That thou hast her...

That thou hast her, it is not all my grief,
 And yet it may be said I loved her dearly;
That she hath thee is of my wailing chief,
 A loss in love that touches me more nearly.
Loving offenders, thus I will excuse ye: 5
 Thou dost love her because thou know'st I love her,
And for my sake even so doth she abuse me,
 Suff'ring my friend for my sake to approve her.
If I lose thee, my loss is my love's gain,
 And losing her, my friend hath found that loss: 10
Both find each other, and I lose both twain,
 And both for my sake lay on me this cross.
  But here's the joy: my friend and I are one.
  Sweet flattery! Then she loves but me alone.

I grieve because you have taken away the woman I love, and even more that
she has you. But, if she does love you, then, because you and I are one, she
still only really loves me.

Q: No. 42. The third of three sonnets (with 40 and 41), addressed to a
male who has taken away the poet's female loved one. Dramatic analogy:
Valentine in *The Two Gentlemen of Verona*.

3 **chief** the main cause
7 **abuse** wrong
8 **Suff'ring** allowing
 approve her put her to the test
 (sexually)
9 **my love's gain** a gain to the
 woman I love

10 **losing** if I lose
12 **lay ... cross** inflict this pain on
 me
14 **flattery** delusion, deception

1595–1597

When most I wink . . .

When most I wink, then do mine eyes best see,
    For all the day they view things unrespected;
But when I sleep, in dreams they look on thee,
    And, darkly bright, are bright in dark directed.
Then thou, whose shadow shadows doth make bright,   5
    How would thy shadow's form form happy show
To the clear day with thy much clearer light,
    When to unseeing eyes thy shade shines so!
How would, I say, mine eyes be blessèd made
    By looking on thee in the living day,   10
When in dead night thy fair imperfect shade
    Through heavy sleep on sightless eyes doth stay!
      All days are nights to see till I see thee,
      And nights bright days when dreams do show thee me.

I see better in my dreams, because I see you there, but how much more brightly you would appear in the daytime, if I saw you as I see you at night!

Q: No. 43. Could be addressed to either a male or a female.

1 **wink** shut my eyes
2 **unrespected** uncared about, unvalued
4 **darkly bright** shining in the darkness
5 **shadow . . . bright** image lightens darkness

6 **shadow's . . . show** substance make a pleasing sight
8 **unseeing eyes** (i.e. of the dreamer)
11 **imperfect shade** insubstantial shadow

1595–1597

If the dull substance . . .

If the dull substance of my flesh were thought,
   Injurious distance should not stop my way;
For then, despite of space, I would be brought
   From limits far remote where thou dost stay.
No matter then although my foot did stand   5
   Upon the farthest earth removed from thee;
For nimble thought can jump both sea and land
   As soon as think the place where he would be.
But ah, thought kills me that I am not thought,
   To leap large lengths of miles when thou art gone,   10
But that, so much of earth and water wrought,
   I must attend time's leisure with my moan,
      Receiving naught by elements so slow
      But heavy tears, badges of either's woe.

If only I were made of thought so that I could fly quickly to wherever
you are! But I am only made of heavy elements and must wait for time
to reunite us.

Q: No. 44. The first of two syntactically related sonnets (with 45) about
the four elements. Could be addressed to either a male or a female.

1 **dull** heavy
4 **limits** regions
  where to where
7 **jump** traverse
8 **would** would like to
11 **so . . . wrought** I being
  compounded of so much earth
  and water (the heavy elements)

12 **attend time's leisure** wait on
  time's convenience
14 **badges . . . woe** emblems of the
  woe of earth and water

1595–1597

The other two . . .

The other two, slight air and purging fire,
 Are both with thee wherever I abide;
The first my thought, the other my desire,
 These present-absent with swift motion slide;
For when these quicker elements are gone   5
 In tender embassy of love to thee,
My life, being made of four, with two alone
 Sinks down to death, oppressed with melancholy,
Until life's composition be recured
 By those swift messengers returned from thee,   10
Who even but now come back again assured
 Of thy fair health, recounting it to me.
  This told, I joy; but then no longer glad,
  I send them back again and straight grow sad.

You and I are most connected by the elements of air (my thought) and fire (my desire), and these are constantly on the move between us, cheering me with news of your health, and saddening me when I send them back to you.

Q: No. 45. The second of two syntactically related sonnets (with 44) about the four elements. Could be addressed to either a male or a female.

1 **The other two** (of the poet's four elements)
  slight insubstantial
  purging purifying
4 **present-absent** not present, not absent, but constantly coming and going

5 **quicker** more lively
9 **composition** make-up
  recured restored
10 **swift messengers** i.e. air and fire
14 **straight** immediately

1595–1597

Mine eye and heart . . .

Mine eye and heart are at a mortal war
   How to divide the conquest of thy sight.
Mine eye my heart thy picture's sight would bar,
   My heart, mine eye the freedom of that right.
My heart doth plead that thou in him dost lie,   5
   A closet never pierced with crystal eyes;
But the defendant doth that plea deny,
   And says in him thy fair appearance lies.
To 'cide this title is empanellèd
   A quest of thoughts, all tenants to the heart,   10
And by their verdict is determinèd
    The clear eye's moiety and the dear heart's part,
     As thus: mine eye's due is thy outward part,
     And my heart's right thy inward love of heart.

My eyes and heart are at war over the different claims they have on you,
but my thoughts decide that my eyes see your outward appearance, my
heart your inner loving self.

Q: No. 46. The first in a pair of related sonnets (with 47) about the eyes
and the heart. Could be addressed to either a male or a female. Dramatic
analogy: the spell-crossed lovers in *A Midsummer Night's Dream*.

1 **mortal** deadly	9 **'cide** decide
3 **bar** prohibit	**title** legal right
6 **closet** room or cabinet	**empanellèd** enrolled
pierced with penetrated by	10 **quest** inquest, jury
7 **defendant** i.e. the eye	12 **moiety** share

1595–1597

Betwixt mine eye and heart . . .

Betwixt mine eye and heart a league is took,
   And each doth good turns now unto the other.
When that mine eye is famished for a look,
   Or heart in love with sighs himself doth smother,
With my love's picture then my eye doth feast,   5
   And to the painted banquet bids my heart.
Another time mine eye is my heart's guest
   And in his thoughts of love doth share a part.
So either by thy picture or my love,
   Thyself away art present still with me;   10
For thou no farther than my thoughts canst move,
   And I am still with them, and they with thee;
     Or if they sleep, thy picture in my sight
     Awakes my heart to heart's and eye's delight.

My eyes and my heart help each other in their loving appreciation of you,
which means you are always with me, even when I dream.

Q: No. 47. The second in a pair of related sonnets (with 46) about the
eyes and the heart. Could be addressed to either a male or a female. Dramatic analogy: Helena to Demetrius in *A Midsummer Night's Dream*; Helen
to Bertram in *All's Well That Ends Well*.

1 **league is took** truce is made   10 **still** constantly
6 **painted banquet** illusory feast

1595–1597

How careful was I . . .

How careful was I when I took my way
    Each trifle under truest bars to thrust,
That to my use it might unusèd stay
    From hands of falsehood, in sure wards of trust.
But thou, to whom my jewels trifles are,   5
    Most worthy comfort, now my greatest grief,
Thou best of dearest and mine only care
    Art left the prey of every vulgar thief.
Thee have I not locked up in any chest
    Save where thou art not, though I feel thou art –   10
Within the gentle closure of my breast,
    From whence at pleasure thou mayst come and part;
      And even thence thou wilt be stol'n, I fear,
      For truth proves thievish for a prize so dear.

I am careful to safeguard my possessions but can only carry you in my heart, from which I fear you might be stolen.

Q: No. 48. Could be addressed to either a male or a female. Dramatic analogy: Troilus to Cressida.

1 **took my way** set off	**sure … trust** reliable safe keeping
2 **truest** most reliable	5 **to** compared to
3 **use** profit, benefit	6 **grief** (because absent and at risk)
4 **hands of falsehood** untrustworthy hands	12 **part** depart
	14 **truth** honesty itself

1595–1597

Against that time . . .

Against that time – if ever that time come –
  When I shall see thee frown on my defects,
Whenas thy love hath cast his utmost sum,
  Called to that audit by advised respects;
Against that time when thou shalt strangely pass   5
  And scarcely greet me with that sun, thine eye,
When love converted from the thing it was
  Shall reasons find of settled gravity:
Against that time do I ensconce me here
  Within the knowledge of mine own desert,   10
And this my hand against myself uprear
  To guard the lawful reasons on thy part.
    To leave poor me thou hast the strength of laws,
    Since why to love I can allege no cause.

I am preparing for the end of our loving because I realise that there is nothing of worth about me for you to love.

Q: No. 49. Could be addressed to either a male or a female.

1, 5 **Against** in preparation for
3 **Whenas** when
  cast … sum made its final reckoning
4 **advised respects** well-considered reflection
5 **strangely** as a stranger

8 **of settled gravity** for a dignified reserve; or of well-established seriousness (for leaving me)
9 **ensconce** establish, shelter
12 **guard … part** justify your unimpeachable case

1595–1597

How heavy do I journey . . .

How heavy do I journey on the way,
　　When what I seek – my weary travel's end –
Doth teach that ease and that repose to say
　　'Thus far the miles are measured from thy friend.'
The beast that bears me, tired with my woe,　　　　　5
　　Plods dully on to bear that weight in me,
As if by some instinct the wretch did know
　　His rider loved not speed, being made from thee.
The bloody spur cannot provoke him on
　　That sometimes anger thrusts into his hide,　　　　10
Which heavily he answers with a groan
　　More sharp to me than spurring to his side;
　　　　For that same groan doth put this in my mind:
　　　　My grief lies onward and my joy behind.

I journey away from you sadly, and even my poor horse seems to know that I do not want to leave you.

Q: No. 50. This is the first in a pair of syntactically related sonnets (with 51) written as from a journey on horseback, and which could be addressed to either a male or a female.

1　**heavy** sadly
5　**tired** exhausted; attired

6　**to bear** at bearing
11　**heavily** sadly

1595–1597

Thus can my love . . .

Thus can my love excuse the slow offence
  Of my dull bearer when from thee I speed:
From where thou art why should I haste me thence?
  Till I return, of posting is no need.
O what excuse will my poor beast then find   5
  When swift extremity can seem but slow?
Then should I spur, though mounted on the wind;
  In wingèd speed no motion shall I know.
Then can no horse with my desire keep pace;
  Therefore desire, of perfect'st love being made,   10
Shall rein no dull flesh in his fiery race;
  But love, for love, thus shall excuse my jade:
    'Since from thee going he went wilful-slow,
    Towards thee I'll run and give him leave to go.'

I depart from you slowly, but when I return my horse will not be able to gallop fast enough; in fact, I will let him walk back, and run more quickly back to you on my own.

Q: No. 51. This is the second in a pair of syntactically related sonnets (with 50) written as from a journey on horseback, and which could be addressed to either a male or a female.

1 **slow offence** offence of slowness
2 **dull bearer** (his horse)
4 **posting** riding quickly
6 **swift extremity** extreme speed
7 **though** even if I were

11 **rein** curb
12 **for love** for love's sake
13 **wilful-slow** i.e. wilfully, bloody-mindedly slowly
14 **go** walk

1595–1597

So am I as the rich …

So am I as the rich whose blessèd key
  Can bring him to his sweet up-lockèd treasure,
The which he will not ev'ry hour survey,
  For blunting the fine point of seldom pleasure.
Therefore are feasts so solemn and so rare   5
  Since, seldom coming, in the long year set
Like stones of worth they thinly placèd are,
  Or captain jewels in the carcanet.
So is the time that keeps you as my chest,
  Or as the wardrobe which the robe doth hide,   10
To make some special instant special blest
  By new unfolding his imprisoned pride.
    Blessèd are you whose worthiness gives scope,
    Being had, to triumph; being lacked, to hope.

You are like precious treasure to me: I look at you occasionally, and on those occasions when I am reunited with you, the treasure is even more special.

Q: No. 52. Could be addressed to either a male or a female, and alludes to a sexual relationship. Dramatic analogy: Bassanio to Portia in *The Merchant of Venice*.

1 **So am I** I am just like
  rich rich man
4 **For** so as to avoid
  seldom occasional
5–7 **Therefore … are** (cf. *1 Henry IV*, 1.2.201–3: 'If all the year were playing holidays, / To sport would be as tedious as to work; / But when they seldom come, they wished-for come')
6 **seldom coming** (also suggesting infrequent orgasm)
7 **stones of worth** jewels (also suggesting testicles)

thinly placèd are spaced thinly out
8 **captain** chief
  carcanet jewelled collar
9 **keeps** detains
  as my chest like my jewel-case
12 **his** its (the time's)
  imprisoned pride concealed splendour (also suggesting erection)
13 **gives scope** enables me
14 **Being had** when you are present (also suggesting sexual intercourse)
  triumph exult (also suggesting orgasm)
  being lacked when you are absent

1595–1597

What is your substance . . .

What is your substance, whereof are you made,
    That millions of strange shadows on you tend?
Since every one hath, every one, one shade,
    And you, but one, can every shadow lend.
Describe Adonis, and the counterfeit   5
    Is poorly imitated after you.
On Helen's cheek all art of beauty set,
    And you in Grecian tires are painted new.
Speak of the spring and foison of the year:
    The one doth shadow of your beauty show,   10
The other as your bounty doth appear;
    And you in every blessèd shape we know.
        In all external grace you have some part,
        But you like none, none you, for constant heart.

There is something supernatural about you: your beauty surpasses that of all creation and art, past and present. But no heart is as constant as yours.

Q: No. 53. Could be addressed to either a male or a female.

2 **strange** remarkable, unfamiliar
   shadows spirits, images
   tend attend
3 **shade** shadow
4 **but … lend** being only one can
   cast all shadows reflectively
5 **Adonis** (one of the most beautiful
   men in Greek mythology)
   counterfeit image, description

7 **Helen's cheek** (one of the
   most beautiful women in Greek
   mythology; cf. *As You Like It*, 3.2.142:
   'Helen's cheek, but not her heart')
8 **tires** attire
9 **foison** harvest-time
12 **blessèd shape** divinely created
   thing
   know recognise

1595–1597

O how much more . . .

O, how much more doth beauty beauteous seem
    By that sweet ornament which truth doth give!
The rose looks fair, but fairer we it deem
    For that sweet odour which doth in it live.
The canker-blooms have full as deep a dye   5
    As the perfumèd tincture of the roses,
Hang on such thorns, and play as wantonly
    When summer's breath their maskèd buds discloses;
But for their virtue only is their show
    They live unwooed and unrespected fade,   10
Die to themselves. Sweet roses do not so;
    Of their sweet deaths are sweetest odours made:
        And so of you, beauteous and lovely youth,
        When that shall fade, by verse distils your truth.

Your faithfulness makes you like a scented rose and, when your beauty fades, my poetry, like perfume, distils your true essence.

Q: No. 54. Addressed to a male (a 'youth', line 13).

2 **By** as a result of
  truth fidelity
3 **deem** judge it to be
5 **canker-blooms** dog-roses
  (unscented)
6 **tincture** colour
7 **such** similar
  wantonly playfully
8 **maskèd** concealed
  discloses opens up

9 **for … show** since their only merit
  is their appearance
10 **unrespected** unvalued
11 **Sweet roses** scented roses
12 **sweet deaths** i.e. because perfume
  is made from their petals (also
  orgasms)
  odours perfumes
14 **truth** i.e. beauty and loveliness

1595–1597

Not marble nor the gilded . . .

Not marble nor the gilded monuments
    Of princes shall outlive this powerful rhyme,
But you shall shine more bright in these contents
    Than unswept stone besmeared with sluttish time.
When wasteful war shall statues overturn,   5
    And broils root out the work of masonry,
Nor Mars his sword nor war's quick fire shall burn
    The living record of your memory.
'Gainst death and all oblivious enmity
    Shall you pace forth; your praise shall still find room   10
Even in the eyes of all posterity
    That wear this world out to the ending doom.
      So, till the judgement that yourself arise,
      You live in this, and dwell in lovers' eyes.

Nothing will outlive my rhyme and the way it immortalises you, until you yourself are resurrected from the dead.

Q: No. 55. Could be addressed to either a male or a female.

3 **these contents** the contents of this poem
4 **besmeared with** sullied by
  sluttish dirty, uncaring
6 **broils** battles
  the work of masonry stoneworkers structures
7 **Nor Mars his** neither Mars's (the god of war's)
9 **all oblivious enmity** all (other) forces including oblivion
10 **pace forth** stride out, live on
  find room gain admittance
12 **ending doom** Day of Judgement
13 **judgement … arise** Judgement Day when you will be resurrected
14 **this** i.e. this poem

1595–1597

Sweet love, renew thy force . . .

Sweet love, renew thy force. Be it not said
   Thy edge should blunter be than appetite,
Which but today by feeding is allayed,
   Tomorrow sharpened in his former might.
So, love, be thou; although today thou fill   5
   Thy hungry eyes even till they wink with fullness,
Tomorrow see again, and do not kill
   The spirit of love with a perpetual dullness.
Let this sad int'rim like the ocean be
   Which parts the shore where two contracted new   10
Come daily to the banks, that when they see
   Return of love, more blessed may be the view;
      Or call it winter, which, being full of care,
      Makes summer's welcome, thrice more wished, more
      rare.

Let our time away from each other be full of appetite and anticipation.

Q: No. 56. Addressed to the spirit of love (lines 1–4), and to either a male
or a female (to whom the poet imagines being newly betrothed: line 10).
Dramatic analogy: Cleopatra to Antony.

1 **love** spirit of love	9 **int'rim** period between our
3 **allayed** satisfied	meetings
4 **his** its	10 **contracted new** newly betrothed
5 **love** the loved one	12 **love** the loved one
6 **wink** close (in sleep)	14 **rare** precious
8 **dullness** lethargy	

1595–1597

Being your slave . . .

Being your slave, what should I do but tend
   Upon the hours and times of your desire?
I have no precious time at all to spend,
   Nor services to do, till you require;
Nor dare I chide the world-without-end hour   5
   Whilst I, my sovereign, watch the clock for you,
Nor think the bitterness of absence sour
   When you have bid your servant once adieu.
Nor dare I question with my jealous thought
   Where you may be, or your affairs suppose,   10
But like a sad slave stay and think of naught
   Save, where you are, how happy you make those.
     So true a fool is love that in your will,
     Though you do anything, he thinks no ill.

I am your slave and have nothing better to do than to wait around for you.
My love for you will excuse anything you do.

Q: No. 57. Could be addressed to either a male or a female. This is the first
in a pair of related sonnets (with 58) about the slavery of love. Dramatic
analogy: Kate to Petruccio in *The Taming of the Shrew*.

1 **tend** attend, wait
5 **chide** rebuke
  world-without-end interminable
10 **your affairs suppose** guess what
    you are doing

13 **true** loyal
  will desire (also pun on the poet's
  first name: cf. Sonnets 22, 89, 134,
  135, 136, and 143)

1595–1597

That god forbid …

That god forbid, that made me first your slave,
　I should in thought control your times of pleasure,
Or at your hand th' account of hours to crave,
　Being your vassal bound to stay your leisure.
O let me suffer, being at your beck,　　　　　　　　　　5
　Th' imprisoned absence of your liberty,
And patience, tame to sufferance, bide each check,
　Without accusing you of injury.
Be where you list, your charter is so strong
　That you yourself may privilege your time　　　　　10
To what you will; to you it doth belong
　Yourself to pardon of self-doing crime.
　　I am to wait, though waiting so be hell,
　　Not blame your pleasure, be it ill or well.

As your slave, I have no right to expect anything from you, but I do seek to endure my lack of freedom, without blaming you.

Q: No. 58. Could be addressed to either a male or a female. This is the second in a pair of related sonnets (with 57) about the slavery of love. Dramatic analogy: Kate to Petruccio in *The Taming of the Shrew*.

4 **vassal** slave
　stay wait upon
5 **beck** beck and call
7 **patience … sufferance** (cf. *Troilus and Cressida*, 1.1.27–8: 'Patience herself, what goddess e'er she be, / Doth lesser blench at suff'rance than I do')

bide each check put up with every rebuke
9 **list** please
　charter privilege
10 **privilege** authorise
11 **to … belong** you have the right

1595–1597

If there be nothing new …

If there be nothing new, but that which is
   Hath been before, how are our brains beguiled,
Which, labouring for invention, bear amiss
   The second burden of a former child!
O that record could with a backward look   5
   Even of five hundred courses of the sun
Show me your image in some antique book
   Since mind at first in character was done,
That I might see what the old world could say
   To this composèd wonder of your frame;   10
Whether we are mended or whe'er better they,
   Or whether revolution be the same.
     O, sure I am the wits of former days
     To subjects worse have given admiring praise.

I bet you are the best subject for a love poem since ever thought was first expressed in words.

Q: No. 59. Could be addressed to either a male or a female.

2 **beguiled** tricked
3 **invention** creativity
  amiss by mistake
5 **record** memory
6 **courses … sun** years
8 **mind … done** thought was first expressed in words

10 **composèd … frame** wonderful composition of your form
11 **mended** improved
12 **revolution** the revolving of the ages
13 **wits** sages, clever writers

1595–1597

Like as the waves ...

Like as the waves make towards the pebbled shore,
　So do our minutes hasten to their end,
Each changing place with that which goes before;
　In sequent toil all forwards do contend.
Nativity, once in the main of light,　　　　　　　　　　5
　Crawls to maturity, wherewith being crowned
Crookèd eclipses 'gainst his glory fight,
　And time that gave doth now his gift confound.
Time doth transfix the flourish set on youth,
　And delves the parallels in beauty's brow;　　　　　10
Feeds on the rarities of nature's truth,
　And nothing stands but for his scythe to mow.
　　And yet to times in hope my verse shall stand,
　　Praising thy worth despite his cruel hand.

Our minutes pass, and time destroys everything that it once made beautiful. But my poetry will survive, praising you.

Q: No. 60. A meditation on the power of poetry to transcend time. Lines 1–4 allude closely to Ovid's *Metamorphoses*, book 15.178–85.

1 **Like** just	9 **transfix the flourish** pierce and
3 **changing ... with** replacing	destroy the ornament (beauty)
4 **In ... contend** toiling after	10 **parallels** wrinkles
each other all struggle	11 **rarities** delicacies
forwards	**truth** perfection
5 **Nativity** the newborn child	12 **but ... mow** that time's scythe will
main broad expanse	not mow
7 **Crookèd** malignant	13 **in hope** in the future
8 **confound** destroy	14 **his** Time's

1595–1597

If we offend . . .

[QUINCE] (*as Prologue*)
If we offend, it is with our good will.
That you should think: we come not to offend
    But with good will. To show our simple skill,
That is the true beginning of our end.
    Consider then we come but in despite.   5
We do not come as minding to content you,
    Our true intent is. All for your delight
We are not here. That you should here repent you
    The actors are at hand, and by their show
    You shall know all that you are like to know.   10

1596: A Midsummer Night's Dream, 5.1.108–17

Nervously introducing the play within the play, Peter Quince garbles this foreshortened sonnet (he does not pay proper attention to its punctuation) with the result that he says the opposite of what he means.

4 **end** aim, intention   5 **in despite** in contempt

1598–1600

❀

1598–1600

What fire is in mine ears?

BEATRICE
What fire is in mine ears? Can this be true?
   Stand I condemned for pride and scorn so much?
Contempt, farewell! and maiden pride, adieu.
   No glory lives behind the back of such.
And, Benedick, love on; I will requite thee,   5
   Taming my wild heart to thy loving hand:
If thou dost love, my kindness shall incite thee
   To bind our loves up in a holy band.
     For others say thou dost deserve, and I
     Believe it better than reportingly.   10

1598: Much Ado About Nothing, 3.1.107–16. Beatrice's women friends have been trying to trick her into falling in love with Benedick by allowing her to overhear them saying that he is in love with her. As she comes out of concealment, she speaks a foreshortened sonnet.

5 **requite** repay   7 **incite** summon

1598–1600

So oft have I invoked thee . . .

So oft have I invoked thee for my muse
    And found such fair assistance in my verse
As every alien pen hath got my use,
    And under thee their poesy disperse.
Thine eyes, that taught the dumb on high to sing   5
    And heavy ignorance aloft to fly,
Have added feathers to the learnèd's wing
    And given grace a double majesty.
Yet be most proud of that which I compile,
    Whose influence is thine and born of thee.   10
In others' works thou dost but mend the style,
    And arts with thy sweet graces gracèd be;
      But thou art all my art, and dost advance
      As high as learning my rude ignorance.

Other poets are now being inspired by you because of me, and their work is getting even better, but you are everything to my poetry and make it fly.

Q: No. 78. Could be addressed to either a male or a female. The first of nine sonnets (with 79–86) which refer to other poets writing about the loved one.

3 **As** that
  every alien pen other, unfamiliar (also foreign) writers
  got my use adopted my practice
4 **under thee** under your patronage or influence
5 **on high** aloud

7 **added ... wing** helped learned poets to fly even higher
8 **grace** excellence
9 **compile** put together, compose
11 **mend** improve
12 **arts** (their) skill and learning
14 **rude** crude

1598–1600

Whilst I alone did call . . .

Whilst I alone did call upon thy aid
   My verse alone had all thy gentle grace;
But now my gracious numbers are decayed,
   And my sick muse doth give another place.
I grant, sweet love, thy lovely argument   5
   Deserves the travail of a worthier pen,
Yet what of thee thy poet doth invent
   He robs thee of, and pays it thee again.
He lends thee virtue, and he stole that word
   From thy behaviour; beauty doth he give,   10
And found it in thy cheek: he can afford
   No praise to thee but what in thee doth live.
     Then thank him not for that which he doth say,
     Since what he owes thee thou thyself dost pay.

It used to be only me that wrote about you, but now someone else does, too. But do not be taken in by his invention, because everything he writes comes from who and how you are.

Q: No. 79. Could be addressed to either a male or a female. The second of nine sonnets (with 78, and 80–6) which refer to other poets writing about the loved one. 'He' (from line 8) refers to another (unidentifiable) poet.

3 **numbers** verses
4 **give another place** yield place to another
5 **thy lovely argument** the theme of your loveliness
6 **travail** labour
8 **pays ... again** pays it back to you
11 **afford** offer

1598–1600

O, how I faint …

O, how I faint when I of you do write,
　　Knowing a better spirit doth use your name,
And in the praise thereof spends all his might,
　　To make me tongue-tied, speaking of your fame!
But since your worth, wide as the ocean is,   5
　　The humble as the proudest sail doth bear,
My saucy barque, inferior far to his,
　　On your broad main doth wilfully appear.
Your shallowest help will hold me up afloat
　　Whilst he upon your soundless deep doth ride;   10
Or, being wrecked, I am a worthless boat,
　　He of tall building and of goodly pride.
　　　　Then if he thrive and I be cast away,
　　　　The worst was this: my love was my decay.

Although I am discouraged because another, better poet is also writing about you, I will continue to do what I can and, if I fail, at least I can say I have failed for love's sake.

Q: No. 80. Could be addressed to either a male or a female. The third of nine sonnets (with 78–9 and 81–6) which refer to other poets writing about the loved one. In this one, which (with 81) forms a pair of syntactically related sonnets, the poet makes direct comparison between his creative endeavours and those of another (unidentifiable) poet.

2 **better spirit** a more worthy poet
　use your name i.e. write about you
7 **saucy barque** cheeky little boat
8 **main** open sea
　wilfully stubbornly
9 **shallowest** slightest
10 **soundless** unfathomable
11 **being** if I am
12 **pride** splendour (also sexual potency)
14 **my decay** (source of) my ruin

1598–1600

Or I shall live . . .

Or I shall live your epitaph to make,
 Or you survive when I in earth am rotten.
From hence your memory death cannot take,
 Although in me each part will be forgotten.
Your name from hence immortal life shall have,   5
 Though I, once gone, to all the world must die.
The earth can yield me but a common grave
 When you entombèd in men's eyes shall lie.
Your monument shall be my gentle verse,
 Which eyes not yet created shall o'er-read,   10
And tongues to be your being shall rehearse
 When all the breathers of this world are dead.
  You still shall live – such virtue hath my pen –
  Where breath most breathes, even in the mouths of
  men.

We do not know who will die first, but you will survive longer than me because my verse will immortalise you and make you live again in readers' breaths and mouths.

Q: No. 81. Could be addressed to either a male or a female. The fourth of nine sonnets (with 78–80 and 82–6) which refer to other poets writing about the loved one. This sonnet, syntactically related to 80, imagines future readers and affirms the confidence the poet has in the power of his own work.

1 **Or** either
3 **hence** i.e. the world
4 **in … part** each of my qualities
8 **entombèd** enshrined in a splendid monument

11 **rehearse** describe
13 **still** for ever
 virtue power

1598–1600

I grant thou wert not ...

I grant thou wert not married to my muse,
    And therefore mayst without attaint o'erlook
The dedicated words which writers use
    Of their fair subject, blessing every book.
Thou art as fair in knowledge as in hue,   5
    Finding thy worth a limit past my praise,
And therefore art enforced to seek anew
    Some fresher stamp of these time-bettering days.
And do so, love; yet when they have devised
    What strainèd touches rhetoric can lend,   10
Thou, truly fair, wert truly sympathized
    In true plain words by thy true-telling friend;
        And their gross painting might be better used
        Where cheeks need blood: in thee it is abused.

I do not have exclusive rights over you, but when you have seen others write, you will find that my poetry is truer than theirs.

Q: No. 82. Could be addressed to either a male or a female. The fifth of nine sonnets (with 78–81 and 83–6) which refer to other poets writing about the loved one. This sonnet is the first in a pair (with 83) which criticises the 'gross painting' (line 13, i.e. the exaggerated rhetoric) of others.

2 **attaint** dishonour
  o'erlook read
3 **writers** i.e. other writers
5 **hue** appearance
8 **fresher stamp** more recent imprint
  (by others)
  time-bettering progressive

10 **What** such
  strainèd laboured
11 **sympathized** represented
12 **true-telling friend** i.e. the poet
  (Shakespeare)
13 **painting** i.e. flattery
14 **abused** wasted

1598–1600

I never saw that you …

I never saw that you did painting need,
    And therefore to your fair no painting set.
I found – or thought I found – you did exceed
    The barren tender of a poet's debt;
And therefore have I slept in your report: 5
    That you yourself, being extant, well might show
How far a modern quill doth come too short,
    Speaking of worth, what worth in you doth grow.
This silence for my sin you did impute,
    Which shall be most my glory, being dumb;   10
For I impair not beauty, being mute,
    When others would give life, and bring a tomb.
      There lives more life in one of your fair eyes
      Than both your poets can in praise devise.

You do not need flattery any more than you need make-up, so I have refrained from singing your praises. Even just one of your lovely eyes has more life in it than either of your poets could write about.

Q: No. 83. Could be addressed to either a male or a female (since both sexes could wear make-up, the 'painting' of line 1). The sixth of nine sonnets (with 78–82 and 84–6) which refer to other poets writing about the loved one. This sonnet is the second in a pair (with 82) about flattery ('painting', line 2), and refers specifically to two poets ('both', line 14), one being the author of this sonnet.

1 **painting** cosmetics
2 **fair** beauty
  painting flattery
4 **tender** offering
5 **slept … report** neglected to sing your praise
6 **That** since
  extant present

7 **modern** commonplace
  come too short (cf. Regan criticising her sister's loving words in *The Tragedy of King Lear*, 1.1.72, 'Only she comes too short.')
8 **Speaking of worth** in speaking of values of the worth that
11 **impair** diminish

1598–1600

Who is it that says most . . .

Who is it that says most which can say more
 Than this rich praise: that you alone are you,
In whose confine immurèd is the store
 Which should example where your equal grew?
Lean penury within that pen doth dwell   5
 That to his subject lends not some small glory;
But he that writes of you, if he can tell
 That you are you, so dignifies his story.
Let him but copy what in you is writ,
 Not making worse what nature made so clear,   10
And such a counterpart shall fame his wit,
 Making his style admirèd everywhere.
  You to your beauteous blessings add a curse,
  Being fond on praise, which makes your praises worse.

You alone are you, and any poet needs simply to copy what is already in you. But, alas, you like praise too much.

Q: No. 84. Could be addressed to either a male or a female. The seventh of nine sonnets (with 78–83 and 85–6) which refer to other poets writing about the loved one.

1 **says most** speaks most fulsomely	6 **his** its
3 **confine** boundaries	7 **he** the one
immurèd confined, shut-up	10 **clear** obvious, glorious
4 **example** i.e. provide the example	11 **fame his wit** make his talent famous
where … grew to produce your equal	14 **fond on** fond of, made foolish by
5 **Lean penury** mean poverty	

1598–1600

My tongue-tied muse ...

My tongue-tied muse in manners holds her still
  While comments of your praise, richly compiled,
Reserve thy character with golden quill
  And precious phrase by all the muses filed.
I think good thoughts whilst other write good words,   5
  And like unlettered clerk still cry 'Amen'
To every hymn that able spirit affords
  In polished form of well-refinèd pen.
Hearing you praised I say ''Tis so, 'tis true,'
  And to the most of praise add something more;   10
But that is in my thought, whose love to you,
  Though words come hindmost, holds his rank before.
    Then others for the breath of words respect,
    Me for my dumb thoughts, speaking in effect.

I hold back in praising you, but agree with what other poets write – even
adding more (but in my thoughts only). Others praise you in words; I in
the action of my thoughts.

Q: No. 85. Could be addressed to either a male or a female. The eighth of
nine sonnets (with 78–84 and 86) which refer to other poets writing about
the loved one. Dramatic analogy: Cordelia in *King Lear*.

1 **in ... still** politely remains silent
3 **Reserve thy character** store up
   your features
4 **filed** polished
6 **unlettered clerk** an ignorant
   parish clerk
   still always
7 **able spirit affords** a competent

   person offers you
8 **well-refinèd** a highly skilful
10 **most of** highest
12 **hindmost** last (and are lowliest)
   rank before place in front
13 **others ... respect** regard other
   people for their words
14 **in effect** in action

1598–1600

Was it the proud full sail . . .

Was it the proud full sail of his great verse
    Bound for the prize of all-too-precious you
That did my ripe thoughts in my brain inhearse,
    Making their tomb the womb wherein they grew?
Was it his spirit, by spirits taught to write   5
    Above a mortal pitch, that struck me dead?
No, neither he nor his compeers by night
    Giving him aid my verse astonishèd.
He nor that affable familiar ghost
    Which nightly gulls him with intelligence,   10
As victors, of my silence cannot boast;
    I was not sick of any fear from thence.
      But when your countenance filled up his line,
      Then lacked I matter; that enfeebled mine.

My rival's ambition and his encouragement from others did not hold my own poetry back; rather, it was when I realised you were in his every line.

Q: No. 86. Could be addressed to either a male or a female. The last of nine sonnets (with 78–85) which refer to other poets writing about the loved one. This one refers specifically to the work of an enigmatically unidentifiable rival and his associates, or collaborators.

1 **his** (another poet's)
2 **prize** booty
3 **inhearse** bury
6 **pitch** height
7 **compeers** associates, collaborators
8 **astonishèd** struck dumb

9 **affable familiar ghost** friend who haunts him
10 **gulls** misleads
   intelligence information
13 **countenance** appearance, favour

1598–1600

Thus far with rough ...

CHORUS
Thus far with rough and all-unable pen
   Our bending author hath pursued the story,
In little room confining mighty men,
   Mangling by starts the full course of their glory.
Small time, but in that small most greatly lived   5
   This star of England. Fortune made his sword,
By which the world's best garden he achieved,
   And of it left his son imperial lord.
Henry the Sixth, in infant bands crowned king
   Of France and England, did this king succeed,   10
Whose state so many had the managing
   That they lost France and made his England bleed,
      Which oft our stage hath shown - and, for their sake,
      In your fair minds let this acceptance take.

1599: *Henry V*, Epilogue

Immediately after the uniting of England with France, a Chorus appears
to anticipate the breaking up of the union, which led to the Wars of the
Roses, already dramatised by Shakespeare.

2 **bending** bowing, respectful
3 **room** space
4 **starts** short bursts of action
6 **star of England** Henry V
7 **world's best garden** i.e. France

9 **infant bands** swaddling clothes
(he came to the throne as an
infant)
13 **oft ... shown** (in the three plays
about the reign of Henry VI)

1598–1600

Hang there, my verse . . .

ORLANDO

Hang there, my verse, in witness of my love;
  And thou thrice-crownèd queen of night, survey
With thy chaste eye from thy pale sphere above
  Thy huntress' name that my full life doth sway.
O Rosalind, these trees shall be my books,   5
  And in their barks my thoughts I'll character
That every eye which in this forest looks
  Shall see thy virtue witnessed everywhere.
    Run, run, Orlando; carve on every tree
    The fair, the chaste, and unexpressive she.   10

1599: *As You Like It*, 3.2.1–10. Orlando, lovesick for Rosalind, hangs on trees
in the Forest of Ardenne poems addressed to her. His speech describing
this takes the form of a foreshortened sonnet, as he runs eagerly away.

2 **thrice-crownèd … night** i.e.
  Diana, goddess of the moon,
  chastity, and the night
4 **huntress'** Rosalind's (thought of
  as a follower of the goddess of the
  hunt)

full entire
sway control
6 **character** inscribe, carve
10 **unexpressive** inexpressible

1600–1609

❦

1600–1604

To me, fair friend ...

To me, fair friend, you never can be old;
   For as you were when first your eye I eyed,
Such seems your beauty still. Three winters cold
   Have from the forests shook three summers' pride;
Three beauteous springs to yellow autumn turned   5
   In process of the seasons have I seen,
Three April perfumes in three hot Junes burned
   Since first I saw you fresh, which yet are green.
Ah yet doth beauty, like a dial-hand,
   Steal from his figure, and no pace perceived;   10
So your sweet hue, which methinks still doth stand,
   Hath motion, and mine eye may be deceived.
     For fear of which, hear this, thou age unbred:
     Ere you were born was beauty's summer dead.

You never seem any older to me than when we first met three years ago, even though I know time does not stand still.

Q: No. 104. Could be addressed to either a male or a female.

4 **pride** splendour
6 **process** the progression
8 **yet** still
  green fresh, youthful
9 **dial** time-piece: clock, watch, sundial
10 **figure** i.e. the number on the time-piece
11 **hue** appearance
  methinks it seems to me
  stand remain unaltered

1600–1604

Let not my love . . .

Let not my love be called idolatry,
  Nor my belovèd as an idol show,
Since all alike my songs and praises be
  To one, of one, still such, and ever so.
Kind is my love today, tomorrow kind,   5
  Still constant in a wondrous excellence.
Therefore my verse, to constancy confined,
  One thing expressing, leaves out difference.
'Fair, kind, and true' is all my argument,
  'Fair, kind, and true' varying to other words,   10
And in this change is my invention spent,
  Three themes in one, which wondrous scope affords.
    Fair, kind, and true have often lived alone,
    Which three till now never kept seat in one.

My love is not idolatrous, only constant and consistent, as is my loved
one, and expresses itself through variations of 'fair', 'kind', and 'true'.

Q: No. 105. A meditation on love and poetry.

3 **Since** even though
4, 6 **still** continually
8 **difference** variety (of theme)
9 **argument** theme

11 **invention spent** inventiveness
  expended
12 **scope** range of subject
14 **kept seat** dwelt permanently

1600–1604

When in the chronicle . . .

When in the chronicle of wasted time
   I see descriptions of the fairest wights,
And beauty making beautiful old rhyme
   In praise of ladies dead and lovely knights;
Then in the blazon of sweet beauty's best,   5
   Of hand, of foot, of lip, of eye, of brow,
I see their antique pen would have expressed
   Even such a beauty as you master now.
So all their praises are but prophecies
   Of this our time, all you prefiguring,   10
And for they looked but with divining eyes
    They had not skill enough your worth to sing;
      For we which now behold these present days
      Have eyes to wonder, but lack tongues to praise.

When I read the poetry of the past, praising the most beautiful people, I realise that they were really describing you but could never do so adequately – nor can we.

Q: No. 106. Could be addressed to either a male or a female.

1 **wasted** past	10 **prefiguring** pre-shaping (through poetry)
2 **wights** people	
5 **blazon** catalogue	11 **for** because
7 **antique** old	**divining** prophetic
8 **master** possess, control	

1600–1604

Not mine own fears …

Not mine own fears nor the prophetic soul
   Of the wide world dreaming on things to come
Can yet the lease of my true love control,
   Supposed as forfeit to a confined doom.
The mortal moon hath her eclipse endured,   5
   And the sad augurs mock their own presage;
Incertainties now crown themselves assured,
   And peace proclaims olives of endless age.
Now with the drops of this most balmy time
   My love looks fresh, and death to me subscribes,   10
Since spite of him I'll live in this poor rhyme
   While he insults o'er dull and speechless tribes;
      And thou in this shalt find thy monument
      When tyrants' crests and tombs of brass are spent.

No one knows how long love will last, but these times of peace are encouraging, my love fresh, and, through this poem, you and I shall survive death.

Q: No. 107. Could be addressed to either a male or a female. This exceptionally cryptic poem appears to have meanings that are lost to time.

3 **lease** term
4 **forfeit** subject to
  confined doom limited time
  (before expiry or judgement)
5 **mortal moon** moon, which is
  subject to mortality
  her eclipse endured has survived
  or suffered eclipse (sometimes
  taken as a reference to the eclipse
  of 1595, or to the death in 1603 of
  Queen Elizabeth)
6 **augurs** prophets
  presage prophecy
8 **olives** olive branches (symbolic of

peace)
  endless age that will endure
  perpetually
  peace … age (cf. 2 *Henry IV*,
  4.3.87: 'peace puts forth her olive
  everywhere')
9 **drops** (of 'balm')
10 **subscribes** submits
11 **him** death
12 **he** death
  dull … tribes stupid and
  inarticulate masses
14 **spent** wasted away

1600–1604

What's in the brain . . .

What's in the brain that ink may character
    Which hath not figured to thee my true spirit?
What's new to speak, what now to register,
    That may express my love or thy dear merit?
Nothing, sweet boy; but yet like prayers divine   5
    I must each day say o'er the very same,
Counting no old thing old, thou mine, I thine,
    Even as when first I hallowed thy fair name.
So that eternal love in love's fresh case
    Weighs not the dust and injury of age,   10
Nor gives to necessary wrinkles place,
    But makes antiquity for aye his page,
        Finding the first conceit of love there bred
        Where time and outward form would show it dead.

I cannot put my love for you into words, except to repeat myself as though at prayer, generating renewed expressions of love that transcend time.

Q: No. 108. Addressed to a 'boy'. Dramatic analogy: Orsino to Cesario (who is Viola in disguise) in *Twelfth Night, or What You Will*.

1 **character** put into writing	9 **case** covering, expression
2 **figured** represented	10 **Weighs not** is unconcerned about
3 **register** record	11 **place** priority
4 **express** represent	12 **antiquity** old age (or 'the writings
8 **hallowed** blessed (as in the Lord's	of the ancients')
Prayer: 'Hallowed be thy name';	**for aye** forever
perhaps with a pun on the fox-	**page** page-boy (with a pun on the
hunting cry 'hallooed'; cf. *Twelfth*	written page of a book)
Night, or What You Will, 1.5.261:	13 **conceit** thought
'Halloo your name.')	

1600–1604

O, never say that I was false …

O, never say that I was false of heart,
   Though absence seemed my flame to qualify –
As easy might I from myself depart
   As from my soul, which in thy breast doth lie.
That is my home of love. If I have ranged,   5
   Like him that travels I return again,
Just to the time, not with the time exchanged,
   So that myself bring water for my stain.
Never believe, though in my nature reigned
   All frailties that besiege all kinds of blood,   10
That it could so preposterously be stained
   To leave for nothing all thy sum of good;
     For nothing this wide universe I call
     Save thou my rose; in it thou art my all.

I have never been unfaithful to you; my love lives in you. I would never give you up for anything insignificant, because you are everything in the world to me.

Q: No. 109. Could be addressed to either a male or a female. The first in a series of four sonnets (with 110, 111, and 112) about temporary absences and distractions.

2 **my … qualify** to moderate my ardour
5 **ranged** strayed
7 **Just … time** faithfully punctual **with … exchanged** changed by time
8 **for** to cleanse
10 **blood** disposition
12 **To** as to
13 **For nothing** in exchange for something insignificant

1600–1604

Alas, 'tis true . . .

Alas, 'tis true, I have gone here and there
　　And made myself a motley to the view,
Gored mine own thoughts, sold cheap what is most dear,
　　Made old offences of affections new.
Most true it is that I have looked on truth　　　　　　　5
　　Askance and strangely. But, by all above,
These blenches gave my heart another youth,
　　And worse essays proved thee my best of love.
Now all is done, have what shall have no end;
　　Mine appetite I never more will grind　　　　　　　10
On newer proof to try an older friend,
　　A god in love, to whom I am confined.
　　　　Then give me welcome, next my heaven the best,
　　　　Even to thy pure and most most loving breast.

I have been foolish in following my attraction to others, but I will never
be distracted from you again, my greatest love.

Q: No. 110. Could be addressed to either a male or a female. The second in
a series of four sonnets (with 109, 111, and 112) about temporary absences,
and distractions.

2 **motley** jester, laughing stock
3 **Gored** savaged; dishonoured
4 **old offences** long-standing
　resentments
　affections new new attachments
5 **truth** fidelity
6 **Askance** disdainfully
　strangely coldly, with reserve
7 **blenches** swervings

heart love (for you)
8 **essays** experiments
9 **have no end** take what is eternal
　(my love)
10–11 **grind ... proof** sharpen on
　new experience
11 **try** test (my love for)
13 **next ... best** second only to
　heaven

1600–1604

O, for my sake . . .

O, for my sake do you with fortune chide,
   The guilty goddess of my harmful deeds,
That did not better for my life provide
   Than public means which public manners breeds.
Thence comes it that my name receives a brand,   5
   And almost thence my nature is subdued
To what it works in, like the dyer's hand.
   Pity me then, and wish I were renewed,
Whilst like a willing patient I will drink
   Potions of eisel 'gainst my strong infection;   10
No bitterness that I will bitter think,
   Nor double penance to correct correction.
     Pity me then, dear friend, and I assure ye
     Even that your pity is enough to cure me.

Blame fortune for the way I sometimes behave, because of the public nature of my work. But your pitying me will cure me.

Q: No. 111. Could be addressed to either a male or a female. The third in a series of four sonnets (with 109, 110, and 112) about temporary absences, and distractions.

1 **do you** may you
   chide rebuke
4 **means** i.e. (since this is
   Shakespeare) employment (as an
   actor and playwright)
   public manners the behaviour of a
   public figure

5 **brand** stigma
7 **dyer's hand** i.e. differently
   coloured, depending on the dye
8 **renewed** restored
10 **eisel** vinegar (used as a medicine)
12 **correct correction** cure me twice
   over

1600–1604

Your love and pity . . .

Your love and pity doth th' impression fill
   Which vulgar scandal stamped upon my brow;
For what care I who calls me well or ill,
   So you o'er-green my bad, my good allow?
You are my all-the-world, and I must strive   5
   To know my shames and praises from your tongue –
None else to me, nor I to none alive,
   That my steeled sense or changes, right or wrong.
In so profound abyss I throw all care
   Of others' voices that my adder's sense   10
To critic and to flatterer stoppèd are.
   Mark how with my neglect I do dispense:
     You are so strongly in my purpose bred
     That all the world besides, methinks, they're dead.

Your love and pity can remove the stigma of my reputation. You alone are everything to me, and I only care about what you have to say.

Q: No. 112. Could be addressed to either a male or a female. The fourth in a series of four sonnets (with 109, 110, and 111) about temporary absences, and distractions.

1 **th' impression fill** efface the scar (made by the 'brand' of Sonnet 111, line 5)
4 **o'er-green** cover (as with fresh green growth), camouflage
allow give credit for
8 **steeled sense** confirmed disposition
9 **abyss** a bottomless pit
10 **adder's sense** deaf ears (adders being proverbially deaf)
12 **my ... dispense** I excuse my neglect (of others' voices)
13 **in ... bred** engrafted in my plans

1600–1604

Since I left you …

Since I left you mine eye is in my mind,
  And that which governs me to go about
Doth part his function and is partly blind,
  Seems seeing, but effectually is out;
For it no form delivers to the heart   5
  Of bird, of flower, or shape which it doth latch.
Of his quick objects hath the mind no part,
  Nor his own vision holds what it doth catch;
For if it see the rud'st or gentlest sight,
  The most sweet favour or deformèd'st creature,   10
The mountain or the sea, the day or night,
  The crow or dove, it shapes them to your feature.
    Incapable of more, replete with you,
    My most true mind thus makes mine eye untrue.

Since I left you my imagination controls my eyesight, and I see you in everything I look at.

Q: No. 113. This is the first in a pair of syntactically related sonnets (with 114). Could be addressed to either a male or a female.

2 **that … about** i.e. my real sight
3 **part his** divide its
4 **effectually is out** in effect is blind
6 **latch** catch sight of
7 **his quick objects** its fleeting impressions

8 **Nor … holds** nor does the eye's vision retain
  catch apprehend
9 **rud'st** roughest
12 **shapes … feature** makes them look like you

1600–1604

Or whether doth my mind …

Or whether doth my mind, being crowned with you,
    Drink up the monarch's plague, this flattery,
Or whether shall I say mine eye saith true,
    And that your love taught it this alchemy,
To make of monsters and things indigest   5
    Such cherubins as your sweet self resemble,
Creating every bad a perfect best
    As fast as objects to his beams assemble?
O, 'tis the first, 'tis flatt'ry in my seeing,
    And my great mind most kingly drinks it up.   10
Mine eye well knows what with his gust is 'greeing,
    And to his palate doth prepare the cup.
        If it be poisoned, 'tis the lesser sin
        That mine eye loves it and doth first begin.

It is flattery rather than a magic learnt from your love that is affecting my eyesight.

Q: No. 114. This is the second in a pair of syntactically related sonnets (with 113). Could be addressed to either a male or a female. Dramatic analogy: Queen Gertrude in *Hamlet*.

1 **Or whether** (introducing alternatives)
4 **your love** love of you
  alchemy transformative power
5 **indigest** shapeless, chaotic
6 **cherubins** angelic forms

10 **great** (because crowned with you)
11 **his gust** its taste
12 **to his palate** to suit its taste
14 **doth first begin** drinks first (like a king's taster)

1600–1604

Those lines that I before have writ . . .

Those lines that I before have writ do lie,
    Even those that said I could not love you dearer;
Yet then my judgement knew no reason why
    My most full flame should afterwards burn clearer.
But reckoning time, whose millioned accidents   5
    Creep in 'twixt vows and change decrees of kings,
Tan sacred beauty, blunt the sharp'st intents,
    Divert strong minds to th' course of alt'ring things –
Alas, why, fearing of time's tyranny,
    Might I not then say 'Now I love you best',   10
When I was certain o'er incertainty,
    Crowning the present, doubting of the rest?
        Love is a babe; then might I not say so,
        To give full growth to that which still doth grow.

My earlier poems do not do you justice. I should not fear time, but rather simply say 'Now I love you best' and let love grow like a baby.

Q: No. 115. Could be addressed to either a male or a female.

5 **reckoning** calculating	12 **Crowning** glorifying
6 **'twixt vows** between vows and their fulfilment	13 **Love** (Cupid)
	say so i.e. 'now I love you best'
7 **Tan** darken, coarsen	14 **give** attribute
11 **o'er** beyond	

1600–1604

Let me not to the marriage ...

Let me not to the marriage of true minds
    Admit impediments. Love is not love
Which alters when it alteration finds,
    Or bends with the remover to remove.
O no, it is an ever fixèd mark   5
    That looks on tempests and is never shaken;
It is the star to every wand'ring barque,
    Whose worth's unknown although his height be taken.
Love's not time's fool, though rosy lips and cheeks
    Within his bending sickle's compass come;   10
Love alters not with his brief hours and weeks,
    But bears it out even to the edge of doom.
      If this be error and upon me proved,
      I never writ, nor no man ever loved.

True minds in love know that love never changes but lasts forever, and, if I am wrong, I have never written anything, nor been in love.

Q: No. 116. A meditation about love with no direct addressee.

2 **Admit impediments** (alluding to the Christian wedding service)
5 **mark** sea mark (aid to navigation)
9 **fool** plaything
10, 11, **his** (Time's)
10 **bending** curved
14 **nor ... loved** nor has anyone ever loved (or, possibly, I have never loved a man)

1600–1604

Accuse me thus …

Accuse me thus: that I have scanted all
   Wherein I should your great deserts repay,
Forgot upon your dearest love to call
   Whereto all bonds do tie me day by day;
That I have frequent been with unknown minds,   5
   And given to time your own dear-purchased right;
That I have hoisted sail to all the winds
   Which should transport me farthest from your sight.
Book both my wilfulness and errors down,
   And on just proof surmise accumulate;   10
Bring me within the level of your frown,
   But shoot not at me in your wakened hate,
     Since my appeal says I did strive to prove
     The constancy and virtue of your love.

You are right to accuse me of inconstancy and neglect, but I was only testing you.

Q: No. 117. Could be addressed to either a male or a female.

1 **scanted** neglected	9 **Book** record
5 **unknown minds** strangers	10 **on … accumulate** add what you
6 **given to time** wasted	suspect to what you can prove
dear-purchased right justified	11 **level** range
calls upon me	13 **appeal** plea
8 **should** would, were likely to	

1600–1604

Like as, to make our appetites . . .

Like as, to make our appetites more keen,
　With eager compounds we our palate urge;
As to prevent our maladies unseen
　We sicken to shun sickness when we purge:
Even so, being full of your ne'er cloying sweetness,　　　5
　To bitter sauces did I frame my feeding,
And, sick of welfare, found a kind of meetness
　To be diseased ere that there was true needing.
Thus policy in love, t'anticipate
　The ills that were not, grew to faults assured,　　　10
And brought to medicine a healthful state
　Which, rank of goodness, would by ill be cured.
　But thence I learn, and find the lesson true:
　Drugs poison him that so fell sick of you.

I tried to purge myself of a love-sickness that was more anticipated than real, but ended up poisoning myself because I was not really sick.

Q: No. 118. Could be addressed to either a male or a female. This sonnet is the first in a series of three (with 119 and 120) about sickness in love.

1 **Like** just
2 **eager** sharp, piquant
　urge stimulate
3 **prevent** forestall, ward off
5 **cloying** overly rich; sickly
6 **frame my feeding** direct my diet

7 **sick of welfare** made ill by good food
　meetness suitability
8 **To be** in being
11 **brought to** treated with
12 **rank of** sickened by

1600—1604

What potions have I drunk ...

What potions have I drunk of siren tears
  Distilled from limbecks foul as hell within,
Applying fears to hopes and hopes to fears,
  Still losing when I saw myself to win!
What wretched errors hath my heart committed   5
  Whilst it hath thought itself so blessèd never!
How have mine eyes out of their spheres been fitted
  In the distraction of this madding fever!
O benefit of ill! Now I find true
  That better is by evil still made better,   10
And ruined love when it is built anew
  Grows fairer than at first, more strong, far greater.
    So I return rebuked to my content,
    And gain by ills thrice more than I have spent.

It is as though I am returning to health after feeling poisoned, and, after realising my mistakes, I am building up a stronger love from a damaged one.

Q: No. 119. A meditation (possibly alluding to a female because of 'siren tears', line 1). This sonnet is the second in a series of three (with 118 and 120) about sickness in love.

1 **siren** temptingly harmful (as of a seductive, mythological mermaid)
2 **limbecks** apparatuses used in distillation
4 **Still** always

saw myself expected
7 **spheres** sockets
  fitted driven by fits
8 **madding** maddening
13 **content** what made me happy

1600–1604

That you were once unkind . . .

That you were once unkind befriends me now,
  And for that sorrow which I then did feel
Needs must I under my transgression bow,
  Unless my nerves were brass or hammered steel.
For if you were by my unkindness shaken   5
  As I by yours, you've passed a hell of time,
And I, a tyrant, have no leisure taken
  To weigh how once I suffered in your crime.
O that our night of woe might have remembered
  My deepest sense how hard true sorrow hits,   10
And soon to you as you to me then tendered
  The humble salve which wounded bosoms fits!
    But that your trespass now becomes a fee;
    Mine ransoms yours, and yours must ransom me.

We have both hurt each other and now need to excuse each other.

Q: No. 120. Could be addressed to either a male or a female. This sonnet
(with 118 and 119) is the last in a series of three about sickness in love.

2 **for** because of
3 **bow** stoop penitently
4 **nerves** sinews
8 **weigh** consider
9 **remembered** reminded
11 **tendered** offered
12 **humble salve** salve of humility,
  apology

fits becomes, suits
13 **that your trespass** that offence of
yours
fee compensation, benefit
14 **ransoms** redeems, excuses

1600–1604

'Tis better to be vile …

'Tis better to be vile than vile esteemed
  When not to be receives reproach of being,
And the just pleasure lost, which is so deemed
  Not by our feeling but by others' seeing.
For why should others' false adulterate eyes   5
  Give salutation to my sportive blood?
Or on my frailties why are frailer spies,
  Which in their wills count bad what I think good?
No, I am that I am, and they that level
  At my abuses reckon up their own.   10
I may be straight, though they themselves be bevel;
  By their rank thoughts my deeds must not be shown,
    Unless this general evil they maintain:
    All men are bad and in their badness reign.

One cannot expect other people to look kindly on how one behaves in love, but they are not blameless and should not be judging me.

Q: No. 121. This sonnet is a meditation on being judged by others about one's own loving inclinations. Dramatic analogy: Iago in *Othello*.

2 **being** being so	**frailer spies** more blameworthy spies
3 **just** fit, appropriate	
3 **so** i.e. vile	8 **wills** evil desires
5 **adulterate** corrupted	9 **level** aim
6 **Give … blood** look kindly on my amorous inclinations	10 **reckon up** count up
	11 **bevel** crooked
7 **frailties** weaknesses	14 **reign** prosper

1600–1604

Thy gift, thy tables …

Thy gift, thy tables, are within my brain
    Full charactered with lasting memory,
Which shall above that idle rank remain
    Beyond all date, even to eternity;
Or at the least so long as brain and heart   5
    Have faculty by nature to subsist,
Till each to razed oblivion yield his part
    Of thee, thy record never can be missed.
That poor retention could not so much hold,
    Nor need I tallies thy dear love to score;   10
Therefore to give them from me was I bold,
    To trust those tables that receive thee more.
        To keep an adjunct to remember thee
        Were to import forgetfulness in me.

My memories of you are in the forefront of my mind forever, so I do not
need to keep any notes or memoranda about you.

Q: No. 122. Could be addressed to either a male or a female. Dramatic
analogy: Hamlet on the Ghost.

1 **tables** memoranda (i.e. notes I
    have taken about you)
2 **charactered** written
3 **idle rank** worthless state
6 **faculty … subsist** power to
    survive
7 **razed** i.e. which obliterates
8 **missed** lost
9 **poor retention** inadequate
    container (my memory)

10 **tallies** counting sticks
    score reckon
11 **them** my notes about you
12 **those tables** i.e. my memories
    receive hold
13 **adjunct** aid (my notes)
14 **import** imply

1600–1604

No, time, thou shalt not boast . . .

No, time, thou shalt not boast that I do change!
   Thy pyramids built up with newer might
To me are nothing novel, nothing strange,
   They are but dressings of a former sight.
Our dates are brief, and therefore we admire   5
   What thou dost foist upon us that is old,
And rather make them born to our desire
   Than think that we before have heard them told.
Thy registers and thee I both defy,
   Not wond'ring at the present nor the past;   10
For thy records and what we see doth lie,
   Made more or less by thy continual haste.
     This I do vow, and this shall ever be:
     I will be true despite thy scythe and thee.

Time: you are fickle, and there is nothing reliable about what we think of as ancient, but I promise to be faithful.

Q: No. 123. A meditation on time and personal loyalty.

2 **pyramids** modern versions of classical monuments and architectural features
  with newer might by more modern means
3 **nothing** not at all
4 **dressings … sight** reconstructions of things already seen
5 **dates** lifespans
7 **make … desire** consider them created to suit us
9 **registers** records
12 **more or less** more or less impressive
14 **true** faithful

1600–1604

If my dear love . . .

If my dear love were but the child of state
    It might for fortune's bastard be unfathered,
As subject to time's love or to time's hate,
    Weeds among weeds or flowers with flowers gathered.
No, it was builded far from accident;   5
    It suffers not in smiling pomp, nor falls
Under the blow of thrallèd discontent
    Whereto th' inviting time our fashion calls.
It fears not policy, that heretic
    Which works on leases of short-numbered hours,   10
But all alone stands hugely politic,
    That it nor grows with heat nor drowns with showers.
    To this I witness call the fools of time,
    Which die for goodness, who have lived for crime.

My love is not subject to changing chance, or the indifferences of time, but stands and flourishes independently.

Q: No. 124. An enigmatic meditation on the vulnerability of the poet's love.

1 **but … state** only the result of circumstances
2 **for … unfathered** have no father but fortune
5 **accident** chance
6 **suffers** alters
  smiling pomp favourable splendour
7 **thrallèd** enslaved
9 **policy** expediency
10 **leases … hours** short-term contracts

11 **hugely politic** prudent in the long term
12 **That** with the result that
  heat prosperity
  showers bad times
13 **I witness call** I call as witnesses
  fools playthings
14 **Which … goodness** who die repentant, or in a good cause
  for crime i.e. the ravages of time

1600–1604

Were 't aught to me . . .

Were 't aught to me I bore the canopy,
    With my extern the outward honouring,
Or laid great bases for eternity
    Which proves more short than waste or ruining?
Have I not seen dwellers on form and favour   5
    Lose all and more by paying too much rent,
For compound sweet forgoing simple savour,
    Pitiful thrivers in their gazing spent?
No, let me be obsequious in thy heart,
    And take thou my oblation, poor but free,   10
Which is not mixed with seconds, knows no art
    But mutual render, only me for thee.
        Hence, thou suborned informer! A true soul
        When most impeached stands least in thy control.

I do not seek public honours or external shows of affection, and want
only to be true and sincere to you, whatever anyone else says.

Q: No. 125. Could be addressed to either a male or a female.

1 **Were 't … me** would it matter to
me if (or 'that')
  bore the canopy carried the
canopy of state (at a public
ceremony)
3 **bases for eternity** foundations for
everlasting monuments
4 **proves** turn out to be
5 **dwellers on** those who attach
importance to
6 **paying … rent** i.e. overdoing their
obligations
7 **For … savour** i.e. giving up simple

sincerity for elaborate flattery
9 **obsequious** dutiful
10 **oblation** offering
  free freely given
11 **seconds** i.e. the second-rate
  art artifice, craft
12 **render** surrender
13 **suborned informer** paid spy (a
critical onlooker of the poet's
love)
  A true soul i.e. the poet himself,
and his loved one
14 **impeached** accused

1600–1604

O thou my lovely boy . . .

O thou my lovely boy, who in thy power
  Dost hold time's fickle glass, his sickle-hour;
Who hast by waning grown, and therein show'st
  Thy lovers withering as thy sweet self grow'st –
If nature, sovereign mistress over wrack,   5
  As thou goest onwards still will pluck thee back,
She keeps thee to this purpose: that her skill
  May time disgrace, and wretched minutes kill.
Yet fear her, O thou minion of her pleasure!
  She may detain but not still keep her treasure.   10
Her audit, though delayed, answered must be,
  And her quietus is to render thee.
        (   )
        (   )

My beautiful boy: you control time through your looks and lovers, and are the darling of nature: but you should fear her because she will eventually surrender you to time.

Q: No. 126. Addressed to a boy. It is uncertain whether the parentheses derive from the author, a scribe, or the printer. Their actual significance is obscure (see Introduction, p. 38).

2 **fickle glass** capricious hour-glass; or a mirror showing changing shapes
  sickle-hour reaping-time
3 **by waning grown** grown more youthful with age
5 **wrack** ruin, decay
6 **goest onwards** becomest older
8 **disgrace** dishonour
9 **minion** darling, favourite
11 **audit** account (nature's to time)
12 **quietus** means of settlement
  render surrender

1600–1609

Words, vows, gifts, tears . . .

CRESSIDA
Words, vows, gifts, tears, and love's full sacrifice
　　He offers in another's enterprise;
But more in Troilus thousandfold I see
　　Than in the glass of Pandar's praise may be.
Yet hold I off. Women are angels, wooing: 　　　　　　　5
　　Things won are done. Joy's soul lies in the doing.
That she beloved knows nought that knows not this:
　　Men price the thing ungained more than it is.
That she was never yet that ever knew
　　Love got so sweet as when desire did sue. 　　　　　10
Therefore this maxim out of love I teach:
　　Achievement is command; ungained, beseech.
　　　Then though my heart's content firm love doth bear,
　　　Nothing of that shall from mine eyes appear.

1602: *Troilus and Cressida*, 1.2.278–91. Pandarus has been lavishing praise of
Troilus to Cressida.

4 **glass** mirror
7 **she** woman
8 **price** value, prize
　is i.e. is worth

9 **she** woman
10 **sue** act as a suitor
12 **beseech** beggary

1600–1609

Our remedies oft in ourselves . . .

Our remedies oft in ourselves do lie
    Which we ascribe to heaven. The fated sky
Gives us free scope, only doth backward pull
    Our slow designs when we ourselves are dull.
What power is it which mounts my love so high,   5
    That makes me see and cannot feed mine eye?
The mightiest space in fortune nature brings
    To join like likes and kiss like native things.
Impossible be strange attempts to those
    That weigh their pains in sense and do suppose   10
What hath been cannot be. Who ever strove
    To show her merit that did miss her love?
      The King's disease – my project may deceive me,
      But my intents are fixed and will not leave me.

1605: *All's Well That Ends Well*, 1.1.212–225. The orphan Helen, a physician's daughter, meditates on the distance between her and Bertram, Count of Roussillon, with whom she is in love.

2 **fated sky** heavens empowered by destiny
4 **dull** unambitious
5 **mounts ... high** makes me love above my station
6 **feed mine eye** satisfy my desire
7–8 **The ... things** natural instinct overcomes the greatest discrepancy in rank to bring affinities together and to form natural unions
10 **weigh ... sense** assess obstacles rationally
12 **miss** fail to win

1600–1609

I am Saint Jaques' pilgrim . . .

HELEN

'I am Saint Jaques' pilgrim, thither gone.
   Ambitious love hath so in me offended
That barefoot plod I the cold ground upon
   With sainted vow my faults to have amended.
Write, write, that from the bloody course of war   5
   My dearest master, your dear son, may hie.
Bless him at home in peace, whilst I from far
   His name with zealous fervour sanctify.
His taken labours bid him me forgive;
   I, his despiteful Juno, sent him forth   10
From courtly friends, with camping foes to live,
   Where death and danger dogs the heels of worth.
     He is too good and fair for death and me;
     Whom I myself embrace to set him free.'

1605: *All's Well That Ends Well*, 3.4.4–17. Reynaldo, the steward, reads to the Countess this letter addressed to her by the heroine, Helen, now her daughter-in-law, declaring her intention to go on a pilgrimage so that her reluctant husband, Bertram, may feel free to return home from the wars.

1 **Saint Jaques' pilgrim** i.e. a pilgrim to the shrine of St James (Santiago de Compostela, Spain)
2 **Ambitious love** (because she is lower in station than Bertram)
4 **sainted vow** i.e. a vow to a saint
6 **hie** hasten back
8 **sanctify** make holy (by repeating it in her prayers)
9 **taken** undertaken
10 **despiteful** cruel
    Juno (the goddess whose enmity caused Hercules to undertake his labours)
11 **camping** encamped
14 **Whom** i.e. death

1600–1609

Now sleep y-slackèd ...

GOWER
Now sleep y-slackèd hath the rout,
  No din but snores the house about,
Made louder by the o'erfed breast
  Of this most pompous marriage feast.
The cat with eyne of burning coal   5
  Now couches fore the mouse's hole,
And crickets sing at th' oven's mouth
  As the blither for their drouth.
Hymen hath brought the bride to bed,
  Where by the loss of maidenhead   10
A babe is moulded. Be attent,
  And time that is so briefly spent
    With your fine fancies quaintly eche.
    What's dumb in show, I'll plain with speech.

1608: *Pericles*, scene 10.1–14. The poet John Gower (1330–1408), who narrates the play, introduces a dumb-show in which Pericles receives a letter bringing news of the death of Antiochus and his daughter.

1 **y-slackèd** laid to rest	9 **Hymen** god of marriage
rout company	11 **moulded** formed
2 **din** noise	**attent** attentive
4 **pompous** ceremonial	13 **fancies** imaginations
5 **eyne** eyes (an archaic form suited	**quaintly** skilfully
to Gower)	**eche** fill out
8 **blither** happier	14 **plain** explain
drouth dryness	

1600–1609

My temple stands in Ephesus . . .

DIANA
My temple stands in Ephesus. Hie thee thither,
    And do upon mine altar sacrifice.
There when my maiden priests are met together,
    At large discourse thy fortunes in this wise:
With a full voice before the people all,   5
    Reveal how thou at sea didst lose thy wife.
To mourn thy crosses, with thy daughter's, call
    And give them repetition to the life.
      Perform my bidding, or thou liv'st in woe;
      Do 't, and rest happy, by my silver bow.   10

1608: *Pericles*, scene 21.225–35. Prince Pericles has a vision in a dream of
the goddess Diana who speaks these instructions to him in the form of a
foreshortened sonnet.

1	**Hie thee** Go there quickly	7	**crosses** trials, troubles
3	**maiden priests** virgin priestesses	8	**repetition** narration
4	**At large** at length	9	**silver bow** Diana was the goddess
	discourse tell		of hunting
	wise manner		

1610—1613

☙

1610—1613

No more, you petty spirits of region low . . .

JUPITER

No more, you petty spirits of region low,
    Offend our hearing. Hush! How dare you ghosts
Accuse the thunderer, whose bolt, you know,
    Sky-planted, batters all rebelling coasts?
Poor shadows of Elysium, hence, and rest   5
    Upon your never-withering banks of flowers.
Be not with mortal accidents oppressed;
    No care of yours it is; you know 'tis ours.
Whom best I love, I cross, to make my gift,
    The more delayed, delighted. Be content.   10
Your low-laid son our godhead will uplift.
    His comforts thrive, his trials well are spent.
Our Jovial star reigned at his birth, and in
    Our temple was he married. Rise, and fade.
He shall be lord of Lady Innogen,   15
    And happier much by his affliction made.
This tablet lay upon his breast, wherein
    Our pleasure his full fortune doth confine.

He gives the ghosts a tablet which they lay upon Posthumus' breast.

1610: *Cymbeline*, 5.5.187–204. While the sleeping Posthumus is visited by the spirits of his family, the god Jupiter descends on a golden eagle and speaks this extended sonnet-prophecy.

1 **of region low**. The spirits are in Elysium, the classical heaven, which seems 'low' to Jupiter on Mount Olympus

3 **thunderer** Jupiter, the god of thunder

4 **Sky-planted** located in the heavens

5 **shadows of** ghosts from

Elysium the classical heaven
7 **accidents** events
10 **delighted** (the more) delighted in
11 **son** (Posthumus)
  our … uplift i.e. I will raise up

12 **well are spent** have a good outcome
13 **Our Jovial star** Our majestical
  planet Jupiter
17 **tablet** inscribed document

1610–1613

'Tis ten to one this play . . .

EPILOGUE

'Tis ten to one this play can never please
    All that are here. Some come to take their ease,
And sleep an act or two; but those, we fear,
    We have frighted with our trumpets; so, 'tis clear,
They'll say 'tis naught: others, to hear the city   5
    Abused extremely, and to cry 'That's witty!'
Which we have not done neither: that, I fear,
    All the expected good we're like to hear
For this play at this time, is only in
    The merciful construction of good women,   10
For such a one we showed 'em: if they smile,
    And say ''Twill do', I know, within a while
        All the best men are ours – for 'tis ill hap
        If they hold when their ladies bid 'em clap.

1613: *All Is True* (*Henry VIII*), with John Fletcher. Epilogue (probably by Fletcher).

5 **naught** worthless
6 **Abused** insulted, satirised
11 **such a one** i.e. Queen Katherine, Henry VIII's misused wife

13 **ours** i.e. on our side
    ill hap bad luck
14 **hold** hold back

Textual Notes

The following substantive changes have been made to the 1609 edition; the original reading is given to the right of the bracket.

12.4 ensilvered o'er] or siluer'd ore
13.7 Yourself] You selfe
17.14 twice: in it] twise in it,
20.2 master-mistress] Master Mistris
23.14 with … wit] wit…wiht
24.13 art:] art
25.9 might] worth
26.12 thy] their
27.10 thy] their
28.12 gild'st the even] guil'st th'eauen
28.14 strength] length
29.14 kings'] kings
31.8 thee] there
34.12 cross] losse
35.8 thy … thy] their … their
37.7 thy] their
39.12 doth] dost
43.11 thy] their
44.12 attend] attend,
44.13 naught] naughts
45.12 thy] their
46.3, 8, 13, 14 thy] their
47.10 art] are
50.4 'Thus … friend'] Thus … friend
51.11 rein] naigh
54.14 fade] vade
55.1 monuments] monument,
56.13 Or] As
58.7 patience, tame] patience tame,
65.12 of] or

67.6 seeming] seeing
69.3 due] end
69.5 Thy] Their
69.14 soil] solye
70.1 art] are
70.6 Thy] Their
71.2 Than] Then
73.4 ruined] rn'wd
76.7 tell] fel
77.1 wear] were
77.10 blanks] blacks
82.8 these] the
85.3 thy] their
88.8 losing] loosing
90.11 shall] stall
91.9 better] bitter
99.4 dwells] dwells?
99.9 One] Our
106.12 skill] still
111.1 with] wish
113.6 latch] lack
113.13 more, replete] more repleat
113.14 makes mine eye] maketh mine
117.10 surmise accumulate] surmise, accumilate
118.10 were not,] were, not
121.11 bevel;] beuel
125.6–7 rent, … sweet] rent … sweet;
126.8 minutes] mynuit
127.10 brow] eyes
128.3 sway'st] swayst,

128.11 thy] their
128.14 thy fingers] their fingers
129.10 quest to have,] quest, to
    haue
129.11 a] and
131.9 swear,] sweare
132.6 the east] th'East

137.11 not,] not
138.12 to have] t'haue
140.6 yet, love,] yet loue
140.13 belied] be lyed
144.6 side] sight
146.2 [   ]] My sinfull earth
153.14 eyes] eye

All the Sonnets of Shakespeare:
Literal Paraphrases

Pre-1582
The little love-god . . .

p. 47 Q: No. 154

Once young Cupid, lying asleep, laid by his side his love-inducing torch, while many nymphs who had taken vows of chastity came tripping by; but the most beautiful virgin picked up into her chaste hand the flame that had inflamed many faithful hearts, and thus the commander of amorous desire was disarmed in his sleep by the hand of a virgin. She doused this torch in a cool nearby well which derived perpetual heat from love's fire, becoming a bath and health-giving remedy for sick men. But I, in thrall to my mistress, came there seeking a cure. And by that I demonstrate this: love's fire heats water, but water does not cool love.

Cupid laid by his brand . . .

p. 48 Q: No. 153

Cupid set aside his torch and fell asleep. A female follower of Diana took advantage of this and quickly dipped his love-inducing flame in a cold fountain in a valley of that district, which borrowed an endlessly invigorating warmth, enduring for ever, from this holy fire of love, and became a boiling-hot bath which men still find an infallible cure for foreign diseases. But after love's torch was newly ignited at my mistress's eye, the boy as a test had to touch my breast. Made sick with this, I needed the help of a bath, and went there, a badly diseased guest, but found no cure. The bath that I need lies where Cupid got fresh stimulus – my mistress's eyes.

1582
Those lips that love's own hand. . .

p. 49 Q: No. 145

Her lips made by Cupid himself spoke softly the words 'I hate' to me, when I was love-sick for her. But as soon as she saw how sad this made me, she began to feel merciful, rebuking her tongue which, always sweet, was accustomed to pronounce a mild sentence, and taught it to greet me in this new way: she altered 'I hate' with a sequel that followed it as gentle day follows night who, like a devil, has flown from heaven back to hell. She threw 'I hate' away from 'Hathaway', and saved my life, saying 'not you'.

233

1589–1591
My thoughts do harbour . . .

p. 50 *The Two Gentlemen of Verona*, 3.1.140–9

DUKE 'My thoughts abide with Silvia every night and are slaves to me who send them flying off. O, if only their master could come and go no less speedily, he himself would lie where they are, insensibly, lying. My thoughts are like heralds in your pure bosom while I, their ruler, who send them there, curse the good fortune that has blessed them with so happy a fate, because I myself lack my servants' favour. I curse myself that they are sent by me in that they find a resting place where their lord should be.'

Sweet Cytherea . . .

p. 51 *The Passionate Pilgrim*: No. 4

Fair Venus, sitting beside a brook with young Adonis – handsome, lively, and inexperienced – wooed the young man with many amorous looks – looks such as only the Queen of Beauty could give. She told him stories to please his ear and showed him love tokens to enthral his eye. Trying to win his heart she caressed him here and there – such soft caresses often prove seductive. But whether because his youthfulness lacked understanding, or because he simply refused to accept her implicit suggestion, the intended victim would not fall for her wiles, but smiled and laughed at every amorous hint. Then, beautiful and yielding queen, she threw herself backward. He stood up and ran away – ah, what a gauche innocent!

Scarce had the sun . . .

p. 52 *The Passionate Pilgrim*: No. 6

The sun had only just dried up the morning dew, and the cattle had just retreated to the hedgerow for shade, when lovesick Venus waited longingly for Adonis under a willow tree growing by a brook – a brook where Adonis was accustomed to cool off his hot and bothered state. The day was hot and she, who awaited the arrival of the man who had often been there, was hotter. Eventually he arrives, casts off his robe, and stands stark naked on the green bank of the brook. The sun shone on the earth with glorious light, but not so longingly as this queen on him. He, noticing her, leapt in on the spot. 'O Jove', said she, 'why was I not that water!'

Fair was the morn . . .

p. 53 *The Passionate Pilgrim*: No. 9

It was a beautiful morning when the beautiful queen of love [...] paler with grief than her milk-white dove, took up her stand on a steep hill for the sake of Adonis, a proud and wayward youngster. Soon Adonis comes with his hunting-horn and his hounds. She, poor queen, with the best of loving intentions, forbade the young man to pass over those grounds. 'Once', she said, 'I saw a lovely, handsome young man severely wounded in these brakes by a boar, deep in his thigh, a pitiful sight. Look in my thigh', she said, 'here was the opening.' She showed her thigh; he saw more than one opening, and dashed off, blushing, leaving her all alone.

1590–1595
And let me have her likened . . .

p. 54 1592: *Edward III*, scene 2.322–33

I want to have her compared to the sun: say that she is three times as brilliant as the sun, that her perfections imitate the sun, that she produces delights as abundant as the sun, that she melts cold winter like the sun, that she encourages blooming summer like the sun, that she, like the sun, overpowers anyone who stares at the sun, and in this analogy to the sun, tell her to be as generous and universally benevolent as the sun, which looks as kindly on the lowest of all weeds as it does with love on the perfumed rose.

In the old age . . .

p. 55 Q: No. 127

In the olden days black was not called beautiful – or if it was, it was not considered beautiful. But now blackness has come to be regarded as beautiful by rightful succession, and a fair beauty discredited as illegitimate because, since everyone has usurped natural powers of attraction with cosmetics, making the ugly fair by deceptive appearances achieved by art, pleasing, natural beauty is little regarded, has no shrine, but is desecrated, or at least held in low repute. So my mistress's eyes are raven-black, her brow similarly dressed, and they seem like mourners for women who, not born beautiful, nevertheless have become so, giving a bad name to others' natural features enhanced artificially. And still they express their mourning in such a manner, glamourising their grief, so that everyone says that is what beauty ought to look like.

How oft, when thou . . .

p. 56 Q: No. 128

As often as you, who are as music to me, make music by blessing that wood, whose mechanism resounds to the touch of your lovely fingers as you sweetly govern the well-strung harmony that astonishes my hearing, do I envy those keys that nimbly leap up to kiss your palm, while my poor lips, which ought to be enjoying that privilege, stand beside you blushing at the keys' audacity! My lips would like to change places with those leaping slivers of wood over which your fingers tread with a gentle movement, making dead wood more graced than living lips. As these cheeky fellows are so privileged in your playing, let them have your fingers, but give me your lips to kiss.

Th' expense of spirit . . .

p. 57 Q: No. 129

Lust indulged is a shameful waste of vital energy, and, until we give way to it, it is dishonest, murderous, brutal, blameworthy, savage, ungoverned, rough, cruel, untrustworthy, no sooner indulged than despised, irrationally sought and no sooner had but irrationally hated, like a bait that has been swallowed which was deliberately laid to make the taker mad, mad being sought, and mad when possessed, extreme when had, when having, and when sought, a joy when being experienced, but a source of grief afterwards, before, an expected joy, afterwards a dream. Everyone knows all of this, but no one is sensible enough to avoid the heaven that only leads them to hell.

My mistress' eyes . . .

p. 58 Q: No. 130

The eyes of my mistress are not at all like the sun; coral is redder than her lips, her breasts are dark grey, rather than being snowy white; the wires of her hair are tarnished black. I have seen dappled, red and white roses, but not in her cheeks, and perfume is more delightful than her breath. I love her voice, but I know that music is far nicer. I admit, I cannot compare her to a goddess, because I have never seen one, but my mistress walks firmly on the ground. But, in heaven's name, I think she is more special than any woman who is misrepresented by false comparison.

Thou art as tyrannous . . .

p. 59 Q: No. 131

You are as tyrannical as those whose pride in their looks makes them cruel, because you know I dote upon you and that to me you are as the most beautiful and treasured jewel. However, to be honest, some who see you say your looks are not that sexy; I am not going to say in public that they are wrong, though I do when I am on my own. And, truly, I know I am not pretending: I can groan a thousand times just thinking about your face, one groan quickly following on from another is testimony that your blackness is most beautiful, as far as I am concerned. Your physical blackness is as nothing compared to the blackness of your behaviour, and that is why others speak ill of you.

Thine eyes I love ...

p. 60 Q: No. 132

I love your eyes, and they, pitying me because you scorn me, are wearing black, like loving mourners, and express a pretty kind of pity for my pain. The sun at dawn does not set off the grey eastern clouds, nor does Venus at sunset complement the dulling western sky as much as those two, mourning eyes do your face. O, that it would become your heart to mourn for me as well, since mourning suits you, then all of your pity for me would be dressed in the same way. If so, then I would swear that beauty is blackness and that anyone who is not like you is ugly.

Beshrew that heart ...

p. 61 Q: No. 133

Curse that heart of yours for making mine ache, because of the deep hurt you give my friend and me. Is it not sufficient for you to torture me alone, without entirely dominating my lovely friend as well? Your cruel looks have made me lose myself, but you have monopolised my closest friend even more cruelly. I have lost myself, my friend, and you, and both of you, similarly tormented, make it a nine-fold loss. Keep me imprisoned in the thrall of your hard heart, but let me bail out my friend's heart with mine. Whoever imprisons me has my heart as my friend's guard, which means you cannot treat me harshly in the prison you have made for me. But I know you will, because I, being enthralled by you, am forced to be only yours, as is everything else of mine, including my friend.

So, now I have confessed ...

p. 62 Q: No. 134

I have now admitted that my friend is yours and that I am legally bound to obey you. I am willing to give myself up entirely to your power, if it means I can remain close to my other self whom you have taken. But you will not give him back, nor does he wish to be free of you; you covet him, and he is good-natured. He has learnt to stand as security for me within the thrall of your beauty. You will take in full the amount I owe you, investing everything, with interest, and thereby suing my friend who has placed himself into your debt because of me. Thus I lose and have lost him through your unkind treatment of me. You now own both of us, and even though he bears the cost of everything, I'm still not free of the debt you hold against me.

Whoever hath her wish ...

p. 63 Q: No. 135

If anyone has what she wants, you have it in your Will, and will in addition, and in an abundance of will. I am more than enough for you in continuing to pester you by wanting to add to your attractive 'will'. But will you, whose capacity for 'will' is so great, allow me, just for once, to conceal my 'will' in yours? Will you welcome the desire of others but not accept my 'will' happily? The seas constantly grow as they receive more and more rain: so might you, already enriched by your will, add to your will that 'will' of mine which will make your large will even bigger. You do not have to be unkind to your other lovers, but only realise that all the 'will' they have for you equals mine.

If thy soul check thee . . .
p. 64 Q: No. 136

If your conscience resists my advances, know deep down that I was the name of your desire, and desire, your conscience knows, is admissible: therefore, dear, let me fulfil my love-suit. My name and desire will fill up the treasury of your love, fill it with many desires, and with my one over-riding, sexual desire. For things of great capacity, it is easy to demonstrate that to receive one thing more is neither here nor there. Though I will increase the tally of your lovers by one, count me as nothing, so long as you regard that nothing as some-'thing' which is pleasant to you. Even if you loved only my name, and loved that continually, then you would love all of me because my name expresses my sexual desire for you: Will.

Thou blind fool love . . .
p. 65 Q: No. 137

Love, you blind fool, what are you doing to my eyes, causing them not to see truly what I look upon? They know what beauty is and can see it, but when they look at the worst they turn it into the best. If my eyes, deluded by glances, dote upon a woman whom every man seems to be enjoying sexually, why have you hooked such false judgement to my heart? Why should I think she is my private property, when I know she is common land? Why should my eyes delude me, and make beauty out of ugliness? My heart and my eyes have mistaken the truth, and have now shifted into a plague of seeing things falsely.

When my love swears . . . (later version)
p. 67 Q: No. 138

When my loved one promises me she is being totally loyal, I say that I believe her, even though I know she is lying, so that she might think of me as some unsophisticated young man, naïve about the world's vain deceits. What vanity: I think she thinks I am younger than I am, even though she knows I am past my prime of life, and I let her get away with lying, so there is no actual truth in our relationship. Why does she not tell me she is being unfaithful, and why do I not say I am old? It is because love is used to the appearance of trust and also does not want to hear the truth about a person's age. So, we lie together, and flatter each other in spite of our imperfections.

O, call not me . . .

p. 68 Q: No. 139

Do not ask me to excuse your hurtful behaviour. Do not give me hurtful looks but speak outright; use your power directly, not in an underhand way. Tell me you love someone else, but, darling, do not flirt with someone else when we are together. Why should you need to use guile to hurt me when your power over me is greater than I can bear? I could excuse you by thinking, 'She knows she no longer looks at me lovingly as she used to, and that's why she's turning away her eyes (as though they were my enemies) from me to someone else.' Stop all this; it's killing me. Just finish me off with those murdering looks, and put me out of my misery.

Be wise as thou art cruel . . .

p. 69 Q: No. 140

Just as you are cruel, be wise: don't try my unspoken patience too disdainfully in case you upset me enough to lead me to speak about the pain and the need for pity that you are making me feel. If I could teach you to be wise it would be better, even if you do not love me, at least, dear, to tell me that you do so – as doctors only give their fretful patients good news, even when they are dying. If you turn me to despair, I'll go mad, and might speak against you. This misinterpreting world has grown so bad that mad slanderers are believed by the mad people who hear them. Avoid this by looking honestly towards me, even though your proud heart looks elsewhere.

In faith, I do not love thee . . .

p. 70 Q: No. 141

Truly, I don't love you because of how I see you, since I notice in you thousands of faults; instead, I love you with my heart in spite of how much I despise what I see you doing. Nor are my ears pleased by your voice, nor is my sense of touch susceptible to fleshly contact; my senses of taste and smell do not want to have anything to do with you either. But neither my intellectual faculties nor my five senses can dissuade my foolish heart from serving you, you who have deserted me, leaving me like the mere semblance of a man, a slave, a hanger-on to your proud heart.

The only consolation for my suffering is that it is caused by the woman who leads me astray.

Love is my sin . . .

p. 71 Q: No. 142

My sin is love, and your virtue is to hate the fact that my sin arises out of loving sinfully. But compare how I am to how you yourself are, and realise that I do not deserve your rebuke. Or, if I do, then not from your lips that have abused their own beauty by being false in love, by committing adultery and by robbing others of the offspring they might have had. Let me be permitted to love you as you love those whom your eyes captivate, just as my eyes try to urge you towards me. Plant pity in your heart so that when it grows the pity you show may win the pity of others. If you seek pity whilst withholding it, then others may treat you after your own example.

Lo, as a care-full housewife . . .

p. 72 Q: No. 143

As an anxious housewife, who runs after a bird which has escaped, puts down her baby and runs as fast as she can after the thing she wants to catch, while her forsaken baby runs after her as well, crying to attract her whose attention is directed in following the bird in front of her, so that she does not care about her child's upset: so you too pursue things that escape you, whilst I, like the baby, run far behind. But, if you obtain what you hope for, turn again towards me; be the 'mother' to my 'baby'; kiss me; be kind to me. Then I will pray that you may satisfy your will, so that you will then turn your attention back to me (your Will) and pacify my crying.

Two loves I have (later version). . .

p. 74 Q: No. 144

I have two loves – one of comfort and one of despair – which tempt me like two spirits. The better of the two is a handsome man, the worse a woman of unpleasing colour. To win me to her hell, my female spirit tempts my better angel away from me, and seeks to corrupt my saint to become a devil, winning over his purity with her ugly lust. Although I suspect that my good angel has been turned into a fiend, I do not actually know, but since both he and she are away from me, and friends with each other, I am assuming that he, my good angel, has been seduced by her. I won't know if my suspicion is true until it becomes clear that she has infected him with her venereal disease.

Poor soul . . .

p. 75 Q: No. 146

O my poor soul, the centre of my sinful self, [rebuke] these rebellious passions that attack you. Why do you dwindle within and suffer famine while adorning your outside so extravagantly? Why, having so short a lease, do you decorate your crumbling mansion at such great cost? Shall worms, heirs to this extravagance, devour your expenditure? Is this how your body will end up? Then, soul, feed upon what your servant loses, and allow that to diminish in order to increase your wealth. Buy a lease of eternal life by selling worthless hours. Be nourished internally, but let your exterior be showy no longer. Thus you will feed on death that feeds on men, and once death is dead, there will be no more dying.

My love is as a fever . . .

p. 76 Q: No. 147

My love for you is like a fever, ever longing for the fever itself to continue, prolonging my sickness, trying to diminish an intermittent appetite. My reason, the doctor to my love-sickness, is cross with me because I am ignoring his advice, and has deserted me; now I am desperate and realise that my desire which refused treatment is fatal. I am beyond treatment, and no longer care how unreasonable I am. I am driven mad with perpetual sleeplessness. My thought and speech are like a madman's, random, uselessly expressing themselves. And all this because I thought you beautiful and attractive, but in fact you are as black as hell and dark as night, in deeds, as well as in your appearances.

O me, what eyes ...

p. 77 Q: No. 148

Alas, the eyes that love has given me misrepresent what they actually see. Or, if they do see truly, I am without judgement because I am misinterpreting true vision. If my false eyes are looking at someone who is beautiful, then the world is contradicting me; if that same someone is not actually beautiful after all, then that just proves that love's way of seeing is not true. But how can love's eyes be true, since they are so frustrated with staying awake and with tears? It is no wonder I see amiss: even the sun cannot see until the sky clears. O, clever love: you keep me blind with tears in case, by seeing properly, I should find out your faults!

Canst thou, O cruel . . .

p. 78 Q: No. 149

Can you, O cruel one, say I do not love you when I take your side against myself? Is it not only you that I think about, when I have forgotten myself, and become a total tyrant over myself because of you? Am I friends with anyone who hates you? Do I like anyone you frown on? And if you look unfavourably on me, do not I take revenge on myself with instant self-censure? What quality do I value in myself that is so proud as to scorn to serve you, when all my best qualities worship your faults – as I am commanded to do by the very movement of your eyes? So, my love, carry on hating me because now I know what you think: you only love those whose judgement is better than mine, and I am blind with love.

O, from what power . . .

p. 79 Q: No. 150

O, from what authority do you derive this powerful ability to influence my heart through your shortcomings, to cause me to deny what is obvious to me, and to swear that brightness does not enhance the day? Where did you get this ability to make ugly things beautiful, with the result that there is such force and guarantee of good workmanship in even the most contemptible of your actions that to me the worst that you can do eclipses the triumphs of others? Who taught you how to make me love you more, the more I hear and see good reason to hate you? O, even if I love what others loathe, you should not, like others, despise my condition. If your faults excited me to love you, the more worthy I am to be loved by you.

Love is too young . . .

p. 80 Q: No. 151

Love is too much of a child to have a sense of right and wrong, but who does not know that such a sense is born of love? So, dear deceiver, do not hold my faults against me, in case your dear self turns out to be guilty of the same faults. For when you cheat on me, I betray what is best in me to the treason of my sinful ¡body. My soul tells my body that he may conquer in love. My flesh needs no more encouragement, but, growing erect at the thought of you, appoints you to be his triumphant conquest. Proud of this erection, he is happy to serve you abjectly, to stand erect in your service and then to droop beside you. Do not think I lack conscience that I call this woman 'love' for whose dear sake I stiffen and slacken.

In loving thee . . .

p. 81 Q: No. 152

You know that in making love to you I have broken my wedding vows, but you are doubly forsworn in swearing love to me, having broken your vow of sexual fidelity by what you have done, and now having broken faith by declaring new hatred after expressing new love. But why do I accuse you of breaking two vows when I break twenty? I am most forsworn because all my vows are simply oaths to betray you, and all the simple faith I had in you is lost. Because I have sworn solemn oaths of your profound kindness, oaths of your love, your truth, your fidelity, and made myself blind to give you light, or made my eyes perjure themselves against the truth of what they see, because I have sworn that you are fair. The more perjured is my sight, to swear so foul a lie against the truth.

1590–1595
But if that I am I . . .

p. 82 *The Comedy of Errors*, 3.2.41–54

ANTIPHOLUS OF SYRACUSE But if I am myself, I know perfectly well that your beautiful sister is not my wife, nor do I owe matrimonial duties to her. I find you far, far more attractive. Dear mermaid, don't lure me with your song to drown me in your sister's flood of tears. Sing, sister, on your own behalf, then I shall dote on you. Spread your golden locks over the silver waves and I'll treat them as a bed and lie there, and in that wondrous delusion think that one who dies in such a way profits by death.

LUCIANA What, are you mad that you talk like this?

ANTIPHOLUS OF SYRACUSE Not mad, but confused – I don't know how.

Study me how to please . . .

p. 83 *Love's Labour's Lost*, 1.1.80–9

BIRON Teach me, I say, how a man may delight his eye by fixing it on a beautiful eye, so that – his eyes being thus bedazzled – that eye will be his lodestar and illuminate the eye that was bedazzled by it. Study is like the glorious sun in the sky which cannot be fathomed with presumptuous glances. Persistent drudges have never won more than second-hand learning from other men's books. These mundane astronomers who give a name to every star in the sky derive no more profit from their starlit nights than those who walk around knowing nothing about them. To know too much is to know nothing but hearsay, and every godfather can think up a name.

Ay, that there is ...

p. 84 *Love's Labour's Lost*, 1.1.159–74

KING Yes, indeed there is. As you know, our court is frequented by a sophisticated visitor from Spain, a man who is familiar with every new fashion, who has a treasure-house of modish phrases in his brain, one whom the sound of his own conceited voice ravishes like the music of the spheres; a man of accomplishment whom right and wrong have selected as a judge to their disputes. This fanciful fellow, known as Armado, will, as a relief from our studies, discourse in high-flown terms about the feats of many knights from sunny Spain lost in warfare. How you enjoy yourselves, my lords, I don't know, but, I am telling you, I love to hear him lie, and I will employ him for my entertainment.

If love make me forsworn ...

p. 85 *Love's Labour's Lost*, 4.2.106–19

NATHANIEL 'If love makes me lie, how can I swear that I love? Ah, faith could never be constant if it were not dedicated to beauty. Even if I betray myself, I will be true to you. Those resolutions that seemed to me to be as firmly established as oak trees now bend before you like willows. The student goes off course and takes your eyes, where dwell all the pleasures that study would seek to fathom, for his text-book. If knowledge is the goal, knowledge of you will encompass it. The tongue that can sing your praises is fully accomplished, and the soul that contemplates you without wondering at you is entirely ignorant. The fact that I admire your virtues is a credit to me. Your eye flashes with Jove's lightning; your voice sounds with his music and delightful enthusiasm. Heavenly as you are, love, pardon this fault that sings praises to heaven with such an earthly tongue.'

So sweet a kiss ...

p. 86 *Love's Labour's Lost*, 4.3.24–39

KING 'The golden sun gives not so sweet a kiss to morning dewdrops on the rose as your eyebeams when their fresh glances have struck the night of dew that flows down on my cheeks. Nor does the silver moon shine half as brightly through the translucent bosom of the ocean as your face shines through my tears. You shine in every tear that I weep. Every teardrop carries you like a coach, so that you ride in triumph over my love-sickness. Just look at the tears that swell up in me, and they will reflect your glory through my grief. But do not love yourself; then you will keep my tears as looking-glasses, and continue to make me weep. O queen of queens, no thought can imagine and no mortal tongue can express how excellent you are.'

Did not the heavenly rhetoric . . .

p. 87 *Love's Labour's Lost*, 4.3.57–70
LONGUEVILLE 'Did not the celestial eloquence of your eye, against which nothing in the world can prevail in argument, persuade my heart to commit this false perjury? Vows broken for you do not deserve punishment. I abandoned a woman, but I will demonstrate that, since you are a goddess, I didn't abandon you. I swore an earthly vow, but you are a heavenly beloved. Gaining your favour redresses all disgrace in me. Oaths are only breath, and breath is only air. Then you, fair sun, breathe out this airy oath. It is in you, so if it is broken, that is not my fault. If I had broken it, what fool is not so wise that he would break an oath to gain a paradise?'

O, never will I trust . . .

p. 88 *Love's Labour's Lost*, 5.2.401–15
BIRON O, I will never put my faith in written speeches, or in a schoolboy's utterances, nor approach my sweetheart in a mask, nor woo in verse, like the song of a blind harpist. Affected phrases, elaborate language, gross exaggeration, super-fine attention, pedantic figures of speech – these irritating tricks have riddled me with flashy tricks of speech. I abjure them, and now I swear by your white glove – how white the hand that wears it, God knows! – that from now onwards my courtship will be phrased in homely agreement and honest, straightforward denials. And to start, wench – God help me!, look – my love for you is wholesome, lacking any fault or weakness.

Two households . . .

p. 89 *Romeo and Juliet*, Prologue
CHORUS Two equally noble households in beautiful Verona, where our scene is set, break out from old resentments to new strife, where blood spilt in civic dispute stains civilised hands. From the death-marked loins of these two enemies a pair of ill-fated lovers have been born, whose luckless and pitiful misfortunes heal their parents' enmity with their deaths. The alarming course of their love that will end in death – and the course of their parents' enmity, which could be overcome only by their children's deaths – is now the two-hours' subject matter of our play; which, if you will patiently attend to it, we will try to heal with our efforts, whatever goes amiss.

If I profane . . .

p. 90 *Romeo and Juliet*, 1.5.92–109

ROMEO If my most undeserving hand should dishonour this holy shrine (your hand), the less reprehensible is this: my lips, like two nervous pilgrims, stand by, ready to make that which is rough smooth with a tender kiss.

JULIET Good pilgrim, you slander your hand too much, which well-mannered act of worship is apparent in this – since saints have hands that pilgrims' hands touch in devotion, and holy pilgrims kiss by joining palms.

ROMEO Do not both saints and holy pilgrims love lips too?

JULIET Yes, pilgrim – lips that they must use for prayer.

ROMEO O then, dear saint, let my lips do what hands do: they pray to kiss you. Give way to me in case my faith should turn to trespass.

JULIET The statues of saints do not move, even though they respond to prayer.

ROMEO Do not move, then, while I take the reward for my prayer.

He kisses her.

JULIET Then my lips are profaned by the sin that they accepted.

ROMEO Sin from my lips? O, a sin that was lovingly provoked. Return my sin.

He kisses her.

JULIET You kiss in an exemplary manner.

Now old desire . . .

p. 91 *Romeo and Juliet*, 2.0

Former desire is now expiring, and a new passion longs to succeed it. The beauty for whom love yearned and would have died to achieve now, compared to Juliet, no longer seems desirable. Now Romeo is loved and returns that love, both are enchanted by the spell cast by beauty. But he has to plead to his supposed enemy, and she to pluck the fruits of love from dangerous hooks. He, thought of as an enemy, is not allowed access that would enable him to offer the kind of vows that lovers are accustomed to swear, and she, no less enamoured, has even less opportunity to meet her new lover anywhere. But their passion gives them the strength of purpose, and time the opportunity, for them to meet, modifying extreme hardships with no less extreme delight.

Is it thy will ...

p. 92 Q: No. 61

Do you mean to keep me awake all night thinking of you? Do you want my eyes to be open, my sleep to be disrupted, while figures that look like you make fun of me? Have you sent your ghost so far away from you to see what I'm up to, to discover things I might be ashamed of, or my idling about: is that how jealous you are? No; your love is impressive, but not as strong as all that. It is my love for you that keeps me awake; my true love that ruins my sleep and makes me behave like a night-constable, ever on the look-out for you. While I stay awake because of you, you are awake somewhere else, far away from me, and all too close to others.

Sin of self-love . . .

p. 93 Q: No. 62

The sin of loving only myself entirely fills how I look at myself, my soul, and every part of my body, and there's no cure for it – it's rooted in my heart. It seems to me that no other face is as pleasing as mine, no other body as well formed, that no one else has as much integrity, or as much value, and so, to satisfy myself I make a full self-evaluation of my worth. But when I look in the mirror and see how I really am – weather-beaten and wrinkled, my skin made leathery with age – I contradict myself: to be entirely self-loving would be wicked. It is you, my other self, that make me praise myself, covering up my age with the beauty of your younger days.

Against my love . . .

p. 94 Q: No. 63

So that I am prepared for when my loved one shall look as I do now, crushed and worn away by time's harmful hands, when the hours have drained his spirit and filled his countenance with creases and wrinkles, when the brightness of his youth has journeyed into the depths of age, and all the attractions of which he's now ruler are disappearing, or have disappeared entirely, furtively hiding away the riches of his youth: in readiness for that time, I am defending myself against the destructive stabs of cruel age, so that my dear loved one's beauty shall never be erased from my memory, even though age will eventually take away his life. My loved one's beauty shall be found in the black lines of my verse, which shall continue to live and keep him ever youthful.

When I have seen . . .

p. 95 Q: No. 64

When I have seen time's cruel hand deface the lavish, showy expense of a worn-away and vanished era; when I see towers that were once tall made ruinous, and things made from brass which should last forever enslaved by destruction; when I have seen the hungry sea take away more of the land's domains, and the solid earth become the ocean's prize, increasing gain through loss, and loss through gain; when I have seen this exchange of territory, and territory itself ruined and decaying, the waste has taught me to meditate like this: the time will come when my loved one is taken away. This thought is like experiencing a death and makes me weep at having something I'm terrified of losing.

Since brass, nor stone . . .

p. 96 Q: No. 65

Since neither brass, nor stone, nor earth, nor the apparently limitless ocean can escape the overruling of death, how can beauty uphold a suit against such destruction, since beauty's efforts are no stronger than a flower? How shall the sweet breath of summer survive the siege of destructive seasons, when even mighty rocks are not so strong, nor are gates of steel, to survive the decay wrought by time? What a terrifying thought! How can the most precious of things avoid being gathered up into time's treasure-chest, or whose hand is so strong that it can slow down time's running or prevent time's ruin of beauty? No one can – unless this miracle can prevail: that in the black ink of my poetry, my loved one may continue to shine brightly.

Tired with all these . . .

p. 97 Q: No. 66

I am tired with all of the following and yearn for the rest that only death can bring: tired with seeing merit being born into beggary, and poverty dressing itself up in cheap finery, and the purest of faiths being abandoned, and apparently splendid honour too embarrassed to act, and young virginity violently prostituting itself, and justified perfection unjustly disparaged, and strength made weak by poor leadership, and learning silenced by the powers that be, and foolishness taking on the air of authority and directing others' abilities, and plain truth misunderstood as being too simplistic, and goodness made a prisoner to an over-controlling rottenness. Tired with all of these, I would like to be gone from them, except that in dying I leave my loved one alone.

Ah, wherefore with infection . . .

p. 98 Q: No. 67

Why should he live amidst the world's moral contamination, and adorn unholiness, letting sin take advantage of him, decorating itself with his fellowship? Why should insincere art try to represent his face and presume to make his lively complexion seem dead? Why should the inferior beauty of art seek to represent fake roses, since the roses in his countenance are real and true? How can he still be alive, since he has taken away all of nature's vitality, depriving nature even of the blood that shows red through living veins, and especially because she has no other treasury apart from him, and (even though nature takes pride in many beauties) she lives upon the interest my loved one earns for her? She keeps him safe to show how wealthy she used to be in the olden days, before these awful times.

Thus is his cheek ...

p. 99 Q: No. 68
And so his face is the epitome of time past, when beauty used to live and die as flowers do, before fake tokens of beauty were worn, or dared to be seen adorning the faces of the living; or before the golden hair of the dead, which should be buried with them, was shaved off and made into wigs, before dead hair of a former beauty was used to make another person attractive. In him can be seen those sacred, olden days, which did not use any decoration, but remained true, did not imitate someone else's beauty, nor steal former fashions to adorn his beauty afresh. He is the guide that nature keeps in order to demonstrate to all false art what beauty used to look like.

Those parts of thee ...

p. 100 Q: No. 69
Your physical characteristics, seen by all, would not be improved by anyone's imagination or desire. Everyone, from deep down, pays you the compliments you truly deserve, even your enemies. So your outward appearance is crowned with public praise, except that those who are complimenting you spoil their praise when they see you more clearly. They look into the beauty of your mind and think they can guess and weigh up your behaviour. Then, these ungracious people, although they looked on you kindly, find something rank among your attractions. And the reason why your inward personality does not correspond to your outward beauty is because you are becoming common and cheap.

That thou art blamed ...

p. 101 Q: No. 70
That you are being blamed is not your fault, because slander always targets something beautiful. Even the appearance of beauty arouses suspicion, like a bird of ill omen flying in a lovely sky. As long as you remain good, any slander only proves your worth even more, time being on your side. Bad practices, like an infecting worm, love the sweetest of buds, such

as yours, in your pure, unblemished spring. You have not yet passed the snares that lie in wait for your youth, nor have they attacked you, nor have you overcome them. But the praise for you cannot prevent the ever-increasing feelings of envy. If only some suspicion of rottenness were not clouding your reputation, then you alone really would own kingdoms full of hearts.

No longer mourn for me . . .

p. 102 Q: No. 71

When I am dead, let your mourning last no longer than the ringing of that lugubrious, solemn bell that will let the world know that I am gone from this contemptible world to dwell among wretched worms. No, if you read this poem, do not recall my hand that wrote it, for I love you in such a way that I would rather be forgotten among your other, pleasing thoughts, if thinking about me then were to make you unhappy. If, I say, you read this verse while I am perhaps being mingled with clay, do not even repeat my pitiable name, but let your love decay like my body – in case the knowing world should question your grief and deride you for loving me, even when I am dead.

O, lest the world . . .

p. 103 Q: No. 72

In case the world requires you, when I'm dead, to talk about the good qualities you loved in me, dear love, just forget me completely. There is no good for you to find in me, unless you are willing to invent a white lie (which would be more than I deserve) to adorn my memory with more praise than the miserly truth would ever allow. In case your love for me seems false, and you speak well of me untruly, just let my reputation be buried with me, rather than be a cause of shame to either of us. I am ashamed of my poetry, and you should be, too, to love something that is worthless.

That time of year . . .

p. 104 Q: No. 73

You can see that time of year in me when it looks as though yellow leaves, or none, or only a few are hanging on the shaking, cold branches of my body, like empty, ruined chancels where the choir boys used to sing. In me you see the twilight, just after sunset, which will soon be overtaken by night, death's agent that closes around everything in a final rest. In me you see the glow of a fire, now choked by the ashes of youth that used to feed it, which will die out soon. Your seeing this makes your love for me stronger, loving well that which you must leave before long.

But be contented . . .

p. 105 Q: No. 74

But be content when I am taken away under that deadly arrest without any chance of bail. My life is still invested in this poem which will remain with you as a memorial. When you re-read it, you will see again that very aspect of me which was dedicated to you. Earth pays its dues to earth, but my spirit is yours, the better part of me. So, when I die, you are only going to lose the remnants of my life to worms; it is only my body that will be stabbed by that coward, death, and that's not worth your remembrance. The value of my body is the spirit that it contains, and it is here in this poem remaining with you.

So are you to my thoughts . . .

p. 106 Q: No. 75

You are to my thoughts as food is to life, or as lovely, seasonable showers of rain are to the earth. And, because of this tranquillity you bring with you, I encounter the kind of conflict a miser does with his wealth. Sometimes I glory in my possessions, then start to fear that someone else will come and steal my treasure; sometimes I think it's best to be alone with you, and then I prefer to be seen with you, so that everyone may see how happy I am. Sometimes I feel satisfied by the attention we give to each other, then I'm entirely famished, and crave your attention. I can neither possess nor pursue pleasure unless it comes, or I take it, from you. And so I fast and surfeit every day, either greedily devouring you, or going without anything.

Why is my verse . . .

p. 107 Q: No. 76

Why is my poetry so lacking in originality, so devoid of decoration, variety, and lively difference? Why don't I glance, as would be fashionable, at new ways of writing compound words? Why do I always write in the same way and use a familiar form of clothing for my work, so that every word (more or less) reveals I am the author, and shows where it came from? Know, my dear love, that everything I write is about you, and both you and love remain my theme, so that the best I can ever achieve is to dress up old words afresh, giving vent to that which is constantly being used up. Just as the sun is new and old every day, so is my love poetry, because I always write about what is already known.

Thy glass will show thee . . .

p. 108 Q: No. 77

Your mirror will show you how your looks are fading, your clock the dwindling of your precious time, the blank pages will preserve your memories, and from this almanac you will be able to learn: the wrinkles in your reflection will remind you of the gaping graves that await us all, the scarcely perceptible movement of your clock reveals the theft of time towards eternity. Whatever you cannot remember, set down on the blank pages, and then you will find that those reflections, like children, born from your mind, will become newly familiar to your intellect. Each time you read over what you've written, you'll profit from it and enhance the reading of your almanac.

Farewell — thou art too dear . . .

p. 109 Q: No. 87

Farewell, you are too precious for me to keep, and you probably know what you are worth. The legal privilege of your value frees you; my ties in love with you are ended. For how can I have any connection with you, but by your giving me permission, and how do I deserve such treasure? I no longer have the right to such a beautiful gift as you. You gave yourself to me without knowing your value, or else I misjudged it, so your great gift, which is increasingly misunderstood, is returned to you with better judgement. So I have had you as though in a dream: while asleep I was a king, but now I awake into an altogether different reality.

When thou shalt be disposed . . .

p. 110 Q: No. 88

When you are inclined to undervalue me and hold my merit up to public ridicule, I'll fight on your side against myself, and show you to be virtuous even though you are lying. Since I best know my weaknesses, I can invent an account for you about the hidden faults of which I am guilty, so that in setting me free you will earn praise. And I will gain too, because in turning all my thoughts of love towards you, any hurt I feel in helping you will double my own sense of worth. My love is such, and I belong to you so much, that I will carry the pain of all the wrong you do me for your advantage.

Say that thou didst forsake me . . .

p. 111 Q: No. 89

Let's suppose you were to leave me because you said I had done something wrong. I would support you in what you claim. If you were to mention my physical, emotional, and literary disabilities, I would immediately start exaggerating these with no attempt at self-defence. My love, you could not dishonour me half as much as I would dishonour myself in telling me how you would like me to change my behaviour. I will choke all sense of familiarity with you, and estrange myself, not frequent your usual haunts, and no longer mention your lovely, loving name, in case I sully it and, by accident, start talking about our relationship. For your sake I will commit myself to strife against myself, because I must never love the one whom you hate.

Then hate me when thou wilt . . .

p. 112 Q: No. 90

So, hate me whenever you will, and, if ever you do, hate me now, while everyone seems determined to thwart me; join fortune's present punishment of me in making me behave like a servant, and do not swoop down to thwart me later. No, do not, when my heart has escaped this unhappiness, attack me from behind; don't follow a windy night with a morning of rain, and stretch out the already intended defeat. If you are going to leave me, do not leave me hanging on, after lots of small sadnesses have already punished me, but thwart me all at once, so that I may take the worst of fortune's blows up front. Then any other kinds of sorrow which might come my way, compared to losing you, will not seem like sorrows at all.

Some glory in their birth . . .

p. 113 Q: No. 91

Some take pride in their breeding, some in their talent, some in their riches, some in their physical strength, some in their clothing (even if only cheaply fashionable), some in their hawks and hunting-dogs, some in their horses, and every kind of taste has its accompanying pleasure which it enjoys above everything else. But these different pursuits are not what make me happy; I have something better than all these. Your love exceeds high breeding, is of more value than wealth, is more impressive than expensive clothing, and more delightful than any hawks or horses, and having you as mine makes me the proudest of all men. I am poor in only one thing: that you might take everything away from me and make me the poorest of all.

But do thy worst . . .

p. 114 Q: No. 92

But even if you do your worst and remove yourself from me, you are mine for the duration of my life, and my life will not last any longer than your love, for it depends on your love. So, I do not need to fear the worst that might happen, since my life would end because of the slightest wrong you might commit against me. I can see my condition is better than if it depended simply on your temperament. You cannot frustrate me with your unreliability, because if you committed such a wrong against me I would surely die. What happiness I am in possession of: happy to love you, happy to die! But is anyone blessed by beauty who fears no taint? You may be being unfaithful without my being aware of it.

So shall I live . . .

p. 115 Q: No. 93

Therefore I will go on believing you are faithful, like a husband who is being deceived by his wife. As a result, love's appearance may still look like love to me, even though it is altered: you appear to be attentive to me while your feelings are elsewhere. Since there can be no hatred in your eyes, I shall not be able to know if you are changed. In many people's faces, the story of their heart's deception is written in their moods, frowns, and insincere looks, but in creating you heaven ordained that love's beauty should always be in your face, that whatever you might be thinking about, or feeling, your expressions should only ever be beautiful. How like forbidden fruit will your beauty become, if the way you seem is not backed up by your good behaviour.

They that have power . . .

p. 116 Q: No. 94

The people who can hurt others but choose not to, who do not do what they seem most likely to do, who, affecting others, remain themselves unemotional, collected, cold, and not easily tempted, they do indeed inherit heaven's favour and manage their natural gifts prudently. They are the lords and masters of their countenances, unlike others who are only like hired managers in comparison to their excellence. The summer's flower is beautiful in summer but lives and dies only for itself, yet if that flower becomes diseased, even the worst weed surpasses it in fine outward appearance. The most beautiful people can turn most ugly by what they do, just as lilies that grow putrid smell a lot worse than weeds.

How sweet and lovely . . .

p. 117 Q: No. 95

How beautiful and lovely do you make that dishonour which, like a canker-worm in a sweet-scented rose, infects the beauty of your flowering reputation! How you hide your sins in pleasant appearances and behaviour! Anyone talking about you, who makes lewd remarks about your fooling around, cannot actually defame you because your name itself evokes a kind of fame and even turns gossip into a kind of blessing. What a splendid dwelling those vices have that chose you to live in, since your beauty covers over every disgrace and makes everything seem attractive. Be careful, dear one, of your great freedom; if you use it ill-advisedly, it will lose its potency.

Some say thy fault is youth . . .

p. 118 Q: No. 96

Some people blame your youth, some your lechery; some say your youth and fooling around are graceful. Both your blessings and your errors are admired by people of all rank, and you turn any errors that come your way into blessings. As the poorest jewel in the ring of an enthroned queen will be highly praised, so your mistakes are transformed into admired actions. How many lambs might a cruel wolf capture if he could look like a lamb himself! How many admirers might you deceive if you were to wield the full force of your commanding power! But do not do this, because I love you in such a way that, since you are mine, I can vouch for your good reputation.

How like a winter . . .

p. 119 Q: No. 97

My absence from you has felt like winter, such is the pleasure of the changeable year! I have felt frozen, the days have been dark, and everything has been bare and felt old, like December. But my time away from you was during the summer and the fertile autumn, burgeoning with fruit, storing the carefree plenty of the spring, like the wombs of widows after their husbands' deaths. But this abundant harvest seemed as helpless as orphans or illegitimate children because summer and its joys are always where you are, and, with you away, even the birds are silent, or if they do sing, it is in so dull a mood that the leaves look faded, fearing winter is on its way.

From you have I been absent . . .

p. 120 Q: No. 98

I have been away from you in the spring, when April, splendidly varied in colour and finery, filled everything with a spirit of youth, and so much so that even melancholy Saturn laughed and frolicked with him. But neither the birdsong, nor the lovely scent of flowers, various in both scent and colour, could encourage me to look forward to the summer, or pick them from the splendid spring earth. Nor did I find wonder in the whiteness of the lily, or praise the deep red of the rose: they were merely lovely, no more than likenesses of delight, based on pictures of you, you their model. Yet even while I played with the spirit of you in the spring around me, with you away it still felt like winter.

The forward violet . . .

p. 121 Q: No. 99

I spoke sternly to a presumptuous violet: 'Lovely thief, where did you steal your scent if it wasn't from my loved one's breath? The splendour of your purple complexion only comes from you having dyed my loved one's blood in the first place.' The lily I discredited for stealing the whiteness of your hand; some buds of marjoram had stolen your hair; some roses stood nervously on their thorns, one blushing, another drip-white, and a third, neither red nor white, had stolen something from both of them, and to this added your breath. But, because of its theft, and in spite of his splendour, it was diseased and dying with a canker-worm. I saw more flowers than these but could see none that had not stolen your scent and colour.

Where art thou, muse . . .

p. 122 Q: No. 100

Where are you, my muse, that you have so long forgotten to speak of that which gives you all your power? Are you wasting your poetic energies on some trivial composition, sullying your strengths by lending them to the betterment of unworthy subjects? Come back to me, forgetful muse, and make good in honourable lines of poetry the time you have spent frivolously away. Sing to my ear that values your songs and gives impetus to both your subject matter and direction. Awake, lazy muse, and look carefully at my loved one's lovely face to see if time has engraved any wrinkles in it. If there are any, then inspire me to write a satirical poem about decay to make time's wastefulness universally despised. Make my loved one famous faster than time wastes our lives, and, in so doing, you will anticipate and outstrip time's cunning knife.

O truant muse . . .

p. 123 Q: No. 101

O, my truant muse, what compensation can you make for neglecting to inspire poetry about truth suffused in beauty? The reputations of both truth and beauty depend on my loved one, and so do you, because that is where your dignity comes from. Answer me, muse. Will you not perhaps say: 'Truth needs no embellishment, once the truth is fixed; beauty requires no paint-brush in order to apply its truth. They are best if never mixed with anything else'? Since he, my loved one, does not need any praise, will you remain dumb? Do not make such excuses for your silence because you have the power in you to make my loved one's reputation far outlive an ornate tomb, and to be praised through the ages. Then, do your work, my muse, inspire me, and I'll teach you how to make my loved one seem no different in the distant future from the way he appears now.

My love is strengthened . . .

p. 124 Q: No. 102

My love is stronger than it used to be, even though it seems weaker. I do not love any less than I did, though I am making less of a show of it.

That love is too commercialised whose value the poet's pen publishes all over the place. Our love was new, only just burgeoning, when I used to welcome it with my songs, like a nightingale at the start of summer, who stops singing when summer ripens. Not that summer is less pleasing now than when the nightingale's mournful melodies quietened the night, but that the kind of poetic music that seems natural, weighs down every branch, and delights that become too usual stop being delightful. So, like the nightingale, I sometimes choose to remain silent because I do not want to take the edge off my song for you by over-repetition.

Alack, what poverty . . .

p. 125 Q: No. 103

O, dear: how impoverished my muse is that, having such a range of possibilities to show off what she can do, the subject matter is entirely bare and of no more value than when I added my uninspired praise to it! Do not blame me if I cannot write any longer! Just look in your mirror and the face that appears there supersedes all my unsophisticated poetic powers, taking the edge off my writing and disgracing my efforts. Is it not wrong then, in trying hard to improve the subject of a poem, actually to make it worse? My poetry has no other purpose than to celebrate your graces and your gifts. And your own mirror shows you far more of those than ever I could place within my poetry.

1595–1597
From fairest creatures . . .

p. 126 Q: No. 1

We long for the most beautiful human beings to procreate so that the best bloom of beauty might not be lost to death, but rather, as the older beauties will die in time, their young successors may carry their memory. You, however, betrothed to your own shining eyes, feed on your own force with self-supporting energy, creating starvation amid plenty; you are your own enemy, and too cruel to your lovely self. Right now, you are creation's most vibrant adornment, the chief announcer of the joyful spring, but you bury your happiness (and future children) in all of your beauty's promise, and, gentle wretch, you waste your expenditure in being miserly. You should have more pity on the world, or else be greedy, by consuming what you owe to the world in keeping potential children within yourself, and therefore the grave.

When forty winters . . .

p. 127 Q: No. 2

By the time forty winters have laid siege to your forehead and dug deep trenches in the field of your beauty, your youth's splendid uniform, now admired by onlookers, will be little more than shabby clothing, not worth very much. When you are then asked where your beauty has gone, where is the treasure of your once-vigorous days, to reply only in your own tired-looking eyes would be truly shameful and a worthless kind of praise. Your beauty's investment deserves better praise than that, especially if you could answer, 'This beautiful child of mine shall present the balance of my account with beauty, and justify my old age', thereby establishing his beauty as your successor. To do this would be to remake yourself in your old age, and to see your blood warm again, even though you will be feeling the cold.

Look in thy glass . . .

p. 128 Q: No. 3

Look in your mirror, and tell the face you see that it is high time that face should make another like it. If you do not refresh its youthful condition, you will be cheating the world and depriving a future mother. Would any woman think herself so beautiful that she would scorn you by withholding her unseeded womb from the cultivation of your being a husband to her? Or is any man so foolish that he would allow his self-absorption to be the death of him and to put an end to breeding? You are the double of your mother, and in you she recalls the sweet April of her own flourishing; in the same way, through your own aged eyes, and in spite of your wrinkles, you will be able to see your own golden age in the face of your child. But if you live without remaking yourself, by dying single, then your looks die as well.

Unthrifty loveliness . . .

p. 129 Q: No. 4

O, wasteful lovely one, why do you squander the inheritance of your beauty on yourself? Nature doesn't bequeath anything; she only lends for profit, and only to those who are willing to be generous. So, beautiful miser, why do you abuse the large bounty you have been given? Worthless money-lender, why do you deal in such impressive amounts, but do not thrive? By only trading with yourself, you defraud yourself of your own self's loveliness. If so, when it is time for you to die, what positive reckoning can you leave behind? Your left-over beauty will be buried with you, but any that you invest will live on in your heir.

Those hours that with gentle work . . .

p. 130 Q: No. 5

All those hours of careful craftsmanship that set off the beautiful looks that captivate everyone else's will become a tyrant and make unbeautiful that which now excels everything else in beauty. Time never stands still, moves summer into winter, and destroys him — sap frozen, lively leaves all gone – beauty covered with snow, and everything barren. So, unless some essence of summer were to remain, held and contained in a vial, the outcome of beauty would be deprived of beauty, and neither beauty nor any memory of it would survive. But flowers made into scent, even though they encounter winter, lose only their appearance; their fragrant essence survives.

Then let not winter's ragged hand . . .

p. 131 Q: No. 6

Then do not allow ruinous winter to despoil the summertime of your life before preserving the essence of yourself! Fill some vial, enrich some place with the treasure of your beauty before it is destroyed by your self-absorption. There is nothing illegal in a loan which makes happy those who repay it. That will happen if you replicate yourself by begetting a child, or ten (if the interest is ten to one). Ten times you would be happier than you on your own – and if ten of yourself in ten children replicated you, what could death do if you were to die, leaving you still alive in your descendants? Do not be self-centred, for you are far too beautiful to be conquered by death and to bequeath yourself to worms.

Lo, in the orient . . .

p. 132 Q: No. 7

Look! When the benevolent sun raises his fiery head high in the east, everyone below pays homage to the freshly presented vision, displaying subservience to his sacred majesty; and then, when the sun, has reached the highest point of heaven, like strong youth in the prime of life, we humans continually pay him homage and follow in his footsteps like pilgrims. But when the sun, from his highest point, in a tired chariot, weak with age, falls away from daylight, those eyes, once loyal, now turn away from the sun's sinking journey and look elsewhere. This is like you who, leaving behind the best of yourself in middle age, will die without anyone's regard – unless you beget a son.

Music to hear . . .

p. 133 Q: No. 8

When music sounds, why does it make you sad? Delights do not conflict with delights, but rather joy finds delight in joy. Why do you love things that make you unhappy, or take pleasure in things that trouble you? If the harmony of properly tuned notes in combined unison offends your hearing, they are only rebuking you charmingly, because you, being single, ruin the music by not playing all the notes you should. Look how one string, the pleasant sustainer of another, is being struck along with all the rest, interdependently, like a father, a child, and a happy mother, and all within one instrument, like one family, singing the same delightful note. The strings' music, without words, combines different notes but sounds like one, and sings to you: 'On your own, you are nothing.'

Is it for fear . . .

p. 134 Q: No. 9

Is it because you are afraid to make somebody a widow that you waste yourself in singleness? If you die without having children, the world will mourn you as though she were your mateless wife. The world itself will become your widow and continually mourn the fact that no one who looks like you survives you, whilst every other widow would normally be able to recall her husband's appearance by looking in her children's eyes. Whatever a prodigal spends is only ever for himself, and the world will continue to indulge him, but the wasting of beauty finally comes to an end, and, if beauty is not used, the beautiful person loses it forever. There is no room for loving others in such a heart that dishonourably kills itself.

For shame deny . . .

p. 135 Q: No. 10

You should feel ashamed to admit that you do not love anybody, you, who do not know what is best for you. At least allow that many others love you, even though it is obvious you do not love anyone. You are so consumed with self-hatred that you have no hesitation in plotting to ruin your body by not starting a family, which should be your priority. O, change the way you think, so that I may change my opinion! Shall hate be more at home with you than tender loving? You should behave as you appear: giving and humane, or at least behave like that towards yourself. Beget a child out of love for me, so that your beauty will live on.

As fast as thou shalt wane . . .

p. 136 Q: No. 11

As quickly as you diminish with age, so quickly in your child could you be growing young again, the new, young blood you could call your own, just as you yourself turn away from youth. Wisdom, beauty, and profit are to be found in making children, without which everything is pointlessness, old age, and comfortless death. If everyone thought like you, the human race would end, and sixty years would bring about the end of the world. Let those whom nature did not intend to have children, the common, unattractive, ugly, waste away without offspring, but for those to whom she gave her best gifts she gave plenty, which you should make the most of by being bountiful, and by having children. Nature figured you for her own authoritative, wax impression and intended you to replicate yourself, not let yourself die out.

When I do count the clock . . .

p. 137 Q: No. 12

When I notice time passing and see the splendid day submerged in terrible night; when I see violets past their best, and black hairs turning white; when I see proud trees stripped of their leaves, which used to provide shade for cattle; and when I see summer's harvest all tied up in bundles, carried on a funeral-like cart, and the heads of the grain looking like old-age with a white beard: then I ask questions about your beauty, because you, too, will experience the desolating effects of time, and because delights and beauties leave themselves behind, and perish as quickly as others take their place. And nothing can survive time's mowing, except the procreation of children to defy time when he takes you away.

O that you were yourself . . .

p. 138 Q: No. 13

If only you had full possession of yourself! But, my love, you are yourself for no longer than you are alive. You should prepare for death by bequeathing your good looks to someone else. Then, the lease you hold for your beauty would not expire, and you would remain yourself after your death, in the lovely child who would preserve your appearance and possibly produce a grandchild. Who would allow so handsome a house as yours to go to wrack and ruin, when honourable management might maintain it against the winter storms of life, and the desolating anger of death's cold eternity? No one but prodigals, my dear love, you know that. You yourself had a father: let your son say the same.

Not from the stars . . .

p. 139 Q: No. 14

I do not obtain my knowledge from the stars, yet I know about astrology, and I cannot predict good or bad happenings, such as plagues, blights, or what the weather will be like; neither can I look ahead to what might be happening in the next few minutes and control their different moods, nor say whether certain rulers will have good fortune, by looking up into the skies for predictions. But my knowledge comes from your eyes, and in them, like constant stars, I learn that truth and beauty would flourish together – if you would turn your attention towards breeding and providing for the future. If not, then I predict this for you: that truth and beauty will end with your death.

When I consider . . .

p. 140 Q: No. 15

When I think that all living things are perfect for only a short time, and that this universe is nothing more than a theatre which the stars mysteriously influence and talk about; when I understand that humans grow like plants, urged on and restrained under that very same course of stars, exulting in their youthful energy, diminishing with old age, wearing out even the memory of how splendid they once were: then such fanciful imagining about this unreliable existence places your rich youthfulness before my eyes, where desolating time argues with decay to turn your youthful brightness into polluted darkness. And I am at war with time over loving you: as he diminishes you, I put new life into you with my writing.

But wherefore do not you . . .

p. 141 Q: No. 16

But why do you not choose a more powerful method of war against this blood-thirsty tyrant, time, and strengthen yourself, even as you diminish, with more fruitful methods than my unproductive verse? You are now in your prime, and there are many young virgins who, like unseeded gardens, would quite properly long to carry the flowers of your offspring (who would be more like you than any artistic representation). Then would life itself renew your life, which neither the artists of this age nor my inexperienced writing can do, and make your inner and outward beauty live in the eyes of the world. In the giving of yourself you will perpetuate yourself, and therefore you will continue to live, re-figured by your own love-making.

Who will believe my verse . . .

p. 142 Q: No. 17

Who will believe my verse in the future if it were full of your supreme merits? As yet, heaven knows, it is like a tomb that covers you and does not even show half of your attributes. If only I could convey how beautiful your eyes are, and in new rhythms beat out all of your gifts, the people of the future would say, 'This poet is lying: such divine qualities were never to be found in human features.' Then would my manuscripts, turned yellow with age, be rejected, like elderly men who are all words and no matter, and then would the praise due to you be labelled poetic folly, an exaggerated form of an old-fashioned song. But, if your child were to be alive then, you would live again: in it, and in my poetry.

Shall I compare thee . . .

p. 143 Q: No. 18

Shall I make comparison between you and a day in summer? You are lovelier and more moderate. In May, strong winds disturb the adorable buds, and the time allowed for summer is nowhere near long enough. Sometimes the sun is too hot, and its golden beauty is often clouded over, just as every beautiful creature eventually diminishes in beauty, by accident, or else it is stripped bare of ornament by its movement through the seasons. But your ever-lasting summer shall never lose its glow, nor shall you lose the beauty which you own; nor shall death be able to boast that you wander in his shadows, while you are being turned into everlasting poetry, and live alongside – and outlive – time. Even as long as humans can breathe and see, this sonnet will live and give you life.

Devouring time . . .

p. 144 Q: No. 19

All-consuming time: make the lion's claws blunt, and bury everything that the earth produces; take away the teeth of ferocious tigers, and incinerate the phoenix in her fullness of vigour. Make the seasons happy or melancholy as you fly by; do whatever you want to do to the whole wide world and all mortal loveliness. But I forbid you one most terrible crime: do not chisel wrinkles into my loved one's beautiful forehead, or draw any other lines there with your well-worn pen. Let him remain unblemished by your passage, the ideal form of beauty for everyone who comes after him. But do the worst you can, old time; for all your depredation, my loved one will be forever young in my verse.

A woman's face . . .

p. 145 Q: No. 20

Your face looks naturally female; you are the male-female lover of my overpowering emotions. Your feelings are gentle, like a woman's, but you show no signs of inconstancy, as not-to-be-trusted women do. Your looks are brighter than theirs; your glances are less flirtatious, superficially enriching (as theirs do) whatever you look at. You are a man in form, and enthral all other forms, catching the eyes of other men, and overwhelming women's spirits. And you were initially created female until nature – even as she was making you – became besotted, and added something which put you beyond me: she gave you a penis, which I have no use for. So, since she decked you out for women to enjoy, I can love you, but your love-making is really for women to prize.

So is it not with me ...

p. 147 Q: No. 21

I am not like those poets who need an overly-made-up, beautiful subject for inspiration, who draw on heaven itself for poetic imagery and compare their beloved to everything that is beautiful, making a link in proud comparison with the sun and moon, the earth, and the sea's treasures, with April's first flowers, and every rare thing that exists on this planet under heaven. Let me, who am true in love, simply tell the truth, and then, believe me, my loved one is as beautiful as anyone else, even though not as bright as the stars. Let people who like rumour exaggerate; I will not praise, am not a salesman, and do not intend to sell you.

My glass shall not persuade ...

p. 148 Q: No. 22

My mirror will not make me think that I am old as long as you are youthful; but when I see wrinkles on your brow I realise that I shall die, because all the beauty that adorns you is just the appropriate clothing for my heart, which lives in your breast as yours lives in me. How then can I be older than you? So, my love, look after yourself just as I will, not for my own sake but because I carry your heart, which I will look after as lovingly as a careful nurse guards her baby against harm. Do not expect to get your heart back after mine is dead; you gave me yours for keeps.

As an unperfect actor ...

p. 149 Q: No. 23

Like an ill-prepared actor who forgets his lines because of stage fright, or like a wild animal that is so enraged that its ferocity inhibits action, so I, lacking confidence, fail to express my love adequately and seem unable to express its strength because of its overwhelming power. So, let what I write silently give voice to my inward thought, pleading for love and hoping for a greater reward than can be expressed in words. Learn to read what voiceless love has written; love has the capacity to hear through the eyes.

Mine eye hath played the painter ...

p. 150 Q: No. 24

My eyesight has acted like a painter and has portrayed your beauty on the canvas of my heart. My body is the frame that encloses your beauty, and seen from the right angle it is like a great painter's work of art because it is through my eyes that you may see his skill and discover where your real likeness is portrayed: that hangs continually in the workshop that is my breast, whose windows are glazed with your eyes. See now what favours eyes have done for eyes: my eyes have portrayed you, and yours give access to my breast, through which the sun loves to peer so as to contemplate you. Nevertheless, eyes lack this skill which would enhance their artistry: they portray only what they see, not its inmost being.

Let those who are in favour . . .

p. 151 Q: No. 25

Let those on whom the stars shine favourably boast of public honour and proud titles, while I, who do not have such luck, take unexpected pleasure in what I honour most greatly. People who are favoured by great men flourish only in the way that marigolds do when the sun shines, and their splendour remains hidden because their glory fades as soon as they fall out of favour. If once a conscientious soldier famous for his conquests is defeated, he is instantly dishonoured, and all the triumphs that he achieved are forgotten. How happy then am I, who love and am loved indestructibly.

Lord of my love . . .

p. 152 Q. No. 26

Lord of my love, to whom your merits have tied my duty in servitude, I send you this written message to bear witness to my respect for you rather than to display my skill — such great respect that skill as poor as mine may make seem worthless because of my lack of eloquence to display it, except that, I hope, some favourable understanding on your part will grace my skill, bare as it is, until whatever star guides my course may look favourably upon me and clothe my threadbare homage in such a way that I may appear worthy of your loving favour. Then I shall be so bold as to make public my love for you; until then, I shall not dare to appear where you may put me to the test.

Weary with toil . . .

p. 153 Q: No. 27

Exhausted by my labour, I go straight to bed, the welcome resting place for overworked limbs. But then, when my bodily labour is over, a journey in my head begins to trouble my brain, because then my thoughts set off from my distant place of rest upon a devout pilgrimage to you and keep my eyelids wide open, looking on darkness which is what blind people see, except that my soul's powers of imagination transmit to my unseeing mind your image, which, like a shining jewel hung in terrifying darkness, makes darkness beautiful and rejuvenates her appearance. So, both my limbs by day and my mind by night experience no rest, either for you, or for me.

How can I then return . . .

p. 154 Q: No. 28

So how can I, lacking the benefits of rest, come happily back, when daytime labour is not relieved by sleep, but day is oppressed by night and night by day, and each of them – although they are opposed to one another – conspires to torture me, one by making me work, the other by making me complain how far away I work, always farther away from you? I tell the day that you are bright to please him and that you grace him even when clouds darken the sky. Similarly, I flatter the dark night – 'when twinkling stars peep not, you gild the evening sky'. But daytime constantly lengthens my sorrows, and every night, night deepens my sadness.

When, in disgrace . . .

p. 159 Q: No. 29

When, out of favour with fortune and in reputation, I am grieving alone over my loneliness and appealing to unresponsive heaven with my useless complaints, thinking about myself and cursing my fate, wishing I had more to hope for, like such and such a one, had someone else's looks and were rich in friends like yet another person, envying such and such a one's skill and another's range, least contented with what I enjoy most – still, almost despising myself in these thoughts, by chance I happen to think of you, and then my spirit, rising like a lark at dawn from the dark earth, sings hymns at the gate of heaven; because the memory of your kind love enriches me so greatly that then I feel that I would not change place with kings.

When to the sessions . . .

p. 156 Q: No. 30

When, sitting in happy and peaceful contemplation, I call up memories of the past, I sigh for the absence of many things I desired, and, along with old griefs, bewail anew the wasting of my precious time. Then can I weep unaccustomed tears for dear friends lost in oblivion, and renew debts of grief that I paid off long ago, and deplore the loss of many sights that I shall see no more. Then can I grieve at long-past causes of sadness and unhappily reassess the cost of griefs that I have already lamented, which I pay afresh as if I had not paid them before. But if while doing this I think of you, dear friend, all that I have lost is restored, and all my griefs come to an end.

Thy bosom is endeared . . .

p. 157 Q: No. 31

Your breast is made precious by all the hearts of those whom, because they are no longer around, I have supposed to be dead, and in it reigns love, and all that goes along with love, and all the friends whom I believed to be buried. What a lot of sacred tokens of grief has dedicated love wrung from me as if due to the dead, which actually turn out to be simply absences concealed in you! You are like a grave, adorned with relics of my past lovers, who endowed you with everything that they took from me, with the result that what was due to many is now yours alone. I see in you images of all those whom I have loved and you, made up of all of them, possess all of me.

If thou survive . . .

p. 158 Q: No. 32

If you survive the inevitable day when grim death will bring about my dissolution, and then happen to look over these unpolished lines of your dead lover, compare them with the superior ones of that time, and then, even though they will be outshone by every other poet's, hang on to them for my sake, rather than for their technical skill, exceeded by that of more able men. O, then just lovingly think this about me: 'If my lover's skill had developed commensurately with time, his love would have brought to birth a finer poem than this to march in the ranks of better-endowed poets. But because he is dead, and poets grow in skill, I will read their poems for their technique, his for his love'.

Full many a glorious morning . . .

p. 159 Q: No. 33

I have seen many a glorious morning shine regally upon the mountain tops, kissing the green fields with its golden face and turning pale streams gold with celestial alchemy, then soon allow the darkest clouds to pass in a disfiguring mass over his heavenly face and hide it from the dismayed world, stealing westward with this disgrace. Similarly, early one morning my sun shone on me with overwhelming splendour. But, alas, he was mine for only one hour – the high clouds have obscured him from me now. Even so, my love does not reject that sun for this: worldly suns may cast a shadow when heaven's sun does.

Why didst thou promise . . .

p. 160 Q: No. 34

Why did you promise such a beautiful day and make me go out without my cloak, only to let dark clouds overtake me, hiding your splendour with their foul vapours? It is no compensation that you break through the cloud to dry the rain on my storm-beaten face, since no one speaks well of an ointment that heals a wound but does not remove the scar. Nor can your penitence cure my grief – even though you are sorry, I still suffer.

Penitence does not do much to help the one who suffers. Still, the tears that your love causes you to shed for me are rich pearls and atone for all offences.

No more be grieved . . .

p. 161 Q: No. 35

Do not grieve any longer for what you have committed: roses have thorns and silver fountains mud. Clouds and eclipses darken both the moon and the sun, and detestable cankerworms live in even the most beautiful buds. Everyone commits sins, as I do in this, justifying your offence with comparisons, corrupting myself by palliating your misdeed, making greater excuses for your sins than they require – because I invoke common sense to plead on behalf of your sensual fault (your opponent is your defending lawyer), and bring forward a lawful plea against myself. There is such an opposition within me between my love and my hatred that I inevitably stand as an accomplice to the dear thief who sourly robs from me.

Let me confess . . .

p. 162 Q: No. 36

I have to admit that we two must be separate individuals even though our love unites us, so responsibility for the offences that I commit must be borne by me alone, without your help. There is only one focus of attention in our love for one another, even though in our lives there is a vexatious cause of separation which, though it does not alter love's single-minded effect, nevertheless reduces the time during which we can enjoy love's pleasures. I cannot always acknowledge you in case my lamented sense of doing wrong puts you to shame, nor can you honour me with public kindness without dishonouring yourself. But do not do that. I love you in such a way that, because you are mine, praise of you relates also to me.

As a decrepit father . . .

p. 163 Q: No. 37

As an aged father loves to see his active child perform youthful feats, so I, lamed by fortune's direst cruelty, take all my comfort from your ability and your loyalty, because whether beauty, high birth, wealth, or intelligence, or any of these, or all of them, or more, are enrolled among your good qualities, I engraft my love upon this abundance (of good qualities). Thus I am not lame, poor, or despised as long as this idea attains such reality that I benefit from your abundance and bask in a share of all your glory. I wish you whatever is best, and if that wish is granted I shall be ten times the happier.

How can my muse . . .

p. 164 Q: No. 38

How can my muse lack subject matter to write about as long as you are alive – you who instil into my verses the theme of your sweet self, too excellent for every commonplace piece of writing to set forth? O, thank yourself if anything I write that is worth reading withstands your scrutiny, for who is so inarticulate that he cannot write in praise of you, when you yourself inspire composition? May you be the tenth of the muses, ten times more inspiring than the nine that mere rhymesters call upon, and let whoever invokes you create immortal verses to live forever. If my feeble inspiration pleases these critical times, let the labour be mine, but yours the praise.

O, how thy worth . . .

p. 165 Q: No. 39

O, how can I extol your excellence with due modesty when you are the better part of myself? What can my praise say about myself, and what am I doing but praising myself when I praise you? Because of this, let us live apart, and let our dear love lose the reputation of unity so that by this separation I may give you that which you deserve on your own. O absence, what torment would you cause were it not that the bitter time you create gave us the leisure to while away the time with loving thoughts, which sweetly deceives both time and thoughts; and that you teach how to make one person two, by praising the author of this poem who stays away!

Take all my loves . . .

p. 166 Q: No. 40

Take all my love and my loved ones, my love, yes, take them all. What more do you then have than you did previously? No love, my love, that you can call true love – because all of my love was yours before you took away even more from me. Then, if for love of me you have taken away my loved one as well, I cannot blame you for making love to my love – but you are still to blame if you deceive this self by lustful use in another of what you refuse in me. I forgive your theft, noble robber, if you steal what little I own – and yet, love knows it is a greater cause of sorrow to have to endure love's deception than to suffer the wrongs brought about by avowed hatred. Oversexed charmer, in whom all faults look well, kill me with outrageous behaviour, but still we must not be enemies.

Those pretty wrongs . . .

p. 167 Q: No. 41

Those engaging little wrongs that freedom commits when I am occasionally absent from your heart entirely befit your beauty and your years, because temptation follows inevitably wherever you go. You are well-born and therefore desirable; you are beautiful and therefore liable to be wooed, and when a woman woos what man will cruelly reject her, until he has got his way? Ah yes, but even so you might keep away from my patch, and rebuke your beauty and your easily tempted youthfulness which lead you in debauchery, even to the extent that you feel compelled to break a double pledge – hers, by your beauty tempting her to you, and yours, by your beauty being unfaithful to me.

That thou hast her …

p. 168 Q: No. 42

That you have won her is not my only cause of sadness, and yet it may be truly said that I loved her dearly. That she has you is the main cause of my sadness, a loss in love that touches me more nearly. Loving offenders, here is how I shall excuse you: you love her because you know I love her, and similarly she wrongs me for my sake, allowing my friend to put her to the test sexually for my sake. If I lose you, my loss is a gain to the woman I love, and if I lose her, my friend has found what I lost. Both find each other, and I lose both of them, and both of them, for my sake, inflict this pain on me. But here's my consolation: my friend and I are one. Sweet delusion! – then she loves only me.

When most I wink …

p. 169 Q: No. 43

When my eyes are most closely shut, they see best, because all the day long they see unvalued things, but when I am asleep they look on you in my dreams, and, shining in the darkness, are brightly directed in the dark. Then you, whose image lightens darkness – what a pleasing sight would your substance form to the unclouded day with your much clearer light when, even to the unseeing eyes (of a dreamer), your shadow shines so! How blessed, I say, would my eyes be made by looking on you in bright daylight when in the dead of night your fair but insubstantial shadow rests on unseeing eyes! All days are like nights until I see you, and nights are bright days when you come to me in my dreams.

If the dull substance …

p. 170 Q: No. 44

If the heavy substance of my flesh were thought, harmful distance would not stand in my way, because then, in spite of distance, I would be transported from remote regions to where you are staying. Then it would not matter even if my foot stood on the plot of land furthest away from you, since quick thought can overleap both sea and land as easily as it can imagine the place where it would like to be. But O, thought kills me because I am not thought, with the power to overleap great distances when you are away, but that I, being compounded of so much earth and water, must sadly attend upon time's convenience to reunite us, receiving nothing from such slow elements except heavy tears, emblems of the woe of earth and water.

The other two . . .

p. 171 Q: No. 45

The other two elements, insubstantial air and purifying fire, are both with you wherever I may be, the first my thought, the other my desire – these, neither present nor absent, are constantly coming and going with swift movement. So, when these more lively elements have gone on a tender embassy of love to you, my life – which is composed of four elements – oppressed with melancholy, sinks down towards death until the make-up of life's elements is restored by the swift messengers of air and fire received from you, which immediately come back again, reassured of your good health, telling me about it. On hearing this I rejoice – but then, no longer joyful, I return them to you and immediately grow sad.

Mine eye and heart . . .

p. 172 Q: No. 46

My eye and heart are engaged in deadly combat about how to share out the spoils of the sight of you. My eye wants to prohibit my heart from seeing you, and my heart wants to debar my eye from that right. My heart – a cabinet never penetrated by bright eyes – pleads that you lie within him. But the defendant denies that plea, claiming that your beautiful appearance lies within him. A jury of thoughts, all of them reporting to my heart, is enrolled to pronounce upon this case, and by their verdict the share of your bright eye and the dear heart is deter-mined thus: your exterior is due to my eye, and your intimate heart's love belongs to my heart.

Betwixt mine eye and heart . . .

p. 173 Q: No. 47

A truce is made between my eye and heart, and now each does good turns to the other. When my eye is famished for a look, or my loving heart is stifled with sighs, then my eye feasts upon the image of my love and in-vites my heart to the illusory feast. At another time, my eye is my heart's guest and shares some of its thoughts of love. So you are always with me through either your image or my love, since you cannot move away from my thoughts, and I am constantly with them and they with you. Or if they sleep, your image in my sight awakens my heart to the joy of both heart and eye.

How careful was I . . .

p. 174 Q: No. 48

How careful I was when I set off to place even my least valuable possessions under the most secure bars so that they might remain in reliable safe keeping away from untrustworthy hands! But you, compared to whom my most precious possessions are mere trifles – my greatest comfort but now, because of your absence, my greatest source of grief – you, dearest of all, and the one I care for most, are left as a prey for every common thief! I have not locked you up in any chest except the one where you are not present even though I feel you are – within the loving enclosure of my breast, from which you may come and go as you wish – and I fear you will be stolen even from there, because honesty itself proves thievish for so rich a prize.

Against that time . . .

p. 175 Q: No. 49

In preparation for that time – if it ever comes – when I shall see you censure my faults – when your love has made its final reckoning, summoned to that audit by well-considered reflection; in preparation for that time when you will pass me by as by a stranger and scarcely greet me with that sun, your eye; when love, changed from what it was, will find reasons for a dignified reserve: in preparation for that time, I establish myself here within the knowledge of my worth and raise this hand of mine against myself to justify your unimpeachable case. You have a legal right to leave poor me, since I can adduce no reason for you to love me.

How heavy do I journey . . .

p. 176 Q: No. 50

How sadly do I travel when what I journey towards – the goal of my exhausting journey – only makes me realise that the sought-for ease and comfort will say: 'Such and such a distance are you from your friend.' The animal that carries me, wearied with my sadness, plods dully along at bearing such a burden in me, as if the poor thing knew instinctively that his rider did not like the speed that takes him away from you. The blood-stained spur that my crossness sometimes pricks into his flank and to which he responds with a groan, that pains me more than my spurring hurts his side, cannot urge him on, because that groan makes me think 'My sadness lies ahead and my happiness behind.'

Thus can my love ...

p. 177 Q: No. 51

Here is how my love for you can excuse the offence of slowness of my plodding bearer when I journey away from you: 'Why should I hasten away from where you are? There's no need to ride quickly till I go back.' What excuse then will my poor beast find when extreme speed can only seem slow? Then I should use my spurs even if I were mounted on the wind. Even in winged speed I shall seem motionless; no horse will be able to keep pace with my desires, so desire, being composed of nothing but love, shall curb no lethargic flesh in its impassioned speed, but love shall find excuses for my horse for love's sake. Because he went bloody-mindedly slowly when he was going away from you, I'll run towards you and let him walk.

So am I as the rich ...

p. 178 Q: No. 52

I am like a rich man whose blessed key can give him access to his precious locked-up treasure which he does not want to look at all the time in case doing so should blunt the fine point of his occasional pleasure. That is why feast days are so solemn and so rare because, coming only at occasional points of the long year, they are, like precious stones or the chief jewels in a jewelled collar, spaced thinly out. So the time that detains you is like my jewel case, or the wardrobe which conceals the robe, by making some special moment specially blessed, by newly revealing its concealed treasure. You are blessed, whose worthiness enables me to exult when you are present and to hope when you are not.

What is your substance ...

p. 179 Q: No. 53

What constitutes you, what are you made of, that causes millions of remarkable spirits and images to attend on you? – because every one, each individual, has its own image, yet you, a single being, can inhabit every shape. Describe Adonis, and the image seems like a poor imitation of you. Artfully depict Helen, and your likeness appears in Greek semblance. Speak of the springtime and of the harvest: one looks like the foreshadowing of your beauty, the other like your abundant self, and we recognise you in every created thing. You have a share of every outwardly beautiful appearance, but no one can match you for inward constancy of heart.

O how much more . . .

p. 180 Q: No. 54

O, how much more beautiful does beauty seem when graced with fidelity! Roses look beautiful, but we think even more of them for the sweet scent that lies within them. Odourless dog-roses are as deeply coloured as sweet-smelling roses, grow on similar thorns, and play no less friskily when summer air causes their closed buds to unfold, but because their merit lies only in their appearance, they live uncared-for and fade unappreciated, die neglected. Scented roses do not so. Appealing perfumes are made from them when they die. Ah, beautiful and handsome youth, when those qualities fade in you poetry will similarly distil your true essence.

Not marble nor the gilded . . .

p. 181 Q: No. 55

Neither marble nor the gold-coloured tombs of princes shall outlive this powerful verse, but you will shine more brightly in what is contained here than in neglected monuments sullied by uncaring time. When devastating warfare topples monuments and battles uproot the stonemason's creations, neither Mars's sword nor the devastations of warfare will extinguish the enduring evidence of your reputation. You will stride out and live on in spite of death and the ravages of oblivion, and your reputation will endure in the eyes of all ages to come, which wear this world out till doomsday. So, till you are resurrected on the Day of Judgement, you live on in my verse and endure in lovers' eyes.

Sweet love, renew thy force . . .

p. 182 Q: No. 56

Dear spirit of love, grow stronger. Let it not be said that your edge should be blunter than desire which one day is satisfied with feeding, but the next day is sharpened to its former force. So, my loved one, be like this too, even if today you feed your hungry eyes till they close with satiety, see again tomorrow and do not quench the spirit of love with everlasting lethargy. Let this sad interval be like the ocean which divides the shores on which two newly engaged lovers resort daily to the banks so that when they see the beloved return, the sight will be even more blessed. Or think of it as winter which, being full of troubles, makes the coming of summer much more desired and more precious.

Being your slave . . .

p. 183 Q: No. 57

Since I am your slave, what ought I to do other than attend constantly upon the occasions and times when you desire anything? I have no time worth speaking of to spend, no services to perform till you have need, nor dare I rebuke the interminable hours whilst – my ruler – I am seeking the chance to serve you, nor think the bitterness of absence from you harsh when once you have said farewell to me, nor dare I wonder with jealous thoughts where you may be, or speculate about what you are doing, but, like an abject slave, hang around and think of nothing but how happy you make those around you. Love is so loyal a fool that whatever you do he never censures it.

That god forbid . . .

p. 184 Q: No. 58

May the god who first made me your slave forbid that I should think of controlling your leisure time, or of seeking from you an account of what you do, since as your slave I am required to wait upon your leisure. O, let me, being at your beck and call, endure the imprisoning effect, especially during absence, of your freedom, and, being meek in endurance, put up with every rebuke without accusing you of cruelty. Go where you like, your privilege is so strong that you yourself may authorise yourself to pass your time as you wish. You have the right to pardon yourself for injuries that you commit against yourself. My place is to wait, even if it is hell to do so, not to blame your choice, whether it be good or bad.

If there be nothing new . . .

p. 185 Q: No. 59

If there is nothing new, but all that is has been before, how are our minds tricked which, striving to create afresh, mistakenly give birth for a second time to a child that has already been born! O that memory, with a look into the past (going back as far as five hundred years, to a time when thought was first expressed in words), could show me your image in some ancient book so that I might see what the ancient world would say to the wonderful composition of your form, whether we have improved or whether they were better, or whether the revolving of the ages makes no difference! O, I am sure that the sages of the past have bestowed admiring praise on less worthy subjects.

Like as the waves . . .

p. 186 Q: No. 60

Just as the waves of the sea flow towards the pebbled beach, so do our minutes hasten to their conclusion, each replacing the one that goes before it; toiling after each other, all struggle forwards. The new-born child, once it emerges into the broad expanse of daylight, crawls towards maturity, and, being crowned with it, malignant forces oppose his success, and time that gave now destroys its own gift. Time pierces and destroys the ornament set on youth, and digs the furrows in beauty's brow, feeds on the delicacies produced by nature's perfection, and nothing endures but for his scythe to mow. And yet my verse shall endure into future times, praising your worth in spite of time's cruel power.

If we offend . . .

p. 187 *A Midsummer Night's Dream*, 5.1.108–17

QUINCE If we cause offence, it is with good intentions that you should believe we have not come to cause offence except with good intentions. To show our simple skill in the true beginning of our ends. Think, then, that we come only to displease. We do not come with the intention of pleasing you. We are not here for your delight. The actors are on hand to cause you to regret, and by their actions you will know everything you are likely to know.

1598–1600

What fire is in mine ears?

p. 188 *Much Ado About Nothing*, 3.1.107–16.

BEATRICE Why are my ears burning? Can what they say be true? Am I really thought so guilty of pride and arrogance? Be off with you, contempt, and farewell pride in maidenhood! Such people deserve no praise. And, Benedick, go on loving me! I will return your love, subduing my wayward spirits to your loving hand. If you are in love, my responsiveness will encourage you to join us together in a holy alliance – because people say you are worthy, and I believe it and more than just by hearsay.

So oft have I invoked thee . . .

p. 189 Q: No. 78

I have so often called upon you as my muse and found such inspiration for my poetry that unfamiliar writers have adopted my practice, and circulate their poetry under your auspices. Your eyes, which taught dumb people to sing aloud and earth-bound ignorance to fly aloft, have helped learned poets to soar even higher and endowed excellence with double grace. Nevertheless, take most pride in what I compose, whose inspiration is yours and inspired by you. In other poets you only improve the style, and their skill and learning are influenced by you, but you are my entire inspiration, and inspire my crude ignorance to heights of creation.

Whilst I alone did call . . .

p. 190 Q: No. 79

While only I invoked you to help me write, my poetry alone had all your noble grace. But now my gracious verses have grown feeble, and my waning powers yield place to another. I admit, dear love, that the theme of your loveliness deserves the labours of a worthier pen than mine, but everything that your poet says about you he derives entirely from you and simply returns it to you. He endows you with virtue, and he stole that term from the way you behave; he gives you beauty, and derived it from your cheek. He can offer no praise to you but what is already in you. So do not thank him for what he says, because he simply endows you with what you already own.

O, how I faint . . .

p. 191 Q: No. 80

O, how feeble I become when I write about you, knowing that a more worthy poet is calling upon your name and spends all his power in praising it, making me inarticulate in what I say about your reputation. But because your value, which is as wide as the ocean, can bear the burden of the humblest as well as of the proudest sail, my cheeky little boat, far less grand than his, stubbornly sails on your wide-open sea. The slightest help you can afford will keep me afloat while he rides on your unfathomed depths, or, if I am wrecked, I am a worthless boat, he tall in construction and of great splendour. So, if he survives and I am destroyed, the worst that can be said is that my love was what brought about my destruction.

Or I shall live . . .

p. 192 Q: No. 81

Either I shall live long enough to write your epitaph, or you will survive when I am decaying in my grave. Death cannot destroy your memory even though all of my qualities will be forgotten. From now onward your name will have immortal life whereas I, once I am dead, must be dead to all the world. The earth can give me only a common grave whereas you will be immortalised. Your monument will be my tender verse, which eyes not yet created will scan, and tongues of the future will describe your beauty when all who are now alive are dead. You will live forever, such power has my pen, where breath breathes most effectively, namely, in men's mouths.

I grant thou wert not . . .

p. 193 Q: No. 82

I admit that you were not married to my muse, and so you may read without dishonour the words of dedication that other writers apply to their admired dedicatees, gracing every book. You are no less graced in learning than in appearance, finding your merits exceeds the capacity of my praise, and so you are obliged to look elsewhere for some more recent endorsement from these progressive times. Do so, my love, but when they have thought up whatever laboured conceits rhetoric can devise, you, genuinely beautiful, would be accurately represented in honest plain terms by your plain-speaking friend, and their gross flattery might be better applied to subjects who need it. It is wasted on you.

I never saw that you . . .

p. 194 Q: No. 83

I could never see that you needed cosmetics, so I applied no flattery to your beauty. I found – or thought I found – that you were worth more than the threadbare offering of a poet's gift, and that is why I have refrained from singing your praises, since yourself, being present, could easily demonstrate how far short a commonplace poetic talent comes, writing about value, in describing what merit grows in you. You thought of this silence as a fault in me, whereas it should be most greatly to my credit, because in being silent I do not diminish your beauty, whereas others, attempting to confer immortality, bury you in oblivion. There is more life in one of your lovely eyes than both your poets can eulogise.

Who is it that says most . . .

p. 195 Q: No. 84

Who is there, however eloquent, who can utter richer praise than this: that you alone are you, within whose boundaries is confined the stock which would be needed to produce your equal? Mean poverty dwells within that pen that does not confer at least some glory upon its subject matter; but whoever writes about you enhances his work simply by doing so. Let him simply set down what is inscribed within you, not obscuring what nature made so clear, and such a transcript will celebrate his skill, making his style universally admired. But alongside the blessings of your beauty, you add one fault: your fondness for praise, which undermines your praiseworthiness.

My tongue-tied muse . . .

p. 196 Q: No. 85

My inarticulate muse holds politely back while comments in praise of you, skilfully put together, store up your features with a golden pen, and in a rich style, polished by all the muses. I think good thoughts about you while others write good words, and like an illiterate parish clerk, I always cry out 'Amen' at the end of every hymn of praise that a competent writer offers up to you as the polished product of a highly skilful pen. When I hear you praised, I say 'That's right, it's true!' and add something more to even the highest terms of praise. But that is only in my thoughts, whose love for you goes foremost even though my words lag behind. So, believe other people for what they say, but me for my silent but effectively eloquent thoughts.

Was it the proud full sail . . .

p. 197 Q: No. 86

Was it the ambitious tenor of his impressive verse aimed at the conquest of your infinitely precious self that buried my well-formed thoughts in my mind, causing them to remain still-born in the place where they were conceived? Was it his spirit, taught by other spirits to write with more than human eloquence, that dumbfounded me? No, neither he nor his nightly associates assisting him rendered me inarticulate. Neither he nor that amiable familiar spirit who misleads him with information every night can claim, like conquerors, to be responsible for my silence. I was not weakened by any fear from that quarter. But when your features and favour formed the subject matter of his verse, that was when I lacked things to write about; that is what weakened my poetry.

Thus far with rough . . .

p. 198 *Henry V*, Epilogue

CHORUS Our humble author has taken the story to this point with his amateurish and incompetent pen, cramming powerful men into a tiny space, bungling with fits and starts the story of their glorious exploits. It did not last long, but within it lived this English hero, loved most gloriously. Fortune forged the sword with which he conquered the world's best garden, leaving his son as its emperor. Henry VI, crowned king as an infant, succeeded his father, and so many men were involved in governing his affairs that they lost France and severely harmed his England — a story that has often been told on our stage — and for their sake, receive the story graciously in your kind imagination.

Hang there, my verse ...

p. 199 *As You Like It*, 3.2.1–10

ORLANDO Hang there, my poem, as witness of my love, and, Diana, triple-honoured queen of night, behold from your solemn orbit in the sky the name of the huntress who dominates my entire life. O Rosalind, these trees will serve as my notebooks, and I will carve my thoughts in their barks so that every eye that looks around in this forest will see your merits celebrated all over the place. Run, run, Orlando! Carve on every tree the name of the beautiful, virtuous, and incomparable maiden.

1600–1609
To me, fair friend ...

p. 200 Q: No. 104

Beautiful friend, you can never seem old to me, because your beauty still seems the same as when I first saw you. Three cold winters have shaken the splendour of three summers from the forests; I have seen three beautiful springs turn to yellow autumn in the progression of the seasons, the scents of three Aprils burned away in three hot Junes, since I first saw you, who are still youthful. Ah, but beauty still moves imperceptibly away from its initial appearance, like the hands on a time-piece. Similarly your fair appearance, which to me seems to stand still, moves on, and my eye may be deceived. For fear of which, let me tell you this, you who are not yet conceived: beauty passed its height of summer even before you were born.

Let not my love ...

p. 201 Q: No. 105

Do not let my love be called idolatry, nor the one I love appear as an idol, even though my songs and expressions of praise are always directed towards one, and are of one – always the same one, and always thus. My loved one is kind today and kind tomorrow, always constant in wonderful excellence. So my verse, consistent in constancy, expressing only one thing, avoids variety. 'Fair, kind, and true' is my constant theme, 'fair, kind and true' expressed in different ways, and in this difference is my invention expended. Three themes in one, which make for a wonderful range of subject matter. 'Fair', 'kind', and 'true' have often existed independently, but never dwelt permanently together until now.

When in the chronicle ...

p. 202 Q: No. 106

When in the chronicle of time long past I read descriptions of the most beautiful people, and of how beauty endows with beauty old verses written in praise of now-dead ladies and of handsome knights, then in the catalogue of the finest attributes of attractive beauty – hand, foot, lip, eye, and brow – I see that their old pens would have given expression to just such beauty as you now possess. So all their eulogies are no more than prophecies of our present time, all of them prefiguring you, and, because they looked only with prophetic eyes, they lacked the ability to sing your praises adequately. For we who live in the present can gaze in admiration but lack eloquence to express our praise.

Not mine own fears . . .

p.203 Q: No. 107

Neither my personal anxieties nor the spirit of prophecy of the wide world musing on what is still to come can determine the duration of my true love, imagined as subject to a limited period of time. The inconstant moon has suffered her eclipse and the melancholy prophets deride their own prophecies. Desired but doubtful possibilities now celebrate their consummation, and peace looks forward to olive branches that will endure forever. Now my love looks fresh with the drops of this most encouraging time, and death submits to me, since I shall live on, in spite of him, in this modest verse, while he exults over the stupid and inarticulate masses. And you will find your memorial in this poem when the emblems and brass tombs of tyrants have wasted away.

What's in the brain . . .

p. 204 Q: No. 108

What is there in the mind that can be written down which has not represented to you my true feelings? What is there original to say, what can be set down, that can express my love or your great merit? Nothing, dear boy, but still I must every day repeat the identical words, like divine prayers, thinking no old things out of date, so long as you are mine, and I yours. Just as when I first called blessings upon your dear name, even so that everlasting love in love's newly renewed expression cares nothing for the damage done by time, nor is troubled by the inevitable signs of age but makes age his page-boy for ever, finding the first thought of love generated in that same place where time and external appearances might be expected to show them dead.

O never say that I was false . . .

p. 205 Q: No. 109

Do not ever say that I was unfaithful even if absence seemed to moderate my ardour. I might as easily stop being myself as part from my soul, which lies in your breast. That is where my love dwells. If I have strayed, I come back again, like a traveller, faithfully punctual, and unchanged by time, so that I myself bring water to cleanse my stain. Never think that, even if every kind of weakness that can undermine every sort of character stained my nature, it could be so absurdly flawed as to abandon your great goodness in exchange for something insignificant – because there is nothing in the whole wide world that I regard as my ideal but you, my rose: you are everything in the world to me.

Alas, 'tis true . . .

p. 206 Q: No. 110

O dear, it is true, I have strayed far and wide, and made myself a laughing stock in everyone's sight, savaged my own opinions, trivialised what is most serious, created long-standing resentment by forming new attachments. It is quite true that I have looked on fidelity disdainfully and coldly. But, by all that is holy, these swervings renewed my love for you, and the worst experiments showed you to be my dearest love. Now that that is all over, take what will last for ever. I will never again sharpen my appetite on new experiences to test my love for an older friend, my god in love, to whom I am exclusively devoted. So, you, whom I adore next to heaven, bid me welcome to your pure and most dearly loving breast.

O, for my sake . . .

p. 207 Q: No. 111

For my sake, rebuke fortune – the goddess who is guilty of the deeds that have harmed me – for having made no better provision for my way of life than giving me a public role which requires me to behave like a public figure. That is why my reputation suffers a stigma, and why my identity is almost diminished to the medium in which it works, like a dyer's hand. Pity me then, wish for me to be restored, while, like a willing patient, I will drink bitter potions to treat my severe infection. I will not regard that as a hardship, or as a double penance designed to cure me twice over. Take pity on me then, dear friend, and I assure you that your pity will be enough to cure me.

Your love and pity . . .

p. 208 Q: No. 112

Your love and pity efface the scar that common opinion stamped upon my brow, for what do I care who speaks well or ill of me so long as you disguise my faults, give me credit for my merits? You are my whole world, and I must try to identify my merits and my demerits from what you say, there being no one else to influence me, and I being susceptible to the influence of no other person that can change my confirmed disposition for better or for worse. I cast all my concern for other people's opinions into so deep an abyss that my deaf ears are oblivious to both praise and criticism. See how I excuse this neglect: you are so deeply involved in my plans that, so far as I am concerned, everyone else is dead.

Since I left you . . .

p. 209 Q: No. 113

Since I left you my eye is in my mind, and the faculty that enables me to go about my business divides its function and is half-blind, seems to be seeing but in effect does not, because it conveys to my heart no form of bird, flower, or any object that it catches sight of. My mind has no sense of its fleeting impressions, nor does the eyes' vision retain what it apprehends, because whether it sees the roughest or the noblest sight, the sweetest impression or the ugliest creature, the mountain or the sea, the day or the night, the crow or the dove, it transforms them all into your appearance. Incapable of anything else, obsessed by you, my profoundly true imagination thus makes my eye untrue.

Or whether doth my mind . . .

p. 210 Q: No. 114

Does my mind, being crowned by you, bask in this flattery – the plague of monarchs – or shall I say my eye tells the truth, and that your love gave it this alchemical power, to transform monsters and half-formed creatures into angelic forms such as resemble your lovely self, transforming every bad thing into perfection as quickly as it comes into your range of vision? O, it is the former – it is flattery in my vision, and my greatly honoured mind laps it up in regal fashion. My eye knows well what suits its taste, and prepares the cup to suit its palate. If the cup is poisoned, then the least harm is done because it is only my eye that loves it, and I drink from it before you.

Those lines that I before have writ . . .

p. 211 Q: No. 115

Those lines that I wrote earlier – even those that said I could not love you more dearly – lie. But, back then, I did not know my ardent flame of love should burn even more brightly. But calculating time (whose millions of mischances creep in between vows and change the decrees even of kings, coarsen sacred beauty and blunt even the sharpest of intentions, weaken strong minds into the status of shifting things) – alas, why, even though I fear time's tyranny, might I not say 'Now I love you best', especially when I used to be certain beyond certainty, glorifying the present, doubting all else? Love is a baby, so why do I not just say that and thereby give full encouragement to growth to one who continues to grow.

Let me not to the marriage ...

p.212 Q: No. 116

Let me not admit any form of impediment to the marriage of constant minds. Love is not true love which alters when it encounters alteration, or shifts affection when it encounters shifting. O no, it is like an immovable sea-mark that encounters storms but is never shaken. It is as a star to every directionless ship, whose value cannot be assessed even when its height above the horizon can be measured. Love is not time's plaything, even though rosy lips and cheeks may suffer under time's curved sickle. Love does not alter with time's short hours and weeks but endures even until the eve of doomsday. If this is wrong, and proved against me, I have never written anything, and no one has ever loved.

Accuse me thus ...

p. 213 Q: No. 117

Bring these accusations against me: that I have neglected every respect in which I should repay your great deservings, forgotten to acknowledge your dearest love to which all obligations tie me daily, that I have often spent time with strangers and wasted your justified calls upon me; that I have allowed myself to be steered by every wind that was likely to take me as far as possible from your sight. Make note of all my wilfulness and mistakes, and add what you suspect to what you can prove; bring me within range of your censure, but do not shoot at me in your newly roused hatred, because my excuse is that I was trying to put the constancy and value of your love to the test.

Like as, to make our appetites ...

p. 214 Q: No. 118

Just as, to sharpen our appetites we stimulate our palates with piquant flavours, and as, to ward off unseen sicknesses we make ourselves sick so as to prevent illness, so I, being full of your never overly rich sweetness, directed my diet towards bitter sauces and, being made ill by good food, found it somehow fitting to make myself sick before there was need for it. So my strategy in love (in order to anticipate a sickness that was not yet present) was to generate a real sickness, and treat with medicine a healthy condition, which, although it is usually made sick by treatment, instead wished to be cured by sickness. But from this I learn, and know the lesson to be true: medicines poison the one who made himself sick because of you.

What potions have I drunk . . .

p. 215 Q: No. 119

What draughts of temptingly harmful potions distilled from infernally foul containers have I drunk, treating hopes with fears and fears with hopes, constantly losing even when I thought I was succeeding! What terrible mistakes has my heart committed, even while it thought it was incomparably blessed! How my eyes have been totally deluded by the distraction of this maddening fever! O benefit resulting from harm! Now I find it to be true that a good state may be improved even by what seemed harmful, and damaged love when it is restored may be happier than it was at first, stronger, much greater. So I return, having learned my lesson, to my previous state of happiness and gain by suffering far more than I lost.

That you were once unkind . . .

p. 216 Q: No. 120

The fact that you were once unkind benefits me now, and because of the grief I felt then I should have to stoop penitently under my wrong-doing, unless my sinews were made of brass or toughened steel. Because if you suffered as much as a result of my unkindness as I did from yours, you must have had a hell of a time, and I, a hard master, have given not a moment's thought to assessing how I once suffered as a result of your ill-doing. O, that our dark time of mutual sadness might have reminded my innermost being what suffering true sorrow causes, and have offered to you as soon as you offered to me the apology that is appropriate for hurt feelings! But that offence of yours now becomes a benefit: mine excuses yours, and yours needs to excuse mine.

'Tis better to be vile . . .

p. 217 Q: No. 121

It is better to be contemptible than to be thought contemptible, when one is reproached for being so, even when one is not, and the appropriate pleasure (which is thought to be vile not by our senses but in other people's eyes) is lost. Because why should other people's false and corrupted eyes look kindly on my amorous inclinations, or why should there be even more blameworthy spies on my weaknesses, who in their evil desires regard as bad what I think of as good? No, I am what I am, and people who take aim at my faults count up their own. I may be blameless even if they go astray. What I do should not be judged by their evil standards – unless they argue that all men are bad and prosper in their badness.

Thy gift, thy tables ...

p. 218 Q: No. 122

Your gift, my memoranda and notes about you, is already inscribed permanently within my memory, and shall remain to the forefront of my otherwise worthless mind, even for all eternity; or at least my records of you can never be lost for as long as my brain and heart have power to survive, till each of them yields its share of you up to obliterating oblivion. Nor do I need physical aids to reckon the memory of your love, so I made so bold as to give them away, putting more trust in my own memory to preserve you. To suppose that I should need material help to remember you would imply that I am forgetful.

No, time, thou shalt not boast ...

p. 219 Q: No. 123

No, time, you cannot boast that I am fickle! Your reconstructions of monuments built with modern techniques are not at all original or wonderful, they are simply replicas of what we have seen already. Our lifespans are short, and so we are inclined to find wonderful whatever you palm off on us as being ancient and rather think it was created to suit us than that we already knew of its existence. I defy both your records and you (time) yourself, not marvelling at either the present or the past, because your records and what we see now are both deceptive, made more or less impressive by your unremitting speed. I swear this oath, and it shall endure forever: I shall be faithful in spite of all your destructive power.

If my dear love ...

p. 220 Q: No. 124

If my love for you were the result only of circumstances, it might have no father but fortune, being equally subject to the vagaries of time, considered either worthless (like weeds) or valuable (like flowers). But no, it is founded upon far more than chance, it does not alter in the face of favourable splendour, nor does it dwindle under the yoke of enslaved rebellion to which these tempting times summon people like us. It does not fear expediency, that heretic which works on short-term contracts, but stands independently, prudent in the long term, so that it neither flourishes in prosperity nor suffers in bad times. As witnesses to this I call time's playthings, who die in a good cause, having lived for a bad one.

Were 't aught to me . . .

p. 221 Q: No. 125

Would it be of any consequence to me if I carried the canopy of state, with my external action doing honour to outward appearances, or if I laid foundations for a supposed eternity which turns out to be briefer than devastation or decay? Have I not seen those who dwell on the significance of appearances and favours lose everything and more by overdoing their obligations, by replacing simple sincerity with elaborate flattery, pathetic in their worthless gain, ruined by external show? No, let me be dutiful to you, and accept my offering, poor but freely tendered, which is not diluted by the second-rate and which admits no artifice other than mutual surrender, just me for you. Go away, you paid spy! An honest person is least at your mercy when most vehemently accused.

O thou my lovely boy . . .

p. 222 Q: No. 126

My beautiful boy, who hold time's hour and looking-glass, and see his reaping time, who have grown more beautiful with age and thus show your lovers fading as your lovely self grows older — if nature, all-powerful mistress over decay, constantly seeks to hold you back in your onward journey, here is why she holds on to you: so that her skill may shame time and make minutes ineffectual. But fear her all the same, you favoured recipient of her graces! Her account, even if delayed, must finally be paid; and her means of doing that is to surrender you.

Words, vows, gifts, tears . . .

p. 223 Troilus and Cressida, 1.2.278–91

CRESSIDA He [Pandarus] offers up words, vows, gifts, and love's complete tribute on another's behalf. But I see a thousand times more in

Troilus than can appear in the image created by Pandarus's eulogy of him. I do not capitulate. Women are angels to their wooers, but when the suit is accomplished their attraction fades. The thrill of the hunt lies in the chase. Any woman who is courted is ignorant unless she knows this: men value what they are pursuing above its true worth. There was never a woman who found love achieved to be as desirable as when it was in prospect. So I recommend this moral out of love: to have won is to be in a position of command: not to have been won is to be a beggar. So, although inwardly my heart is full of love, I shall give no hint of that in my behaviour.

Our remedies oft in ourselves . . .
p. 224. *All's Well That Ends* Well, 1.1.212–25
Often the cure for our problems – which we suppose must rest with the heavens – lies in our own hands. The fateful heavens give us a free rein, and only thwart our dull-witted ambitions when we ourselves lack initiative. What power is it that puts my love on so high a pedestal, that gives me a vision but cannot bring it to reality? Nature causes even things at opposite ends of fortune's scale to join together as if they had a natural affinity, and to embrace as if it were natural for them to do so. Difficult enterprises are hopeless for those who rationally assess the obstacles and who think that what actually has been achieved must be impossible. Was there ever anyone who tried to demonstrate her deserts who failed in love? The King's sickness! – my aim may be unattainable, but my ambition is firm and I will not give up.

I am Saint Jaques' pilgrim . . .
p. 225 *All's Well That Ends Well*, 3.4.4–17
HELEN 'I have gone as a pilgrim to the shrine of St James. My over-weening love has done such harm that I am proceeding there barefooted on the cold ground having vowed to the saint to expiate my sins. Write to implore my dearest master – your dear son – to hasten back from the bloody warfare. Bless him at home in peace, while I pray fervently for him from afar. Ask him to forgive me for the labours I have undertaken for his sake. I, like cruel Juno, caused him to abandon his aristocratic friends to live with encamped enemies, where death and danger threaten noble prey. He is too good and noble for me and for death, which I embrace in the hope of setting him free.'

Now sleep y-slackèd . . .

p. 226 *Pericles*, scene 10.1–14

GOWER Now sleep has laid the company to rest. There is no sound in the house except snoring made louder by the gorged breasts of this extravagant marriage feast. The cat with eyes as bright as burning coals crouches in front of the mouse-hole, and crickets sing in front of the oven as if all the happier for their thirst. Hymen has escorted the bride to her bed where, by the loss of virginity, a baby is conceived. Be attentive and fill out with your thoughts and keen imaginations the time that has passed so quickly. That which is obscure in appearance I will explain in speech.

My temple stands in Ephesus . . .

p. 227 *Pericles*, scene 21.225–35

DIANA My temple is in Ephesus. Go there quickly, and do sacrifices on my altar. When my virgin priestesses are assembled there, tell them what has happened to you like this. Before all the people, announce loudly how you lost your wife at sea. Call on them to grieve for your troubles, and for your daughter's, cry out and describe them vividly. Do as I say, or you will be sorry. Do it, and I swear by my silver bow, you will stay happy.

1610–1613

No more, you petty spirits of region low . . .

p. 228 p. 1610: *Cymbeline*, 5.5.187–204

JUPITER You inferior spirits of a lower region, trouble my ears no longer! Be silent! How dare you spirits accuse the thunder-bearer, whose bolt, you know, stationed in the heavens batters all rebellious shores? Depart, poor shadows, from the heavens, and rest on your everlasting flower-banks. Be not troubled by human events. It is no concern of yours, but, as you know, of mine, I put troubles in the way of those I love so as to cause my favour to be more highly appreciated because delayed. Be satisfied. My divinity will rest on the fortunes of your oppressed son. His well-being is assured, his trials are successfully concluded, my godhead was in the ascendancy at his birth, and he was married in my temple. Rise, and disappear. He shall remain the husband of Lady Innogen and be made much happier as a consequence of his trials. Lay on his chest this happy document in which my will spells out his happy fortune.

'Tis ten to one this play ...

p. 230 *All Is True (Henry VIII)*

EPILOGUE It is ten to one that this play will not please all who have come to see it. Some come to relax and sleep through an act or two. But we fear we have startled them with our trumpets, so it is obvious that they will say it is a flop. Others come to hear the city thoroughly mocked, and to cry 'That's funny!', which we haven't done either. So I am afraid the only praise we are likely to hear for this play at present lies in the charitable interpretation of virtuous women, because we have showed them such a one. If they smile and say 'It's a success', I know that before long all the best men will agree – because it is a poor do if they remain silent when their ladies tell them to applaud.

Numerical Index of *Shakespeare's Sonnets* (1609)

An asterisk indicates the suggestion of a dramatic analogy (see Introduction, pp. 41–2, and the notes for the relevant sonnet).

1 From fairest creatures we desire increase, p. 126.

2 When forty winters shall besiege thy brow, p. 127.

3 Look in thy glass, and tell the face thou viewest, p. 128.

4 Unthrifty loveliness, why dost thou spend, p. 129.

5 Those hours that with gentle work did frame, p. 130.

6 Then let not winter's raggèd hand deface, p. 131.

7 Lo, in the orient when the gracious light, p. 132.

8 Music to hear, why hear'st thou music sadly, p. 133.

9 Is it for fear to wet a widow's eye, p. 134.

10 For shame deny that thou bear'st love to any, p. 135.

11 As fast as thou shalt wane, so fast thou grow'st, p. 136.

12 When I do count the clock that tells the time, p. 137.

13 O that you were yourself! But, love, you are, p. 138.

14 Not from the stars do I my judgement pluck, p. 139.

15 When I consider every thing that grows, p. 140.

16 But wherefore do not you a mightier way, p. 141.

17 Who will believe my verse in time to come, p. 142.

18 Shall I compare thee to a summer's day, p. 143.

19 Devouring time, blunt thou the lion's paws, p. 144.*

20 A woman's face with nature's own hand painted, p. 145.*

21 So is it not with me as with that muse, p. 147.

22 My glass shall not persuade me I am old, p. 148.

23 As an unperfect actor on the stage, p. 149.

24 Mine eye hath played the painter, and hath stelled, p. 150.

25 Let those who are in favour with their stars, p. 151.

26 Lord of my love, to whom in vassalage, p. 152.

27 Weary with toil I haste me to my bed, p. 153.

28 How can I then return in happy plight, p. 154.

29 When, in disgrace with fortune and men's eyes, p. 155.*

30 When to the sessions of sweet silent thought, p. 156.*

31 Thy bosom is endearèd with all hearts, p. 157.

32 If thou survive my well-contented day, p. 158.

33 Full many a glorious morning have I seen, p. 159.

34 Why didst thou promise such a beauteous day, p. 160.

35 No more be grieved at that which thou hast done, p. 161.

36 Let me confess that we two must be twain, p. 162.

37 As a decrepit father takes delight, p. 163.

38 How can my muse want subject to invent, p. 164.

39 O, how thy worth with manners may I sing, p. 165.

40 Take all my loves, my love, yea, take them all, p. 166.*

41 Those pretty wrongs that liberty commits, p. 167.

42 That thou hast her, it is not all my grief, p. 168.*

43 When most I wink, then do mine eyes best see, p. 169.

44 If the dull substance of my flesh were thought, p. 170.

45 The other two, slight air and purging fire, p. 171.

46 Mine eye and heart are at a mortal war, p. 172.*

47 Betwixt mine eye and heart a league is took, p. 173.*

48 How careful was I when I took my way, p. 174.*

49 Against that time – if ever that time come, p. 175.

50 How heavy do I journey on the way, p. 176.

51 Thus can my love excuse the slow offence, p. 177.

52 So am I as the rich whose blessèd key, p. 178.*

53 What is your substance, whereof are you made, p. 179.

54 O how much more doth beauty beauteous seem, p. 180.

55 Not marble nor the gilded monuments, p. 181.

56 Sweet love, renew thy force. Be it not said, p. 182.*

57 Being your slave, what should I do but tend, p. 183.*

58 That god forbid, that made me first your slave, p. 184.*

59 If there be nothing new, but that which is, p. 185.

60 Like as the waves make towards the pebbled shore, p. 186.

61 Is it thy will thy image should keep open, p. 92.

62 Sin of self-love possesseth all mine eye, p. 93.*

63 Against my love shall be as I am now, p. 94.

64 When I have seen by time's fell hand defaced, p. 95.

65 Since brass, nor stone, nor earth, nor boundless sea, p. 96.

66 Tired with all these, for restful death I cry, p. 97.

67 Ah, wherefore with infection should he live, p. 98.

68 Thus is his cheek the map of days outworn, p. 99.

69 Those parts of thee that the world's eye doth view, p. 100.

70 That thou art blamed shall not be thy defect, p. 101.

71 No longer mourn for me when I am dead, p. 102.*

72 O, lest the world should task you to recite, p. 103.

73 That time of year thou mayst in me behold, p. 104.

74 But be contented when that fell arrest, p. 105.

75 So are you to my thoughts as food to life, p. 106.*

76 Why is my verse so barren of new pride, p. 107.

77 Thy glass will show thee how thy beauties wear, p. 108.

78 So oft have I invoked thee for my muse, p. 189.

79 Whilst I alone did call upon thy aid, p. 190.

80 O, how I faint when I of you do write, p. 191.

81 Or I shall live your epitaph to make, p. 192.

82 I grant thou wert not married to my muse, p. 193.

83 I never saw that you did painting need, p. 194.

84 Who is it that says most which can say more, p. 195.

85 My tongue-tied muse in manners holds her still, p. 196.*

86 Was it the proud full sail of his great verse, p. 197.

87 Farewell – thou art too dear for my possessing, p. 109.

88 When thou shalt be disposed to set me light, p. 110.

89 Say that thou didst forsake me for some fault, p. 111.

90 Then hate me when thou wilt, if ever, now, p. 112.

91 Some glory in their birth, some in their skill, p. 113.*

92 But do thy worst to steal thyself away, p. 114.*

93 So shall I live supposing thou art true, p. 115.

94 They that have power to hurt and will do none, p. 116.

95 How sweet and lovely dost thou make the shame, p. 117.

96 Some say thy fault is youth, some wantonness, p. 118.

97 How like a winter hath my absence been, p. 119.

98 From you have I been absent in the spring, p. 120.

99 The forward violet thus did I chide, p. 121.

100 Where art thou, muse, that thou forget'st so long, p. 122.

101 O truant muse, what shall be thy amends, p. 123.

102 My love is strengthened, though more weak in seeming, p. 124.

103 Alack, what poverty my muse brings forth, p. 125.

104 To me, fair friend, you never can be old, p. 200.

105 Let not my love be called idolatry, p. 201.

106 When in the chronicle of wasted time, p. 202.

107 Not mine own fears nor the prophetic soul, p. 203.

108 What's in the brain that ink may character, p. 204.*

109 O never say that I was false of heart, p. 205.

110 Alas, 'tis true, I have gone here and there, p. 206.

111 O, for my sake do you with fortune chide, p. 207.

112 Your love and pity doth th' impression fill, p. 208.

113 Since I left you mine eye is in my mind, p. 209.

114 Or whether doth my mind, being crowned with you, p. 210.*

115 Those lines that I before have writ do lie, p. 211.

116 Let me not to the marriage of true minds, p. 212.

117 Accuse me thus: that I have scanted all, p. 213.

118 Like as, to make our appetites more keen, p. 214.

119 What potions have I drunk of siren tears, p. 215.

120 That you were once unkind befriends me now, p. 216.

121 'Tis better to be vile than vile esteemed, p. 217.*

122 Thy gift, thy tables, are within my brain, p. 218.*

123 No, time, thou shalt not boast that I do change, p. 219.

124 If my dear love were but the child of state, p. 220.

125 Were 't aught to me I bore the canopy, p. 221.

126 O thou my lovely boy, who in thy power, p. 222.

127 In the old age black was not counted fair, p. 55.*

128 How oft, when thou, my music, music play'st, p. 56.

129 Th' expense of spirit in a waste of shame, p. 57.*

130 My mistress' eyes are nothing like the sun, p. 58.*

131 Thou art as tyrannous so as thou art, p. 59.

132 Thine eyes I love, and they, as pitying me, p. 60.*

133 Beshrew that heart that makes my heart to groan, p. 61.

134 So, now I have confessed that he is thine, p. 62.

135 Whoever hath her wish, thou hast thy Will, p. 63.

136 If thy soul check thee that I come so near, p. 64.

137 Thou blind fool love, what dost thou to mine eyes, p. 65.

138 When my love swears that she is made of truth, pp. 66–7.*

139 O, call not me to justify the wrong, p. 68.*

140 Be wise as thou art cruel; do not press, p. 69.*

141 In faith, I do not love thee with mine eyes, p. 70.*

142 Love is my sin, and thy dear virtue hate, p. 71.

143 Lo, as a careful housewife runs to catch, p. 72.

144 Two loves I have, of comfort and despair, pp. 73–4.

145 Those lips that love's own hand did make, p. 49.

146 Poor soul, the centre of my sinful earth, p. 75.

147 My love is as a fever, longing still, p. 76.

148 O me, what eyes hath love put in my head, p. 77.*

149 Canst thou, O cruel, say I love thee not, p. 78.

150 O, from what power hast thou this powerful might, p. 79.

151 Love is too young to know what conscience is, p. 80.

152 In loving thee thou know'st I am forsworn, p. 81.

153 Cupid laid by his brand and fell asleep, p. 48.

154 The little love-god lying once asleep, p. 47.

Index of First Lines

Each first line is followed by the number of the sonnet in the 1609 quarto, or its play reference, and then its page location in this volume.

A woman's face with nature's own hand painted, 20, p. 145.

Accuse me thus: that I have scanted all, 117, p. 213.

Against my love shall be as I am now, 63, p. 94.

Against that time – if ever that time come, 49, p. 175.

Ah, wherefore with infection should he live, 67, p. 98.

Alack, what poverty my muse brings forth, 103, p. 125.

Alas, 'tis true, I have gone here and there, 110, p. 206.

And let me have her likened to the sun, *Edward III*, scene 2.322–33, p. 54.

As a decrepit father takes delight, 37, p. 163.

As an unperfect actor on the stage, 23, p. 149.

As fast as thou shalt wane, so fast thou grow'st, 11, p. 136.

Ay, that there is. Our court, you know, is haunted, *Love's Labour's Lost*, 1.1.159–74, p. 84.

Be wise as thou art cruel; do not press, 140, p. 69.

Being your slave, what should I do but tend, 57, p. 183.

Beshrew that heart that makes my heart to groan, 133, p. 61.

Betwixt mine eye and heart a league is took, 47, p. 173.

But be contented when that fell arrest, 74, p. 105.

But do thy worst to steal thyself away, 92, p. 114.

But if that I am I, then well I know, *The Comedy of Errors*, 3.2.41–54, p. 82.

But wherefore do not you a mightier way, 16, p. 141.

Canst thou, O cruel, say I love thee not, 149, p. 78.

Cupid laid by his brand and fell asleep, 153, p. 48.

Devouring time, blunt thou the lion's paws, 19, p. 144.

Did not the heavenly rhetoric of thine eye, *Love's Labour's Lost*, 4.3.57–70, p. 87.

Fair was the morn when the fair queen of love, *The Passionate Pilgrim*, 9, p. 53.

Farewell – thou art too dear for my possessing, 87, p. 109.

For shame deny that thou bear'st love to any, 10, p. 135.

From fairest creatures we desire increase, 1, p. 126.

From you have I been absent in the spring, 98, p. 120.

Full many a glorious morning have I seen, 33, p. 159.

Hang there, my verse, in witness of my love, *As You Like It*, 3.2.1–10, p. 199.

How can I then return in happy plight, 28, p. 154.

How can my muse want subject to invent, 38, p. 164.

How careful was I when I took my way, 48, p. 174.

How heavy do I journey on the way, 50, p. 176.

How like a winter hath my absence been, 97, p. 119.

How oft, when thou, my music, music play'st, 128, p. 56.

How sweet and lovely dost thou make the shame, 95, p. 117.

I am Saint Jaques' pilgrim, thither gone, *All's Well That Ends Well*, 3. 4. 4–17, p. 225.

I grant thou wert not married to my muse, 82, p. 193.

I never saw that you did painting need, 83, p. 194.

If I profane with my unworthiest hand, *Romeo and Juliet*. 1.5.92–109, p. 90.

If love make me forsworn, how shall I swear to love?, *Love's Labour's Lost*, 4.2.106–19, p. 85.

If my dear love were but the child of state, 124, p. 220.

If the dull substance of my flesh were thought, 44, p. 170.

If there be nothing new, but that which is, 59, p. 185.

If thou survive my well-contented day, 32, p. 158.

If thy soul check thee that I come so near, 136, p. 64.

If we offend, it is with our good will, *A Midsummer Night's Dream*, 5.1.108–17, p. 187.

In faith, I do not love thee with mine eyes, 141, p. 70.

In loving thee thou know'st I am forsworn, 152, p. 81.

In the old age black was not counted fair, 127, p. 55.

Is it for fear to wet a widow's eye, 9, p. 134.

Is it thy will thy image should keep open, 61, p. 92.

Let me confess that we two must be twain, 36, p. 162.

Let me not to the marriage of true minds, 116, p. 212.

Let not my love be called idolatry, 105, p. 201.

Let those who are in favour with their stars, 25, p. 151.

Like as the waves make towards the pebbled shore, 60, p. 186.

Like as, to make our appetites more keen, 118, p. 214.

Lo, as a careful housewife runs to catch, 143, p. 72.

Lo, in the orient when the gracious light, 7, p. 132.

Look in thy glass, and tell the face thou viewest, 3, p. 128.

Lord of my love, to whom in vassalage, 26, p. 152.

Love is my sin, and thy dear virtue hate, 142, p. 71.

Love is too young to know what conscience is, 151, p. 80.

Mine eye and heart are at a mortal war, 46, p. 172.

Mine eye hath played the painter, and hath stelled, 24, p. 150.

Music to hear, why hear'st thou music sadly, 8, p. 133.

My glass shall not persuade me I am old, 22, p. 148.

My love is as a fever, longing still, 147, p. 76.

My love is strengthened, though more weak in seeming, 102, p. 124.

My mistress' eyes are nothing like the sun, 130, p. 58.

My temple stands in Ephesus. Hie thee thither, *Pericles*, scene 21.225–35, p. 227.

My thoughts do harbour with my Silvia nightly, *The Two Gentlemen of Verona*, 3.1.140–9, p. 50.

My tongue-tied muse in manners holds her still, 85, p. 196.

No longer mourn for me when I am dead, 71, p. 102.

No more be grieved at that which thou hast done, 35, p. 161.

No more, you petty spirits of region low, *Cymbeline*, 5.5.187–204, p. 228.

No, time, thou shalt not boast that I do change, 123, p. 219.

Not from the stars do I my judgement pluck, 14, p. 219.

Not marble nor the gilded monuments, 55, p. 139.

Not mine own fears nor the prophetic soul, 107, p. 203.

Now old desire doth in his deathbed lie, *Romeo and Juliet*, 2.0, p. 91.

Now sleep y-slackèd hath the rout, *Pericles*, scene 10.1–14, p. 226.

O, call not me to justify the wrong, 139, p. 68.

O, for my sake do you with fortune chide, 111, p. 207.

O, from what power hast thou this powerful might, 150, p. 79.

O, how I faint when I of you do write, 80, p. 191.

O, how much more doth beauty beauteous seem, 54, p. 180.

O, how thy worth with manners may I sing, 39, p. 165.

O, lest the world should task you to recite, 72, p. 103.

O me, what eyes hath love put in my head, 148, p. 77.

O, never say that I was false of heart, 109, p. 205.

O, never will I trust to speeches penned, *Love's Labour's Lost*, 5.2.401–15, p. 88.

O that you were yourself! But, love, you are, 13, p. 138.

O thou my lovely boy, who in thy power, 126, p. 222.

O truant muse, what shall be thy amends, 101, p. 123.

Or I shall live your epitaph to make, 81, p. 192.

Or whether doth my mind, being crowned with you, 114, p. 210.

Our remedies oft in ourselves do lie, *All's Well That Ends Well*, 1.1.212–25, p. 224

Poor soul, the centre of my sinful earth, 146, p. 75.

Say that thou didst forsake me for some fault, 89, p. 111.

Scarce had the sun dried up the dewy morn, *The Passionate Pilgrim*, 6, p. 52.

Shall I compare thee to a summer's day, 18, p. 143.

Sin of self-love possesseth all mine eye, 62, p. 93.

Since brass, nor stone, nor earth, nor boundless sea, 65, p. 96.

Since I left you mine eye is in my mind, 113, p. 209.

So am I as the rich whose blessèd key, 52, p. 178.

So are you to my thoughts as food to life, 75, p. 106.

So is it not with me as with that muse, 21, p. 147.

So, now I have confessed that he is thine, 134, p. 62.

So oft have I invoked thee for my muse, 78, p. 189.

So shall I live supposing thou art true, 93, p. 115.

Some glory in their birth, some in their skill, 91, p. 113.

Some say thy fault is youth, some wantonness, 96, p. 118.

So sweet a kiss the golden sun gives not, *Love's Labour's Lost*, 4.3.24–39, p. 86.

Study me how to please the eye indeed, *Love's Labour's Lost*, 1.1.80–9, p. 83.

Sweet Cytherea, sitting by a brook, *The Passionate Pilgrim*, 4, p. 51.

Sweet love, renew thy force. Be it not said, 56, p. 182.

Take all my loves, my love, yea, take them all, 40, p. 166.

That god forbid, that made me first your slave, 58, p. 184.

That thou art blamed shall not be thy defect, 70, p. 101.

That thou hast her, it is not all my grief, 42, p. 168.

That time of year thou mayst in me behold, 73, p. 104.

That you were once unkind befriends me now, 120, p. 216.

Th' expense of spirit in a waste of shame, 129, p. 57.

The forward violet thus did I chide, 99, p. 121.

The little love-god lying once asleep, 154, p. 47.

The other two, slight air and purging fire, 45, p. 171.

Then hate me when thou wilt, if ever, now, 90, p. 112.

Then let not winter's raggèd hand deface, 6, p. 131.

They that have power to hurt and will do none, 94, p. 116.

Thine eyes I love, and they, as pitying me, 132, p. 60.

Those hours that with gentle work did frame, 5, p. 130.

Those lines that I before have writ do lie, 115, p. 211.

Those lips that love's own hand did make, 145, p. 49.

Those parts of thee that the world's eye doth view, 69, p. 100.

Those pretty wrongs that liberty commits, 41, p. 167.

Thou art as tyrannous so as thou art, 131, p. 59.

Thou blind fool love, what dost thou to mine eyes, 137, p. 65.

Thus can my love excuse the slow offence, 51, p. 177.

Thus far with rough and all-unable pen, *Henry V*, Epilogue, p. 198.

Thus is his cheek the map of days outworn, 68, p. 99.

Thy bosom is endearèd with all hearts, 31, p. 157.

Thy gift, thy tables, are within my brain, 122, p. 218.

Thy glass will show thee how thy beauties wear, 77, p. 108.

Tired with all these, for restful death I cry, 66, p. 97.

'Tis better to be vile than vile esteemed, 121, p. 217.

'Tis ten to one this play can never please, *All Is True (Henry VIII)*, Epilogue, p. 230.

To me, fair friend, you never can be old, 104, p. 200.

Two households, both alike in dignity, *Romeo and Juliet*, Prologue, p. 89.

Two loves I have, of comfort and despair, 144, pp. 73–4.

Unthrifty loveliness, why dost thou spend, 4, p. 129.

Was it the proud full sail of his great verse, 86, p. 197.

Weary with toil I haste me to my bed, 27, p. 153.

Were 't aught to me I bore the canopy, 125, p. 221.

What fire is in mine ears? Can this be true? *Much Ado About Nothing*, 3.1.107–16, p. 188.

What is your substance, whereof are you made, 53, p. 179.

What potions have I drunk of siren
tears, 119, p. 215.
What's in the brain that ink may
character, 108, p. 204.
When forty winters shall besiege thy
brow, 2, p. 127.
When I consider every thing that
grows, 15, p. 140.
When I do count the clock that tells
the time, 12, p. 137.
When I have seen by time's fell hand
defaced, 64, p. 95.
When, in disgrace with fortune and
men's eyes, 29, p. 155.
When in the chronicle of wasted
time, 106, p. 202.
When most I wink, then do mine
eyes best see, 43, p. 169.
When my love swears that she is
made of truth, 138, pp. 66–7.
When thou shalt be disposed to set
me light, 88, p. 110

When to the sessions of sweet silent
thought, 30, p. 156.
Where art thou, muse, that thou
forget'st so long, 100, p. 122.
Whilst I alone did call upon thy aid,
79, p. 190.
Who is it that says most which can
say more, 84, p. 195.
Who will believe my verse in time to
come, 17, p. 142.
Whoever hath her wish, thou hast
thy Will, 135, p. 63.
Why didst thou promise such a
beauteous day, 34, p. 160.
Why is my verse so barren of new
pride, 76, p. 107.
Words, vows, gifts, tears, and love's
full sacrifice, *Troilus and Cressida*,
1.2. 278–91, p. 223.

Your love and pity doth th'
impression fill, 112, p. 208.